D0443246

On Reading Well

On Reading Well

FINDING THE GOOD LIFE through GREAT BOOKS

KAREN SWALLOW PRIOR

a division of Baker Publishing Group
Grand Rapids, Michigan

Published by Brazos Press
a division of Baker Publishing Group
PO Box 6287, Grand Rapids, MI 49516-6287
www.brazospress.com

Printed in the United States of America

ISBN: 978-1-58743-396-2

Library of Congress Cataloging in Publication Control Number: 2018007015

18 19 20 21 22 23 24 7 6 5 4 3 2 1

In keeping with biblical principles of creation stewardship, Baker Publishing Group advocates the responsible use of our natural resources. As a member of the Green Press Initiative, our company uses recycled paper when possible. The text paper of this book is composed in part of post-consumer waste.

To Roy, who loves me so well

Contents

Foreword

Leland Ryken

In this foreword I have set myself the task of previewing the three things that readers most need to know as they begin to read the book that follows. These three things touch upon the context, the content, and the achievement of the book.

It would be possible for a contemporary reader to revel in this book while being ignorant of the age-old tradition of literary criticism that it represents and also the debate over that tradition in the modern era. The premises that literature makes moral statements, that these statements can strengthen the moral life of a reader, and that literary criticism should explore the moral dimension of literary texts began in classical antiquity and held sway until the twentieth century. For Aristotle, a mark of good literature is that it "satisfies the moral sense."[1]

The Christianized version of this classical tradition reached its climax in the Renaissance author Sir Philip Sidney's treatise *A Defense of Poetry*. Sidney claimed that the very purpose of literature is the "winning of the mind from wickedness to virtue" and inflaming a reader with a "desire to be worthy."[2]

With the Enlightenment and modernity came the collapse of a unified sense of moral standards in the West. Consequently, the idea that literature has moral implications and can influence readers to be virtuous became passé. Morality itself became reduced to Ernest Hemingway's dictum that "what is moral is what you feel good after, and what is immoral is what you feel bad after."[3] This echoed Oscar Wilde's earlier statement that "there is no such thing as a moral or an immoral book. Books are well written, or badly written. That is all."[4]

Reacting against this rejection of moral criteria for literature, a towering literary scholar named F. R. Leavis wrote a famous book entitled *The Great Tradition* (1948). What is this "great tradition" championed by Leavis? It is both a literary tradition, represented by great authors and works that portray the moral life, and a type of literary criticism that explores the moral dimension of literature. Karen Swallow Prior's book is squarely within this great tradition.

I have already hinted at the content of this book. There is a theoretic side in which Prior explains the ethical and literary nature of her enterprise. A pleasant bonus is the primer on ethical theory and moral thinking included in the discussion. Mainly, though, this is a book of literary criticism. It is based on what I call "good old-fashioned example theory," which was particularly prominent in the English Renaissance. What this means is that it is in the nature of literature to place examples before us—examples of virtue to emulate and vice to repudiate. In our day, this is stigmatized as "surely a very simplistic view of literature," to which my comeback is, "Tough—this is demonstrably how literature works." On the self-evident nature of this, I am reminded of C. S. Lewis's comment in regard to Sir Philip Sidney that "the assumption . . . that the ethical is the aesthetic *par excellence* is so basic to Sidney that he never argues it. He thought we would know."[5]

In *On Reading Well*, Prior chooses monuments of Western literature and explores a single virtue embodied in each work. No claim is made that this is all that a reader would wish to do with these works. The result of Prior's moral analysis is that our understanding of virtue is increased and our desire to practice it enhanced. Today in the secular literary guild and public school classroom there is a sustained assault on Christian morality. *On Reading Well* offers a revisionist agenda, which is, of course, nothing less than a return to the great tradition.

As for the achievement of *On Reading Well,* it is of the highest order. The book is a monument to scholarship. Assertions are buttressed with copious research. All of the right sources are incorporated. A particular gift of Prior's is precision of thought and expression. The goal of the book—to enhance both literary appreciation and the moral life of the reader—is a noble one, meeting Sir Philip Sidney's goal of leading a reader to desire to be worthy.

I will confess that as a literary scholar I have always been somewhat resistant to moral criticism of literature because I fear that it will be moralistic. But right from the start, Karen Swallow Prior puts these fears to rest. The moral dimension of literature is only one dimension of literature, she assures us, and it does not exist separate from the aesthetic form of a work. The moral viewpoint of a work is not stated abstractly but embodied in the particulars of the text, especially the characters. And so forth.

It is the nature of scholars to be critical when reading books in their discipline, and it is relatively rare that they end a book feeling that the subject could not have been handled better than it was. I did end *On Reading Well* feeling that nothing was lacking in Prior's treatment of the subject of virtue in literature and that everything essential had been beautifully stated.

Introduction

Read Well, Live Well

> Who is wise and understanding among you? Let them show it by their good life, by deeds done in the humility that comes from wisdom.
>
> —James 3:13

My first book, *Booked: Literature in the Soul of Me*, is a love story, the story of how my deep love of reading slowly meandered into a deep love of God. I retell in the pages of *Booked* how, by reading widely, voraciously, and indiscriminately, I learned spiritual lessons I never learned in church or Sunday school, as well as emotional and intellectual lessons that I would never have encountered within the realm of my lived experience. Most importantly, by reading about all kinds of characters created by all kinds of authors, I learned how to be the person God created me to be.

A central theme of *Booked* is reading promiscuously. This phrase is drawn from one of the books that proved most formative for me, John Milton's *Areopagitica*. In this treatise, published in 1644, the Puritan poet most famous for his epic poem *Paradise Lost* makes an argument that would become a building block for the modern notions of freedom of speech and freedom of the press. In the tract, Milton inveighs against parliamentary licensing orders requiring all publications to be approved by the government before being printed (a legal concept that would later be called prior restraint). Significantly, it was Milton's own political faction that was in power at the time, his own people whom he thought to be in error and hoped to persuade to reject censorship.

Areopagitica makes a deeply theological argument, one that Christians today, particularly those nervously prone to a censoring spirit, would do well to consider. Grounded in Protestant doctrine (as well as the polarized political situation surrounding the English Civil War), Milton associates censorship with the Roman Catholic Church (the political as well as doctrinal enemy of the English Puritans) and finds in his Reformation heritage a deep interdependence of intellectual, religious, political, and personal liberty—all of which depend, he argues, on virtue. Because the world since the fall contains both good and evil, Milton says, virtue consists of choosing good over evil. Milton distinguishes between the innocent, who know no evil, and the virtuous, who know what evil is and elect to do good. What better way to learn the difference between evil and good, Milton argues, than to gain knowledge of both through reading widely: "Since therefore the knowledge and survey of vice is in this world so necessary to the constituting of human virtue, and the scanning of error to the confirmation of truth, how can we more safely, and with less danger, scout into the regions of sin and falsity than by reading all manner of tractates and hearing all manner of reason? And this is the benefit which may be had of books promiscuously read."[1]

But it is not enough to read widely. One must also read well. One must read virtuously. The word *virtue* has various shades of meaning (many of which will unfold in the pages of this book), but in general, virtue can most simply be understood as *excellence*. Reading well is, in itself, an act of virtue, or excellence, and it is also a habit that cultivates more virtue in return.

Literature embodies virtue, first, by offering images of virtue in action and, second, by offering the reader vicarious practice in exercising virtue, which is not the same as actual practice, of course, but is nonetheless a practice by which habits of mind, ways of thinking and perceiving, accrue.

It is not enough to read widely. One must also read well.

Reading virtuously means, first, reading closely, being faithful to both text and context, interpreting accurately and insightfully. Indeed, there is something in the very form of reading—the shape of the action itself—that tends toward virtue. The attentiveness necessary for deep reading (the kind of reading we practice in reading literary works as opposed to skimming news stories or reading instructions) requires patience. The skills of interpretation and evaluation require prudence. Even the simple decision to set aside time to read in a world rife with so many other choices competing for our attention requires a kind of temperance.

If, like me, you have lived long enough to have experienced life—and reading—before the internet, perhaps you have now found your attention span shortened and your ability to sit and read for an hour (or more) nil. The effects on our minds of the disjointed, fragmentary, and addictive nature of the digitized world—and the demands of its dinging, beeping, and flashing devices—are well documented. Nicholas Carr explains in *The Shallows: What the Internet Is Doing to Our Brains* that "the linear mind is being pushed aside by a new kind of mind that wants and needs to take in and dole out information in short, disjointed, often overlapping bursts—the faster, the better."[2] Our brains work one way when trained to read in logical, linear patterns, and another way when continually bouncing from tweet to tweet, picture to picture, and screen to screen. These effects on the brain are amplified by technology developers who intentionally build addictive qualities into programs in order to increase user engagement, as some industry leaders have acknowledged.[3] Whether you feel you have lost your ability to read well, or you never acquired that ability at all, be encouraged. The skills required to read well are no great mystery. Reading well is, well, simple (if not easy). It just takes time and attention.

There is something in the very form of reading—the shape of the action itself—that tends toward virtue.

Reading well begins with understanding the words on the page. In nearly three decades of teaching literature, I've noticed that many readers have been conditioned to jump so quickly to interpretation and evaluation that they often skip the fundamental but essential task of comprehending what the words actually mean. This habit of the mind can be seen in the body. When I ask students to describe or restate a line or passage, often their first response is to turn their eyes upward in search of a thought or an idea, rather than to look down at the words on the page in front of them where the answer actually lies. Attending to the words on the page requires deliberation, and this improves with practice.

To Read Well, Enjoy

Practice makes perfect, but pleasure makes practice more likely, so read something enjoyable.[4] If a book is so agonizing that you avoid reading it, put it down and pick up one that brings you pleasure. Life is too short and books are too plentiful not to. Besides, one can't read well without enjoying reading.

On the other hand, the greatest pleasures are those born of labor and investment. A book that requires nothing from you might offer the same diversion as that of a television sitcom, but it is unlikely to provide intellectual, aesthetic, or spiritual rewards long after the cover is closed. Therefore, even as you seek books that you will enjoy reading, demand ones that make demands on you: books with sentences so exquisitely crafted that they must be reread, familiar words used in fresh ways, new words so evocative that you are compelled to look them up, and images and ideas so arresting that they return to you unbidden for days to come.

Also, read slowly. Just as a fine meal should be savored, so, too, good books are to be luxuriated in, not rushed through. Certainly, some reading material merits a quick read, but habitual skimming is for the mind what a steady diet of fast food is for the body. Speed-reading is not only inferior to deep reading but may bring more harm than benefits: one critic cautions that reading fast is simply a "way of fooling yourself into thinking you're learning something." When you read quickly, you aren't thinking critically or making connections. Worse yet, "speed-reading gives you two things that should never mix: superficial knowledge and overconfidence."[5] Don't be discouraged if you read slowly. Thoughtfully engaging with a text takes time. The slowest readers are often the best readers, the ones who get the most meaning out of a work and are affected most deeply by literature.[6] Seventeenth-century Puritan divine Richard Baxter writes, "It is not the reading of many books which is necessary to make a man wise or good; but the well reading of a few, could he be sure to have the best."[7]

Read with a pen, pencil, or highlighter in hand, marking in the book or taking notes on paper.[8] The idea that books should not be written in is an unfortunate holdover from grade school, a canard rooted in a misunderstanding of what makes a book valuable. The true worth of books is in their words and ideas, not their pristine pages. One friend wisely observed that "readers are not made for books—books are made for readers."[9] (The sheer delight to be found in reading other readers' marginalia is unforgettably rendered in Billy Collins's poem, "Marginalia."[10])

Read books you enjoy, develop your ability to enjoy challenging reading, read deeply and slowly, and increase your enjoyment of a book by writing words of your own in it.

Great Books Teach Us *How* (Not *What*) to Think

My exploration in these pages of a dozen or so great works of literature attempts to model what it means to read well by examining the insights about virtues these works offer. I have selected from among my favorite literary works those that might help us to understand the classical virtues—the cardinal virtues, the theological virtues, and the heavenly virtues (more about these below). Sometimes the virtues are shown through positive examples and sometimes, perhaps more often (given the exploratory nature of great literature), by negative examples. Literary characters have a lot to teach us about *character*.

To read well is not to scour books for lessons on *what* to think. Rather, to read well is to be formed in *how* to think. In *An Experiment in Criticism*, C. S. Lewis argues that to approach a literary work "with nothing but a desire for self-improvement" is to use it rather than to receive it.[11] While great books do offer important truths about life and character, Lewis cautions against using books merely for lessons. Literary works are, after all, works of art to be enjoyed for their own sake rather than used merely for our personal benefit. To use art or literature rather than receive it "merely facilitates, brightens, relieves or palliates our life, and does not add to it."[12] Reading well adds to our life—not in the way a tool from the hardware store adds to our life, for a tool does us no good once lost or broken, but in the way a friendship adds to our life, altering us forever.

Literary characters have a lot to teach us about *character*.

Yet receiving a work of art as an aesthetic experience is indeed "useful," though in a human sense, not merely utilitarian. Thomas Jefferson expresses this idea in a letter written to a friend in 1771:

> Everything is useful which contributes to fix in the principles and practices of virtue. When any original act of charity or of gratitude, for instance, is presented either to our sight or imagination, we are deeply impressed with its beauty and feel a strong desire in ourselves of doing charitable and grateful acts also. On the contrary when we see or read of any atrocious deed, we are disgusted with its deformity, and conceive an abhorence [*sic*] of vice. Now every emotion of this kind is an exercise of our virtuous dispositions, and dispositions of the mind, like limbs of the body acquire strength by exercise. But exercise produces habit, and in the instance of which we speak the exercise being of the moral feelings produces a habit of thinking and acting virtuously.[13]

Here Jefferson gets at the aesthetic aspect of reading literature. While the ethical component of literature comes from its content (its ideas, lessons, vision), the aesthetic quality is related to the way reading—first as an exercise, then as a habit—forms us. Just as water, over a long period of time, reshapes the land through which it runs, so too we are formed by the habit of reading good books well.

Reading as Aesthetic Experience

The virtue—or excellence—of literature cannot be understood apart from its form. To read literature virtuously requires attention to that form, whether the form be that of a poem, a novel, a short story, or a play. To attend to the form of a work is by its very nature an aesthetic experience.

The content of a literary work is what it says; its form is how it is said. Unfortunately, we are conditioned today to focus on content at the expense of form. When we read (or watch a film or view a work of art), we tend to look for themes, worldviews, gripping plots, relatable characters, and so forth, but often neglect the form. Part of this tendency is the fruit born of a culture influenced by a utilitarian emphasis on function and practical use at the expense of beauty and structure. Yet we know from real-life relationships and experience that *how* something is communicated is just as important as, if not more important than, *what* is communicated. Form is what sets literary texts apart from informational texts in the same way that a painting differs from paint that covers a wall: same materials, different form.

Compare, for example, the various ways one might experience an encounter with the content of a literary work: through a *CliffsNotes* summary, a film adaptation, or actually reading it. Each of these experiences differs significantly from the others even though the idea communicated is essentially the same. Reading virtuously requires us to pay attention to both form and content. And because literature is by definition an aesthetic experience, not merely an intellectual one, we have to attend to form at least as much as to content, if not more. Form matters.

One of the earliest works of literary aesthetics—the study of literature's form and how its form affects readers as an aesthetic experience—was Aristotle's *Poetics*. In *Poetics*, Aristotle introduces the notion of literature's cathartic effect, an idea that has had widespread influence, referring to the way literature trains emotions by arousing and then resolving them through the structure of a well-crafted plot, the element of literature that Aristotle identifies as the most important. Aristotle's emphasis on plot also bears fruitful insights into character. This is because plot, according to Paul Taylor in his essay "Sympathy and Insight in Aristotle's *Poetics*," "centers on the fact that the individual actions of characters follow with probability or necessity from a combination of three factors: the characters' humanity, their individual personalities, and their involvement in the circumstances depicted in the plot."[14] In other words, plot reveals character. And the act of judging the character of a character shapes the reader's own character.

Reading virtuously requires us to pay attention to both form and content.

Through the imagination, readers identify with the character, learning about human nature and their own nature through their reactions to the vicarious experience. Even literature that doesn't have character or plot, such as poetry, allows for a similar kind of process: the speaker of the poem is a kind of character whose experience the reader enters into, and the unfolding of the poem in time as it is read is itself a form of plotting.

This is the difference, as Taylor explains, between learning propositional truth through reading history or an argumentative essay and gaining knowledge aesthetically through the process of reading a fictional narrative.[15] Or, in the words of writer George Saunders, "A story means by how it proceeds."[16] The aesthetic experience of literature—its formative quality—differs from its intellectual or informative qualities. Taylor says that "we learn from fiction in something like the way we learn directly from real life."[17] Just as in real life, a work of literature doesn't assert but presents.[18] Thus the act of reading literature invites readers to participate in the experience aesthetically, not merely intellectually. Our desires as human beings are shaped by both knowledge and experience. And to read a work of literature is to have a kind of experience and to gain knowledge. Ultimately, this kind of aesthetic experience—formative, not merely informative—"can help to undermine an idealized picture of human nature—one which self-deception, or plain sentimentality, might otherwise sustain."[19] Visions of the good life presented in the world's best literature can be agents for cultivating knowledge of and desire for the good and, unlike visions sustained by sentimentality or self-deception, the true.

The act of judging the character of a character shapes the reader's own character.

So while reading for virtue means, in part, reading *about* virtue, in a deeper, less obvious way reading literature well is a way to *practice* virtue. Reading literature, to a certain extent, can inform us about many things (the injustices of the nineteenth-century English court system, the persecution of Christians in seventeenth-century Japan, and the manners and morals of the wealthy class in 1920s America, for example). But certainly, literature does not inform on such matters as well as history textbooks and lectures do. Whatever similarities there might be in the content of, say, a documentary on the French Revolution and *A Tale of Two Cities*, the differences between their forms make all the difference in the way we experience them. Reading literature, more than informing us, forms us.[20]

In his important work *A Defense of Poetry*, Renaissance poet and courtier Sir Philip Sidney offers one of the first Christian arguments for the power of poetry, saying that it surpasses the power both of history, which teaches by example, and of philosophy, which teaches by precept. "Now doth the peerless poet perform both, for whatsoever the philosopher saith should be done, he giveth a perfect picture of it by someone by whom he pre-supposeth it was done, so as he coupleth the general notion with the particular example. A perfect picture I say, for he yieldeth to the powers of the mind an image of that whereof the philosopher bestoweth but a wordish description."[21] Since history is restricted to what was and philosophy to what could be, Sidney argues, literature exceeds both by offering a picture of what should be. And because "the end of all earthly learning is virtuous action,"[22] poetry is more likely than either philosophy or history to cultivate virtue.

Reading literature, more than informing us, forms us.

A famous passage on the relationship of virtue, or excellence, to practice comes from Will Durant's *The Story of Philosophy* in his chapter on Aristotle, in which Durant quotes from Aristotle's *Nicomachean Ethics*:

> Excellence is an art won by training and habituation: we do not act rightly because we have virtue or excellence, but we rather have these because we have acted rightly; "these virtues are formed in man by his doing the actions"; we are what we repeatedly do. Excellence, then, is not an act but a habit: "the good of man is a working of the soul in the way of excellence in a complete life . . . for as it is not one swallow or one fine day that makes a spring, so it is not one day or short time that makes a man blessed and happy."[23]

Reading "After Virtue"

We would be remiss to examine virtue without considering that virtue in the ancient world existed within an entirely different context from that of the modern world in which we find ourselves. The Aristotelian philosophy of virtue is tied to a sense of human purpose or *telos*—in other words, humanity's ultimate end or purpose. In this understanding, virtues are parts of a whole that is oriented toward one end. For Aristotle, this end is living well, or (as his Greek term is often translated) happiness. Today we might refer to this as human flourishing. For the Christian, however, the ultimate end or purpose of one's life is to glorify God and enjoy him forever. This end does not always translate to our own happiness or flourishing. Quite the opposite, as the Christians in the novel *Silence* prove, along with a host of believers in the history of the real world.

In fact, a persistent question about virtue arises in most contemporary discussions, a question that will be examined more in chapter 1. This question centers on whether virtue is an end in itself or a means to some other end. The evidence that many think of it as the latter can be seen in the pervasive belief today that if one simply does a certain thing right, the reward will be a particular desired outcome. This way of thinking about virtue owes in part to the fact that we no longer have a sense of our larger purpose. Without knowing what the purpose of a bicycle is, we cannot determine its excellence. Similarly, we can hardly attain human excellence if we don't have an understanding of human purpose. Human excellence occurs only when we glorify God, which is our true purpose. Absent ultimate purpose, we look for practical outcomes.

The modern age that emerged from the Enlightenment stripped humanity of a commonly understood human *telos*, or end, taking with it the shared moral language necessary for agreeing upon and cultivating virtue, as Alasdair MacIntyre explains in *After Virtue*. Apart from a unifying whole, virtues are like lifeless limbs severed from the body that once gave them purpose. Severed from an understanding of human purpose, virtue becomes mere emotivism. MacIntyre describes emotivism as the belief that "moral judgments are nothing but expressions of preference, expressions of attitude or feeling."[24] In other words, without an external, objective source of meaning and purpose, we are left with only our internal and subjective feelings. Emotivism isn't simply having and expressing emotions but being overwhelmingly informed and driven by them. And because emotivism appropriates the language of morality, it appears in the guise of virtue, despite the fact that the true foundation of virtue—a transcendent absolute—has crumbled.[25] Because the language of morality has been hijacked by emotivism, giving us a "simulacra of morality" (a mere image or reflection in place of the real thing), talking about virtue and morality is nearly impossible in a life "after virtue."[26] It's something like when a kid hears an orchestra perform a Beethoven number and thinks it's a riff on his favorite cartoon song.

Similarly, we can hardly attain human excellence if we don't have an understanding of human purpose. Absent ultimate purpose, we look for practical outcomes.

The Virtues of Literary Language

Although now emptied, moral language "was once, too, at the full" (to echo Matthew Arnold in his poem "Dover Beach"). Literary language, inherently resonant with layers of meaning, reminds us what fullness of language looks like. The language of literature can fill this gap between meaningful language about virtue and empty gestures toward it. The ability to understand figurative language, in which "a word is both itself and something else," is unique to human beings and, as one cognitive psychologist explains, "fundamental to how we think" in that it is the means by which we can "escape the literal and immediate."[27] We see this quality most dramatically in satire and allegory. Although very different, both satirical and allegorical language employ two levels of meaning: the literal meaning and the intended meaning. In satire, the intended meaning is the opposite of the stated words; in allegory, the intended meaning is symbolized by the stated words. Satire points to error, and allegory points to truth, but both require the reader to discern meaning beyond the surface level. In this way, allegory and satire—and less obviously, all literary language—reflect the transcendent nature of the human condition and the "double-willed self" described by Paul in Romans 7:19.[28]

Human beings "inhabit language," explains theologian Graham Ward in an article titled "How Literature Resists Secularity." He writes, "Although the best writers of literature demonstrate a phenomenal control over their language, associations escape, rhythms beat out older and more sacred patterns, and words carry memories of previous use."[29] Words carry resonances that spill beyond the bounds of logic and even conscious thought. Ward says of literary texts that "their acts of naming and our acts of reading" cannot but conjure the possibilities of transcendence, "particularly when we attend to experience rather than dictionary definitions, as either a writer or a reader."[30] The fullness of literary language echoes meaning—and reminds us that there is, in fact, *meaning*.

When Emily Dickinson, for example, writes, "I dwell in Possibility— / a fairer House than Prose," the suggestive, layered senses of each word expand the meaning of these lines far beyond a mere nine short words.[31] The metaphor of the house links "possibility" with poetry, which, the lines assert, is fairer than "prose," which is now implicitly linked to the opposite of "possibility." "Dwell" means both *live* and *ponder*. "Fairer" suggests both *beauty* and *justice*. And the word "in" differs meaningfully from other possible word choices such as "with" or "by." These echoing meanings mark only the beginning of the possibilities poetic language opens up. Many more meanings could easily be drawn out of these two lines and the rest that follow in the complete poem. But even this brief examination shows how literary writing—all literary writing, not just poetry—uses language in a way that relies on layers of memory, meaning, and associations that can be objectively supported once explicated.

The fullness of literary language echoes meaning—and reminds us that there is, in fact, *meaning*.

In this way, literary language encourages habits of mind, ways of perceiving, processing, and thinking that cultivate virtue by reminding us of the meaning that cannot be found apart from *telos*. To read a literary work well, one must attend not only to the parts but also to the way in which the parts support the whole and meaning accrues. Literary language, as Sir Philip Sidney says, "figures forth good things."[32] In so doing, it is virtuous in and of itself, and it figures forth virtue in the reader as well. "Figuring forth" refers to the use of the imagination, which in its most literal sense refers to our ability to create a picture or image in our mind's eye. The stories in which we are immersed project onto our imaginations visions of the good life—as well as the means of obtaining it.[33] We must imagine what virtue looks like in order to act virtuously.

All literature—stories most obviously—centers on some conflict, rupture, or lack. Literature is birthed from our fallenness: without the fall, there would be no story. "Only desire speaks," writes Jacques Ellul in *The Humiliation of the Word*. "Satisfaction is silence."[34] Thus it is the nature of literature to express—and cultivate—desire. Marcel Proust says that "it is one of the great and wonderful characteristics of good books . . . to provide us with desires."[35]

But the desires that are cultivated by books (and other forms of stories, including film, songs, and especially commercials) can pull us toward the good life—or toward false visions of the good life (as Gustave Flaubert shows in romance-reading Emma Bovary).[36] Reading well entails discerning which visions of life are false and which are good and true—as well as recognizing how deeply rooted these visions are in language. Mark Edmundson explains in *Why Read?*, "Such visions are easier to derive from words, from writings, in part because for most of us the prevailing medium, moment to moment, is verbal."[37] Bucking the fashions in literary theory that have prevailed for decades, Edmundson (a distinguished professor at the University of Virginia) makes an assertion most of his colleagues would deem quaint at best: "The ultimate test of a book, or of an interpretation, is the difference it would make in the conduct of life."[38]

Certainly, reading great books is not the only way to cultivate virtue and achieve the good life. (Plenty of virtuous people I know and love don't love books.) But literature has a particular power in forming our visions of the good life. "Once past the issue of sheer physical survival, human lives are about feeling, believing, and judging, and stories profoundly map themselves onto this agenda of human concerns, because at the core of every story is a set of invitations to feel, to believe, and to judge as the story dictates," explains Marshall Gregory.[39] Indeed, "Our hearts traffic in stories," James K. A. Smith writes in *Imagining the Kingdom*. "We are narrative animals whose very orientation to the world is fundamentally shaped by stories."[40] We see this storied aspect of our lives in the most mundane, everyday ways—for example, when a loved one relays a funny or interesting incident, not by rushing to the outcome but by re-creating the whole scene, narrating it from start to finish in the form of an entertaining story.

Because we first make sense of the world aesthetically (referring to its root meaning of sensory experience), Smith says, our primary means of processing is "more like poetry than propositional analysis." Just as our first response to the world comes from its physical shape, so too our first response to literature comes from the way its form shapes our experience of it. Training our affect, or emotions, is a way of shaping our very perceptions, of "training people to 'see situations in the right way.'"[41] Developing perceptiveness—the sort that literary reading requires—cultivates virtue because action follows affective response. This connection between literary interpretation and affective response is seen in one study in which participants could retain the meaning of a word better if they used facial expressions to match the emotions conveyed by that word.[42] Our actions, our decisions, and even the very perceptions we register in our consciousness have been primed by the larger story—of our family, our community, our culture—in which we imagine ourselves.[43]

Literary form echoes the form of the virtuous life, teaching us "to live as good characters in a good story do, caring about what happens, resourcefully confronting each new thing . . . search[ing] for truth," according to moral philosopher Martha Nussbaum.[44] Literature conveys not life, but "a sense of life, and of value, a sense of what matters and what does not . . . of life's relations and connections."[45] Echoing Aristotle's argument on the role literature plays in developing virtue, Nussbaum writes:

> We have never lived enough. Our experience is, without fiction, too confined and too parochial. Literature extends it, making us reflect and feel about what might otherwise be too distant for feeling. . . . All living is interpreting; all action requires seeing the world *as* something. So in this sense no life is "raw," and . . . throughout our living we are, in a sense, makers of fictions. The point is that in the activity of literary imagining we are led to imagine and describe with greater precision, focusing our attention on each word, feeling each event more keenly—whereas much of actual life goes by without that heightened awareness, and is thus, in a certain sense, not fully or thoroughly lived.[46]

Great books offer perspectives more than lessons. Literature shows us "how a different character, a situation, an event seems from different angles and perspectives, and even then how inexact our knowledge remains."[47] Literature replicates the world of the concrete, where the experiential learning necessary for virtue occurs. Such experiential learning does not come through technique. "One learns it by guidance rather than by a formula."[48]

Reading and interpreting literature notoriously lacks hard and fast rules. It is this very quality that makes literature exciting for some, frustrating for others. There is no one right reading of a literary text—but there are certainly erroneous readings, good readings, and excellent readings. Similarly, virtue ethics, rather than proffering a rigid set of rules by which to determine decisions (deontological ethics) or considering the likely consequences or outcomes of a decision (pragmatic ethics), relies on moral character, developed through good habits, for the governing of behavior. For the most part, this is the hardest and most challenging course. Cultivating and exercising wisdom is harder than consulting a rule book. As Aristotle says, "Both skill and virtue are always concerned with what is harder, because success in what is harder is superior."[49]

Human virtue, or moral excellence, is a habit of moral character; because it is a habit, it becomes a kind of second nature. In *Nicomachean Ethics,* Aristotle locates virtue, or excellence, between the extremes of excess and deficiency: the virtuous mean.[50] Both the deficiency and the excess of a virtue constitute a vice. For example, the virtue of courage is found between the excess of rashness (a vice) and the deficiency of cowardice (also a vice). Each of the virtues is such a mean. This idea is expressed in the old aphorism "everything in moderation."

Various virtues have been identified and cataloged throughout the history of philosophical thought. The Greeks, Romans, and early Christians all had different but overlapping concepts of virtue as a whole and of specific individual virtues. For this book, I've chosen twelve of the most central virtues and grouped them according to their traditional categories.

The cardinal virtues, the subject of part 1, constitute the most agreed-upon grouping across Greek and early Christian thought. These virtues are prudence, temperance, justice, and courage. They are called cardinal virtues because *cardinal* originally meant "hinge" or "pivot." Philosophers consider these four virtues to be the ones on which all other virtues depend or hinge. And of these, prudence or practical wisdom, the subject of the first chapter, is queen.

The theological virtues—faith, hope, and love—are drawn directly from the Bible. While the Bible mentions other virtues, these three have special significance among the virtues, not only because of the way they are emphasized in 1 Corinthians 13:13, but also because, unlike the other virtues, they occur in their true sense not through human nature but by God's divine power. As we will explore in part 2, the sense of faith, hope, and love as they are discussed in Scripture differs from the abilities and passions that human beings have naturally. In contrast to the other virtues, these virtues can be attained only when granted to us by God through his supernatural grace.

In part 3 we consider what are called the heavenly virtues. There are seven of these (a number of special significance in the Christian tradition, one that symbolizes perfection or completion). These heavenly virtues are charity and temperance (discussed in previous sections of the book), chastity, diligence, patience, kindness, and humility. Traditionally, the heavenly virtues were cataloged as those that specifically countered the seven deadly sins (a list that has also varied throughout church history).

While each chapter can be read alone, connections and comparisons among the virtues are drawn throughout, making reading the book as a whole from start to finish the most fruitful approach. I've tried to write about the literary works in ways that will interest and engage both those who have read the works and those who have not. For those who have not, a warning: spoilers abound. However, because all of the works chosen are literary works of enduring quality, notable for their form as well as their content, I hope that the practices and images of virtue each offers will serve to invite first readings and rereadings alike.

May these and many other works affirm the words of Richard Baxter: "Good books are a very great mercy to the world."[51]

Part One

The Cardinal Virtues

"Tom Foolery"

CHAPTER ONE

Prudence

THE HISTORY OF TOM JONES, A FOUNDLING

by Henry Fielding

I, wisdom, dwell together with prudence;
I possess knowledge and discretion.
—Proverbs 8:12

Rules rule.

We do like our rules. Some rules are strict, some unspoken; some apply to everyone, some to only a few. Some of us like rigid moral rules. Some of us like unwritten rules of political correctness. No matter what, adhering to rules is much easier than exercising wisdom.

A society couldn't exist without the rule of law, of course. And a civilization wouldn't be civil without its informal expectations. The Christian faith is built on laws that Jesus came not to abolish but to fulfill. Yet, because no number of rules or laws could cover every moral or ethical choice we face, virtue picks up where rules leave off. And where rules abound, virtue, like an underused muscle, atrophies.

Virtue requires judgment, and judgment requires prudence. Prudence is wisdom in practice. It is the habit of discerning the "true good in every circumstance" and "the right means of achieving it."[1] In other words, it is "applied morality."[2] A person possesses the virtue of prudence when "the disposition to reason well about what courses of action and emotion will best bring about our own and others' well-being" becomes an acquired habit.[3] Perhaps Cicero puts it most clearly and succinctly in saying, "Prudence is the knowledge of things to be sought, and those to be shunned."[4]

"Prudence is the knowledge of things to be sought, and those to be shunned."

Prudence is considered the mother of the other three cardinal virtues.[5] While temperance, fortitude, and justice are moral virtues, virtues related to doing, prudence is an intellectual virtue, a virtue related to knowing. Prudence is "at the heart of the moral character, for it shapes and directs the whole of our moral lives, and is indispensable to our becoming morally excellent human persons."[6] Prudence measures the other virtues[7] and determines what "makes an action good."[8] It is described as the "charioteer of the virtues," the basis and the measure of all other virtues, helping us to apply general principles to particular situations in ways that avoid evil and accomplish good.[9]

Is Virtue Its Own Reward?

While we hardly even talk about virtue today, in eighteenth-century England, virtue was the center of the biggest literary feud of the age. This debate, carried out on the pages of great books, grappled with the question: Do we practice virtue in hopes of achieving some personal gain, or is virtue, as the saying goes, its own reward?

The furor began in 1740 when an obscure printer's apprentice named Samuel Richardson published a fictitious series of letters titled *Pamela, or Virtue Rewarded*. Written from the perspective of a young servant girl, the letters convey, moment by moment, the girl's severe trials as her wealthy, debauched master attempts to wrest her "virtue" (or virginity) from her by, at turns, guile and force. Ultimately, Pamela wins him to marriage—an unbelievable turn of events at the time because of their vast difference in social class when rigid class divisions were rarely breached, but also an (almost) unbelievable turn of events to readers today because of how hard it is to imagine a woman falling in love with so vile a suitor.

As unrealistic as the novel seems in some respects, however, *Pamela* offered to readers of its day a dramatic turn toward realism in a novel, a departure from the more typical fictional tales that had been popular for centuries. By using a realistic form (letters) and employing realistic language (the vernacular of a common servant girl), Richardson composed a story far more believable than the epics and romances of old. But even more pioneering was his combining of this new kind of realism with a powerful moral message about virtue.

Richardson's literary accomplishment was so significant that he is now called the father of the English novel. *Pamela* was a huge sensation.

Entire villages read it together, and one even rang the church bell upon reading of Pamela's marriage. Preachers extolled the book from the pulpit. An industry of paraphernalia arose, including *Pamela*-themed fans, prints, paintings, cards, and waxworks. And long before *fan fiction* was a term, *Pamela* inspired volumes of spin-offs, sequels, and parodies.

Two of the best of these parodies were penned by Henry Fielding. Parodying the moral philosophy of *Pamela,* Fielding's *Shamela* roundly satirizes what he saw in the novel as a crude commodification of virtue for the sake of worldly gain. In a longer parody, *Joseph Andrews,* Fielding comically reverses the sex roles with a hilarious depiction of a poor, virtuous young man being pursued by an older wealthy woman. He then turned to a work that would counter Richardson's not merely with mockery but with a competing moral and literary aesthetic. *The History of Tom Jones, A Foundling* is Fielding's masterpiece.

The literary battle between Fielding and Richardson changed the course of literature. Their skirmish reflected—and shaped—not only differences in literary form but also the ongoing cultural transition from the classical virtues to modern individualistic morality. The debate reflects a modern cultural shift whereby, as Alasdair MacIntyre explains in *After Virtue,* morality was severed from theology, replacing it with the modern notion of autonomy.[10] *Pamela,* drawing on an earlier tradition of conduct books, promotes individual morality based on what MacIntyre calls "rules of conduct,"[11] while *Tom Jones* is built on what was even then a crumbling theological foundation for virtue.[12] The dispute between the two novelists mirrors the Enlightenment-era debate that has ultimately led to our current state of moral discourse. MacIntyre describes this state as the replacement of a transcendent basis for shared moral principles with mere individualistic emotivism.[13] Paralleling this philosophical development, contemporary Christian practice, particularly as expressed in American evangelicalism, has largely experienced the replacement of orthodox doctrine with what sociologist Christian Smith terms "moralistic therapeutic deism."[14]

A School of Virtue Ethics: *Tom Jones*

While *Pamela* reflects much about modernity and the rise of the individual, *Tom Jones* is a textbook example (literally: I use it as a textbook) of neoclassicism. It is also a veritable school of virtue ethics. Its opening dedication explains that its purpose is to advance "the cause of religion and virtue" by "displaying that beauty of virtue which may attract the admiration of mankind." While philosophers rightly hold that virtue is developed through actual practice—by which habits become tendencies, which become instincts, which then become essential nature—literature provides a vicarious practice of virtue. After all, as Fielding explains further into his dedication, "an example is a kind of picture, in which virtue becomes as it were an object of sight," one that "strikes us with an idea of that loveliness, which Plato asserts there is in her naked charms."[15]

Fielding's high moral purpose for his novel is reflected in many ways throughout the story that unfolds, but most striking is his narrative technique. A highly involved narrator opens each major section of the novel and interjects throughout to offer explicit commentary (as well as humorous asides). One scholar explains that this intrusive narrator is much more than a clever narrative device in that the narrator embodies Fielding's theology concerning the character of a God who intervenes and is active in the affairs of humankind—in other words, God's providence.[16]

In fact, the word *prudence* comes from the word *providence,* which means, literally, the ability to foresee.[17] Cicero, a classical orator held in high regard by the neoclassical Fielding, said that what instinct is for animals, prudence is for human beings; and what prudence is for human beings, providence is for the gods.[18] Because it means foreseeing, *providence* has come to refer to the actions of God based on his all-seeing and all-knowing power. The word *prudence* developed an analogous meaning within the human realm, referring to the actions of human beings based on foreseeing the consequences of a course of action and choosing accordingly. Prudence is in human affairs what God's sovereignty is over all of creation. In *Tom Jones*, prudence becomes the human, finite picture of God's infinite omniscience.[19] Aptly, *Tom Jones* is a book full of surprises and multiple colorful (sometimes bawdy) threads woven together by a masterful author-narrator whose highly visible presence reflects a world-view founded on belief in the active presence of an Author-God in the world of human affairs.

It is fitting that a novel whose theme is the acquisition of prudence is epic in length, taking its hero, along with a rich array of major and minor characters, on an arduous, twisting, adventure-filled sojourn from country to urban setting and back again.

Tom's story begins when the noble Squire Allworthy (noble in both his social class and his moral character) discovers a foundling (the term used at that time for an infant abandoned, then found) and decides to raise him like a son. Allworthy's mercy is remarkable in a time when illegitimate children were not treated kindly. Given the name Tom Jones, the boy develops into a high-spirited young man, full of passion but eminently good-natured. As Tom grows, Allworthy's generosity to the child raises the jealousy of other members of the household, however, and they don't let pass any opportunity to shed a bad light on the boy. The imprudent Tom provides many chances for them to succeed. When Tom finally loses favor with Allworthy through a combination of his own bad behavior and the exaggeration of this by his enemies, his benefactor expels him from the estate—aptly named Paradise Hall—after admonishing Tom that he must learn prudence.

Prudence is a form of wisdom. The ancients distinguished between two kinds of wisdom: speculative wisdom (*sophia*), related to the world of abstract ideas, and practical wisdom (*prudentia*), related to the concrete world of particular actions. As Tom pursues the story's heroine, his beloved Sophia (wisdom), he must also pursue and acquire prudence, or applied wisdom.

Wisdom is so rare today that distinguishing between speculative and practical wisdom seems overly nuanced. But we've all heard advice or a principle that seems right—yet is impossible to apply to a particular situation. One notices this often with pundits and commentators who are wont to spout platitudes that sound wise in theory yet prove disastrous when applied to an actual situation.

I think, for example, of a man I know who, after his wife divorced him to be with another man, was fired from his job assisting a ministry leader. The ministry leader thought it wise not to sully his family-centered ministry's reputation by working so closely with a man whose life didn't live up to the ministry's values. Years later, however, when divorce hit closer to home within the leader's family, his understanding of divorce tempered, and he realized that his views, although seemingly wise in theory, couldn't stand the test of application in the real world. By then it was too late. The man he had fired, who had done no wrong, was embittered and hurt beyond easy repair. Another example is the rule among some male leaders not to meet alone with a woman, which sounds moral and wise but generally becomes impossible to practice without falling into other errors such as disrespect or discrimination. Yet many today assume its prudence and adopt the rule without examination. Prudence is wisdom at work on the ground, doing good and avoiding evil in real-life situations.

Prudence is wisdom at work on the ground, doing good and avoiding evil in real-life situations.

On the other hand, the practical nature of prudence is the very thing that so easily distorts it. Because prudence is concerned with the means to an end,[20] it is easily confused with pragmatism, easily corrupted by justifying the means with the end. Misguided backlash against prudence recasts the cardinal virtue as crass *quid pro quo* (which is exactly how Fielding viewed Richardson's portrayal of "virtue rewarded" in *Pamela*). Consider the contempt for the related word *prude*, which has no positive connotations whatsoever. *Prudery, prudence, prudent*: each in today's usage suggests a narrow-minded, slim-souled, hand-wringing Pollyanna. (Being of a certain age, I can't hear any of these words without remembering Dana Carvey on *Saturday Night Live* imitating George H. W. Bush saying, "Wouldn't be prudent!")

Even as far back as 1749, the year *Tom Jones* was published, prudence was viewed cynically. Its ambiguous status is shown in the way Fielding treats it both seriously and humorously in the novel, demonstrating the transition when moral language began being used pragmatically and manipulatively, obscuring the arbitrary and autonomous basis of moral choices by cloaking personal preference in the language of virtue.[21]

One way the diminishing power of virtue in general can be seen is in the narrowing of its definition such that it was often used synonymously with virginity, as in *Pamela*, a conflation that grounded a significant part of Fielding's objection to Richardson's moral vision. (This is an interesting etymological development given that the Latin root for *virtue* literally means "man" or "manliness.") When *virtue* is used as a euphemism for *virginity*, it's inevitable that the concept of virtue is depleted, its practice diminished, and the virginity for which it stands commodified and fetishized.

This points to a problem in the purity culture popular today in some strains of Christianity. The movement's well-intentioned attempt to encourage believers to remain virgins until marriage unfortunately misses the mark by inadvertently making sexual purity a means to an end (such as alluring a fine marriage partner or being rewarded with a great sex life once married) rather than being a virtue in itself. Furthermore, apart from a more holistic sense of virtue, and in particular the virtue of chastity (the topic of chapter 8), virginity itself means little—as evidenced by the creative ways people maintain their virginity while remaining anything but sexually pure and by a former US president who claimed he'd not committed adultery because he'd engaged in all but intercourse with his mistress, and as further evidenced by situations in which virginity (not chastity) is lost through sexual assault.

Accordingly, in Fielding's view, Richardson's message in *Pamela* is that virtue is not a good in and of itself but is proven in being rewarded—by marriage, wealth, advancement, or praise (or in the case of Pamela, all four). *Pamela* offers a more complicated picture than Fielding gives it credit for, but his reading of the novel effectively demonstrates how easily morality slips into moralism, how finely drawn the line is between the law and legalism, and how readily the promise of blessings is mistaken as a contract for material prosperity.

Satire and Virtue

Such slippage is ripe fodder for satire, and *Tom Jones* is, along with being epic and comic, satirical. Satire is the ridicule of vice or folly for the purpose of correction. It is a harsh way to communicate truth, but pointing to truth—by first pointing to error—is its goal. Satire mocks—but it does so with a moral aim. And that's a problem in an age with few agreed-upon manners or rules. Unlike a lampoon or a parody or other forms of low comedy, satire relies on both a shared moral standard and a shared desire to attain that standard. This makes satire tricky for two reasons: first, agreement on moral standards varies from age to age, and second, some simply don't believe that it's anyone's job to "correct" anyone else's behavior. We live today in times that are hard for satire for both of these reasons. Vice and even folly are more and more seen as being "in the eyes of the beholder." Absent agreement on these, satire just seems mean. On the surface, ridicule doesn't seem kind, of course. But to ridicule what is wicked or foolish in hopes of preventing more of the same is much kinder than letting wickedness or folly continue along their merry, destructive way. Moreover, the sharp bite of satire leads some to think satire must be pessimistic, misanthropic even. Yet the truth is that the satirist, someone who tries so hard to improve the world, must, I think, love people very much. Even God's inspired Word contains plenty of irony and satire, such as when Job mocks the worldly-wise friends who've taunted his faith, saying, "Doubtless you are the only people who matter, and wisdom will die with you!" (Job 12:2). The satirist loves in the way of God, who chastens those whom he loves. There is only one thing worse than being chastened: that is, not being chastened.

The satirist loves in the way of God, who chastens those whom he loves. There is only one thing worse than being chastened: that is, not being chastened.

As with all satire, *Tom Jones* requires readers to distinguish between the narrator's ironic voice and the true one. Sometimes the novel presents an ironic picture of prudence and other times a true one. False prudence is, like irony, a form of misdirection—in this case, directing knowledge toward unjust ends. The burden is on the reader to distinguish between the sincere and the ironic in order to discern what true virtue consists of. (Fielding offers the reader considerable help with his highly obtrusive, and funny, narrator.) Think of this misdirection as a precursor to *Seinfeld*, modern satire at its finest. *Seinfeld* doesn't affirm the shallow, egotistical, trivial characters of Jerry, George, Elaine, and Kramer—it satirizes them. Humor is closely connected to prudence because "morality is not sufficient for virtue; virtue also requires intelligence and lucidity. It is something that humor reminds us of and that prudence prescribes. It is imprudent to heed morality alone, and it is immoral to be imprudent."[22] By forcing us to test our understanding and application of prudence, satire paradoxically deepens our understanding of prudence.

In Pursuit of Prudence

The word *prudence* appears dozens of times throughout *Tom Jones*, and the reader must prudently discern the tone with each use, for the narrator can rarely be taken at face value. Most often, the word is used satirically in order to correct various forms of false prudence. Fielding believed that "it is much easier to make good men wise than to make bad men good."[23] Teasing out what true prudence consists of advances Fielding's hope "to make good men wise."

One early example in the story demonstrates the irony that runs throughout, forcing the careful reader to pause and consider whether true or false prudence is being portrayed. While lecturing her niece on matrimonial affairs, Sophia's aunt tells her that women of the polite world "consider matrimony, as men do offices of public trust, only as the means of making their fortunes, and of advancing themselves in the world."[24] Clearly, this is not virtuous prudence but the vice formed from its excess: cunningness, shrewdness, or conceit. Its opposite vice—negligence, or rashness—is formed from the deficiency of prudence.[25] Prudence, like all virtues, is the moderation between the excess and deficiency of that virtue.

Two of the most comical characters in the novel embody these vices: the household tutors, Thwackum and Square. Thwackum is (as his name hints) a pious legalist who spots sin and corruption everywhere he looks—all of which turns out, not surprisingly, to be a projection of his own vice (cunning) onto everyone else. The negligent Square, on the other hand, ends up being caught, rather imprudently, with his pants down (literally) in the bedroom of Tom's first lover.

Part of prudence is "the ability to govern and discipline oneself by the use of reason."[26] Obviously, self-governance is a positive quality. It requires a kind of knowledge of both oneself and the world, which is what prudence essentially refers to. But when such knowledge is used toward unjust or evil ends, it transforms from the virtue of prudence into the vice of cunning. The word *cunning* is etymologically connected, not coincidentally, to the word *knowledge*. The just use of knowledge that constitutes prudence devolves into mere cunning when that knowledge is used for unjust ends.

When knowledge is used toward unjust or evil ends, it transforms from the virtue of prudence into the vice of cunning.

The excess prudence of cunning and conceit is embodied in the character of Tom's foil, Squire Allworthy's nephew and presumed heir, Blifil. Blifil, whose personality is as limp and lisping as his name, contrasts in every way with the robust, vivacious, and generous Tom. When the novel describes Blifil as "prudent," this is clearly meant in the bad—ironic—way. Sophia, over whom Tom and Blifil vie, observes that Blifil is "prudent," but merely as concerns "the interest only of one single person; and who that single person was the reader will be able to divine without any assistance of ours."[27] While virtuous prudence is characterized by "purity, straightforwardness, candor, and simplicity of character," false prudence relies on the appearance of these as a tactic toward some other end.[28] In this, Blifil excels.

While some of his motive for marrying Sophia is to expand the family estate, Blifil's cunning should not be confused with the vice of covetousness. Covetousness is "immoderate straining for all the possessions which man thinks are needed to assure his own importance and status."[29] Blifil, however, is so dispassionate and lacking in ambition that his selfish ends—his tutors' approval, Allworthy's favor, and the affection of the novel's heroine, the lovely Sophia—seem almost accidental.

This fact points to an interesting quality of vice: it is just as likely to be accidental as intentional. In this way, virtue opposes vice not only in its moral content but in its acquisition as well. Vice is natural to human beings in their fallen state. But virtue must be practiced, become a habit, and be inhabited by a person in order to attain excellence.

Vice is just as likely to be accidental as intentional. In this way, virtue opposes vice not only in its moral content but in its acquisition as well. Vice is natural to human beings in their fallen state. But virtue must be practiced, become a habit, and be inhabited by a person in order to attain excellence.

In contrast to Blifil's, Tom's deficient vices are rashness and negligence. While he does possess an abundance of charity and generosity, his negligence and rashness, despite his good intentions, nullify his virtuous qualities. Such imprudence leads him to engage in poaching, fornication, and selling gifts Allworthy has given him (albeit in order to help a needy neighbor). Furthermore, Tom's robust sexual appetite leads him into extremely imprudent liaisons. His intemperate spirits lead him to drunkenness and other excesses. His lack of prudence renders his good intentions either ineffectual or even harmful, both to others and to himself. In contrast to Tom, the prudent person makes "intelligent judgements regarding the overall trajectory of a flourishing life as well as accurate judgements about how to achieve it."[30]

Despite his vices, Tom demonstrates that prudence is formed by charity, or love.[31] "Prudence is love that chooses with sagacity between that which hinders it and that which helps it."[32] Developing prudence requires Tom to moderate all his passions, including his charitableness, since even love of others must be in proper proportion in order to be just, as Augustine explains in *On Christian Teaching*.[33] Loving oneself in proper proportion is necessary to loving others well. As Allworthy explains to Tom, prudence is "the duty which we owe ourselves. . . . If we will be so much our own enemies as to neglect it, we are not to wonder if the world is deficient in discharging their duty to us; for when a man lays the foundation of his own ruin, others will, I am afraid, be too apt to build upon it."[34] Tom's lack of prudence proves Sophia's observation that Tom is "nobody's enemy but his own."[35]

As "the perfected ability to make decisions in accordance with reality,"[36] prudence requires some knowledge of the world. In classical art, the goddess Prudentia is often depicted with a mirror (to represent self-knowledge or conscience) and a serpent (an ancient symbol of wisdom). The image conveys the understanding that prudence requires knowledge of both universal principles and the particulars of a given situation, along with the idea that, as Aquinas says, a prudent person is one who sees from afar.[37] Prudence concerns the "realities of a life lived within a specific and communal history, wisdom which proceeds to act."[38] It is exercised "within the mix of specific relations and goods that give the moral life of any person its texture. . . . Hence prudence responds specifically to the concrete particularities of one's life."[39] In other words, applying wisdom requires the ability to discern truth and then to act rightly based on truth. This is why John Milton, as we noted in the introduction to this book, distinguishes between virtue and mere innocence. Josef Pieper explains the connection of prudence to reality this way: "There can be false and crooked ways leading even to right goals. The meaning of the virtue of prudence, however, is primarily this: that not only the end of human action but also the means for its realization shall be in keeping with the truth of real things. This in turn necessitates that the egocentric 'interests' of man be silenced in order that he may perceive the truth of real things, and so that reality itself may guide him to the proper means for realizing his goal."[40]

Thus Tom's cultivation of prudence parallels his growth in knowledge of the world as he leaves the rural setting of his birth, travels on the road, and experiences urban life, encountering complex situations and deceptive people along the way. The pickles he gets himself into demonstrate how prudence is an intellectual virtue based in the rational ability, first, to distinguish between competing goods (for Tom, too often, these competing goods are women); then to foresee the consequences of possible actions; and finally, to take the best course of action accordingly. Reading his story allows us to learn about the world along with Tom. Prudence "transforms knowledge of reality into realization of the good."[41] But in the real world, what is good is what is practical, even if it falls short of ideal.[42] In other words, as the saying goes, the enemy of the good is the best. If only the ideal will do, the good will likely never be realized. Perfectionism is the foil of prudence.

One way Tom learns prudence, just as we do in real life, is by observing its lack in others. By observing reality, Tom learns that "folly is self-inflicted, due chiefly to our willingly directing our attention to secondary goods, or evils . . . that oppose the divine concerns."[43] When Tom's companion Mr. Nightingale impregnates his lover and then refuses to marry her because of her loss of reputation (never mind that she lost it to him!), Tom exhorts Nightingale to do the right thing, admonishing him that "when you promised to marry her she became your wife; and she hath sinned more against prudence than virtue."[44] Tom comes by this advice honestly, having found himself in similar straits earlier in the story when, believing he had impregnated a woman, he is humble and responsible enough to do right by the young woman (until fate reveals other surprises). Prudence, in fact, has affinity with the open nature of magnanimity. In contrast to magnanimity, "insidiousness, guile, craft, and concupiscence are the refuge of small-minded and small-souled persons."[45] Tom is an open book, even to a fault, initially.

If only the ideal will do, the good will likely never be realized. Perfectionism is the foil of prudence.

The pages are open, but the cover needs repair. Tom must learn that his natural inward state of goodness should be reflected outwardly by mores and morals. Appearances and reputation are not unnecessary adornments but are prudent in making one's outward behavior and morality conform to one's inward state. As the helpful narrator of the story tells us,

> Prudence and circumspection are necessary even to the best of men. They are indeed as it were a guard to virtue, without which she can never be safe. It is not enough that your designs, nay that your actions are intrinsically good, [but] you must take care they shall appear so. If your inside be never so beautiful, you must preserve a fair outside also. This must be constantly looked to, or malice and envy will take care to blacken it so, that the sagacity and goodness of an Allworthy will not be able to see through it, and to discern the beauties within. Let this, my young readers, be your constant maxim, that no man can be good enough to enable him to neglect the rules of prudence; nor will virtue herself look beautiful, unless she be bedecked with the outward ornaments of decency and decorum.[46]

A Novel of Development

Tom Jones is a traditional bildungsroman, a novel of development. Thus, as Tom's love for Sophia (wisdom) grows, so too does his prudence. Because "the virtue of prudence is dependent upon the constant readiness to ignore the self,"[47] the more Tom puts Sophia's interests ahead of his own, the more he is able to cultivate prudence (such as by learning to decline the wealthy and worldly women who offer themselves to him). Tom eventually applies wisdom by pursuing all its components—seeking counsel, deliberation, judgment, coming to resolution, and action.[48]

The novel paints a vivid picture of Fielding's own belief that a good-natured soul is capable of great good once virtue is cultivated. This question of human nature—whether it is essentially good or corrupt—is a strong undercurrent in the larger debate between Fielding and Richardson and among their contemporaries. Fielding's more liberal theology emerges in *Tom Jones* in his emphasis on Tom's essential good nature, which triumphs over his moral failures. In contrast to Fielding's high-church Anglicanism, Richardson's theological view of human nature was influenced by the Methodism of John Wesley and George Whitefield and thus reflects the doctrine of human depravity. The question of whether human nature is essentially good or bad was a pressing one among Enlightenment philosophers and, not surprisingly, made its way into the most influential literature of the day. This philosophical, and essentially theological, debate played a significant role not only in shaping these novels (e.g., the differences between each side's literary style and overall message) but also in the development of the emerging genre of the novel as a whole. Because of such underlying questions, the novel is, in many ways, the genre best representative of the modern condition.

This debate over the essential goodness or depravity of human nature has continued into the present day and is commonly cited as the fundamental division between conservative and liberal theology and politics. However, a question even more significant than whether human nature is essentially good or bad has emerged, and that is the question of whether such a thing as an essential human nature exists at all. If not, then there can be no *telos* or true end toward which human existence and excellence should be directed. And if there is no purpose for human existence, then there can be no unified, transcendent basis for morality or virtue. This, MacIntyre argues, is what places contemporary humanity in the position of being "after virtue."[49]

But Tom Jones lives in a world in which the foundation of virtue still stands, though crumbling. The story reaches its happy conclusion for Tom (it is a comedy, after all) only when he has recognized and confessed the errors of his ways. In response, Squire Allworthy joyfully tells him, "You now see, Tom, to what dangers imprudence alone may subject virtue (for virtue, I am now convinced, you love in a great degree)."[50] The all-knowing narrator informs us that Tom, "by reflection on his past follies, acquired a discretion and prudence very uncommon in one of his lively parts."[51]

Thus the novel demonstrates that the virtue of prudence is indeed "right reason directed to the excellent human life,"[52] a virtue as uncommon as it is essential to the admirable goal of retaining our lively parts."

"Such Beautiful Shirts"

Chapter two

Temperance

THE GREAT GATSBY

by F. Scott Fitzgerald

And beside this, giving all diligence, add to your faith virtue; and to virtue knowledge; and to knowledge temperance; and to temperance patience; and to patience godliness.

—2 Peter 1:5–6 (KJV)

Some years ago, I joined a weight-loss program with a couple of friends. Mainly, I wanted to spend time with them and support their efforts. But I figured I could benefit from losing a few pounds too. To stay within the stingy allotment of daily food points the program allowed, I gave up three of my favorite things: Chinese buffets, ice cream, and cream in my coffee. It was hard at first. I wasn't used to going hungry—ever—and doing so made me cranky. So to keep hunger at bay, I filled up on more healthful foods. (Fortunately, I like all food, even the healthy stuff.)

Then, a few months into these changed habits, an odd thing happened. One evening, as usual, hunger struck. Immediately, I was seized by a craving . . . for grapes. Grapes! Not lo mein, not gummy bears, not ice cream—but *grapes*. I actually *desired* more than anything else a food that was good for me. It seemed like a miracle. But it wasn't. In changing my habits, I had developed (at least in this one area) the virtue of temperance.

Temperance is unique among the virtues. Unlike other virtues that are revealed under pressure, temperance is "an ordinary, humble virtue, to be practiced on a regular rather than an exceptional basis." It "is a virtue for all times but is all the more necessary when times are good."[1] It is also unlike the other virtues in centering not on actions but on desires. Since we desire what is pleasurable, temperance is "the virtue that inclines us to desire and enjoy pleasures well."[2] It helps us to desire pleasures in a reasonable manner,[3] desiring them neither too much nor too little, the virtuous mean between the vices of self-indulgence and insensibility.[4]

For Aristotle temperance concerned the physical appetites we share with animals: the desires for food, drink, and sex.[5] For both humans and animals, these appetites are necessary to perpetuate life (whether individually or as a species), but they are also the source of pleasure. The Catholic Church, following Aristotle's understanding, teaches that temperance "ensures the will's mastery over instincts and keeps desires within the limits of what is honorable," but expands the role of temperance as governing "the use of created goods."[6]

Temperance is not simply resisting temptation. It is more than merely restraint. Aquinas uses the example of a miser who eschews extravagance because of its expense: such a man is not temperate,[7] for the temperate man would not desire extravagance. One attains the virtue of temperance when one's appetites have been shaped such that one's very desires are in proper order and proportion.

We can learn so much about God's economy, his nature, and the way to human flourishing by observing the marvelous ways in which God has built balance, a form of temperance, into the natural order. Night tempers day. Water relieves earth. The four seasons comprise two pairs that offset each other in the stages of life: birth, fertility, decay, death. Even creating as male and female those who bear forth his image (instead of making humans capable of reproducing from one rather than two, like bacteria) reveals something about how we are to live. Yet, so often in human affairs, balance seems unnatural, prone as we are to careen from one extreme to another, both as individuals and collectively within culture. The ancients showed wisdom in understanding how foundational temperance is to human excellence.

One attains the virtue of temperance when one's appetites have been shaped such that one's very desires are in proper order and proportion.

Temperance is the virtue that helps us rise above our animal nature, making the image of God in us shine more brilliantly. For humans, unlike animals, pleasure is tempered by understanding. Developing desires for the good requires understanding. Human beings are creatures who are rational as well as spiritual and who, as such, do not approach pleasurable activities purely physically. The temperate person is one who "understands these connections between bodily pleasures and the larger human good, and whose understanding actually tempers the desires and pleasures."[8]

Temperance is liberating because it "allows us to be masters of our pleasure instead of becoming its slaves."[9]

But while understanding is necessary for the virtue of temperance, it is not sufficient. Even Paul acknowledges the limits our understanding holds over our desires when he writes, "I do not understand what I do. For what I want to do I do not do, but what I hate I do" (Rom. 7:15).

A History of Intemperance

The difficulty of balancing between excessive and deficient pleasures is evident all around us in many ways, not only in the present, but in human history as well. Two ancient schools of thought that demonstrate the extremes of excess and deficiency in regards to physical pleasures are Stoicism and Epicureanism, one advocating restraint and the other indulgence as the way to the good life. We might not adopt their extremes in such intensely philosophical ways today, but the influence of these approaches is all around us. This ping-ponging between excess and deficiency in the indulgence of our animal appetites manifests in endless ways in American culture today: all-you-can-eat buffets and detox diets, pornography and purity culture, fast food and slow food, the sexual revolution and the death of sex,[10] McMansions and tiny houses, the prosperity gospel and the gospel of self-denial. Even in the longer view of our nation's history, we see this wild pendulum swing: the excesses rampant today are the counter swing to the Puritan roots of our country's beginning. This ongoing tension that has always defined American culture is at the heart of one of the most quintessentially American novels: *The Great Gatsby*.

The defining quality of Gatsby's life is excess. Even the word *great* in the title establishes this (although ironically, as it turns out). We see Gatsby's greatness through the eyes of the first-person narrator, Nick Carraway. A nondescript, struggling businessman who is renting the modest cottage next to Gatsby's lavish mansion, Nick is in every way a foil to Gatsby. The truth Nick slowly uncovers about Jay Gatsby reveals not only the humble origins of a man (whose real name turns out to be James Gatz) but also his excessive efforts both to overcome these beginnings and to suppress the very nature of his past and his identity.

But nature—including human nature—is like a balloon. If squeezed at one end, the air inside simply moves to the other end. If squeezed enough, the balloon will burst. Extremes will eventually out. The virtue of temperance keeps us from bursting at either end.

Aptly, *The Great Gatsby* is set during a time characterized by the impulse to suppress: Prohibition. The historical background to the story exemplifies in itself how excess in one direction can lead to an equal and opposite excess in the other direction.

Prohibition grew out of the more moderate movement called Temperance. The American Temperance Society was founded in 1826 as a call, first, to temper (or moderate) excessive consumption of alcohol, but eventually to total abstinence (teetotalism). The push toward complete prohibition developed as a reaction against another excess: the growing drunkenness (often resulting in domestic violence and familial neglect) that accompanied the Industrial Revolution. In previous ages, it was common, even among some Puritans, to imbibe mild wine, mead, and beers from breakfast till nighttime with little effect. However, what had long been a healthy and relatively harmless social and gustatory custom turned into an addictive and dangerous habit for many when modern means of producing alcohol increased the potency of alcoholic beverages.[11] In addition, the Industrial Revolution's increasingly rigorous and dehumanized systems of labor prompted more workers to seek even more relief in alcohol, and an epidemic began. Alcohol consumption was so rampant in the early decades of the nineteenth century that the average American consumed 7 gallons of pure alcohol each year (compared to 2.32 gallons consumed in America in 2014).[12] Efforts to address the problem culminated in 1920 with the Eighteenth Amendment to the US Constitution, which made the manufacture, transportation, and sale of intoxicating liquor illegal. The law was so intemperate that it could only result in vice. Prohibition was an ill-fated but short-lived social experiment that, in effect, replaced virtue. In 1933, the Twenty-First Amendment repealed Prohibition.

A Corrupted American Dream

This is the setting for *The Great Gatsby*. Written in 1925 and set in 1922, during the time between these two Amendments, the novel presents a society that replaced moderation with excesses on both ends of the spectrum. Self-governance, the principle many observe to be the foundation of the American experiment, diminished, and with it the virtue of temperance to which it is connected. *The Great Gatsby* interrogates, eerily and prophetically, the reckless excesses of American life during the Prohibition era, excesses that would contribute to the economic crash a few years later, bringing about the Great Depression and the tumbling down of the American Dream.

The American Dream takes various forms, of course, and has not vanished entirely. But some forms of that noble ideal are corrupt, as Gatsby's version is. Gatsby's life is essentially a lie, one told in the service of a distorted dream. Not only does this false dream take Gatsby's life, but it prevents him from truly living even when he is alive. His "intemperance has consumed him from his youth," leaving his mind and spirit always "in a constant, turbulent riot." The mad dreams and desires that fill his soul are but "founded securely on a fairy's wing."[13]

Even his sexual appetites were intemperate from the time of his youth: "He knew women early and since they spoiled him he became contemptuous of them, of young virgins because they were ignorant, of the others because they were hysterical about things which in his overwhelming self-absorption he took for granted."[14] Yet Gatsby considers himself "careful" in his liaisons because he refrains from any among the wives of his friends.[15] His intemperance leads him to regard women as objects that either belong to other men or are free for the taking.

Even the mean of an intemperate life is intemperate.

Even the mean of an intemperate life is intemperate.

A poster boy for the American Dream, young Gatsby envisions for himself some vague "future glory." Lacking the patience and humility to work his way up from his job as a college janitor, he chooses to ingratiate himself to a wealthy millionaire to become his heir.

After he has gained wealth and reinvented himself, Gatsby meets Daisy, "the first 'nice' girl he had ever known," who from the start inflames Gatsby's desires more.[16] With their first kiss, Gatsby vows that the act would "forever wed" his immortal dreams to her mortal being, and consequently, "his mind would never romp again like the mind of God."[17]

Conspicuous Consumption

Gatsby's lust for Daisy is not merely sexual, however. Daisy, an upper-class Southern belle, is part of a world Gatsby wants to enter but can never be from. Gatsby's worldview is the product of the new culture of consumer capitalism where, "rather than wealth or political or economic power," *desire* had become democratized. The rising consumerism of these years turned desire into "a spur to effort, forcing people to compete, discipline themselves, and deny present comfort for future pleasures."[18] Thus when Gatsby loses Daisy to a man who comes from long-standing wealth and power, Gatsby devotes his life to accumulating even more wealth in hopes of regaining her. We meet Gatsby five years later when he has succeeded in this goal to a level that can only be called obscene.

His enormous mansion's "purposeless splendor"[19] includes music rooms, salons, a pool room, dressing rooms, period bedrooms, and bathrooms with sunken baths.[20] Preparations for his weekend parties begin each Monday when eight servants and a gardener begin their daily labor. Crates of fruit are delivered from the city each Friday, and each Monday carried out "in a pyramid of pulpless halves." Caterers cover buffet tables with appetizers, meats, salads, and pastries. An orchestra performs as guests arrive in cars parked five deep in the driveway. Fashionable people fill the rooms, and "the air is alive with chatter and laughter and casual innuendo and introductions forgotten on the spot and enthusiastic meetings between women who never knew each other's names."[21]

Gatsby's excessive materialism reflects the culmination of American history decades in the making. Between the end of the Civil War and the turn of the century, capitalist ventures birthed a new ethos in America. This "consumer capitalism" created "a culture almost violently hostile to the past and to tradition, a future-oriented culture of desire that confused the good life with goods . . . one moving largely against the grain of earlier traditions of republicanism and Christian virtue."[22] This old culture, based on values rooted in tradition, community, and religion, was replaced by a new culture that promoted "acquisition and consumption as the means of achieving happiness."[23] A few years before the time of *The Great Gatsby*, the term "conspicuous consumption" originated in economic theory to describe the values of this new culture, in which those who were made wealthy through opportunities offered by the Industrial Revolution sought to acquire and flaunt material possessions as symbols of their new economic power. America became what the turn-of-the-century marketing pioneer John Wanamaker called the "land of desire."[24]

Today conspicuous consumption has spread even more throughout American culture. A recent four-year study, for example, found that the lives of the middle class are "overwhelmed" by stockpiled supplies, clutter, and toys. Three out of four garages are too full to hold cars, and while the United States has 3.1 percent of the world's children, it has 40 percent of the world's toys.[25] Consumerism sells the idea that material things will make us happy. To counteract this excess, an entire industry in minimalism promises to rescue those drowning in stuff. The downside of this excess stuff is more than simply material or financial, however. "Economic plenty seems to impose materialistic limits on imagination and people devote themselves to recreation, entertainment, and physical pleasure. Freedom consequently becomes trivial. . . . Everyone lives in about the same way, and it may be difficult even to think of a different way."[26]

Intemperate consumption and accumulation is something I struggle with in my own life. My grandparents, who lived through the Depression and lifelong poverty, threw nothing away. Whatever potential value even junk might hold was enough value to justify keeping it. My mother, despite rising to the comfortable middle class, was habituated by this upbringing to seek and buy bargains, an example I followed from early on and have continued far past its necessity or even its usefulness. Only in recent years have I slowly begun to shed the irrational sense that not taking advantage of a good deal is a loss, whether I need it or not. In fact, owning far more things than I need has become a great burden. Even so, changing my thinking has proven easier than changing my practices. (Although it is nice to know we will never run out of toilet paper in this house.) Temperance is, for many of us raised in a culture birthed by consumerism, a virtue difficult to attain.

Temperance is, for many of us raised in a culture birthed by consumerism, a virtue difficult to attain.

The Great Gatsby offers a larger-than-life picture of a life spun out of control by excess. If temperance is "selfless self-preservation," then Gatsby is the epitome of intemperance: "self-destruction through the selfish degradation of the powers which aim at self-preservation."[27] Nick recognizes the fatal nature of this intemperate world when he observes that in it "are only the pursued, the pursuing, the busy, and the tired."[28] Consumption does indeed consume us.

An early scene in the novel reveals the suffocating weight of excess consumption. A small, drunken party takes place in an apartment kept by Tom Buchanan, Daisy's husband, in New York City where he and his married mistress, Myrtle Wilson, have their regular rendezvous. The apartment is crammed with people and stuff, "crowded to the doors with a set of tapestried furniture entirely too large for it so that to move about was to stumble continually." The passage brims with words suggesting oversaturation, such as "large" and "full." There is even an "over-enlarged photograph" of a "hen sitting on an enlarged rock." One day, Tom takes Nick there, and Nick drinks excessively for only the second time in his life.[29] The apartment is a microcosm of the larger world Gatsby inhabits, a world riddled with vices: materialism, adultery, drunkenness, organized crime, and domestic violence.

Consumption does indeed consume us.

Temperance and Time

Yet temperance is more than merely restraining from vices. While restraint is one aspect of temperance, there is more to it than simply negation. Inherent to temperance is balance, as evident in the Old English word *temprian*, which means to "bring something into the required condition by mixing it with something else."[30] This is why the process of strengthening a metal is called "tempering." Evenness or balance brought about through mixing diverse elements can be seen in many spheres: the truth spoken in love, vegetation that flourishes in receiving both sun and rain, the one-flesh relationship formed by the marriage of a man and a woman, or the distinct satisfaction of a salty snack chased down by a sweet beverage.

Temprian is derived from the Latin *temperare*, which means to "observe proper measure, be moderate, restrain oneself" or to "mix correctly, mix in due proportion; regulate, rule, govern, manage." This word, in turn, may come from another root, *tempus*, from which we get the word *temporal*, related to time and seasons.[31] (Interestingly, the original meaning of *tempus* is likely "stretch" or "measure." From this comes the word *temple*, a space made sacred by being marked out and marked off.[32])

The motif of time, or tempo, is prominent in *The Great Gatsby* and echoes throughout the novel in several ways. First, tempo characterizes the language of the novel, language sometimes effusive, sometimes economic, often delivered in measured beats that achieve powerful effect. Similarly, heavy use of symbolism compresses time by packing much meaning into few words. Tempo is at play, too, in the many polarities of the novel: ideal and real, myth and truth, hero and anti-hero, the upper and working classes, old money and nouveau riche, East Egg and West Egg, the Old World of Europe and the New World of America, the American Dream as materialist and the American Dream as transcendent, the American West and the American East. The failure of the characters to harmonize the tensions within these pairings is part of what destroys everyone caught between them.

Probably the most significant of these polarities is past and present. The sense of time is, in fact, a prominent theme in the novel, as seen in one of its most famous lines, which occurs when Nick tries to temper Gatsby's expectations regarding his reunion with Daisy:

> "I wouldn't ask too much of her," I ventured. "You can't repeat the past."
> "Can't repeat the past?" he cried incredulously. "Why of course you can!"[33]

The novel makes many such explicit references to time. Gatsby talks of the past often, Nick says, observing Gatsby's longing for something passed: "I gathered that he wanted to recover something, some idea of himself."[34] Gatsby is "never quite still; there was always a tapping foot somewhere or the impatient opening and closing of a hand."[35] Nick feels the oppressive weight of time when he says that the "relentless beating heat was beginning to confuse me."[36] And, of course, the novel's last line closes on this theme: "So we beat on, boats against the current, borne back ceaselessly into the past."[37]

Self-Improvement

But time is not on Gatsby's side. This is the story of time running out. When Gatsby dies, a scant few attend his funeral. One person who does show up is Gatsby's father. He shows Nick an old book Gatsby had as a boy.

> He opened it at the back cover and turned it around for me to see. On the last fly-leaf was printed the word *Schedule*, and the date September 12, 1906, and underneath:

Rise from bed	6.00	A.M.
Dumbbell exercise and wall-scaling	6.15–6.30	"
Study electricity, etc	7.15–8.15	"
Work	8.30–4.30	P.M.
Baseball and sports	4.30–5.00	"
Practice elocution, poise and how to attain it. . .	5.00–6.00	"
Study needed inventions	7.00–9.00	"

GENERAL RESOLVES

No wasting time at Shafters or [a name, indecipherable]
No more smokeing or chewing
Bath every other day
Read one improving book or magazine per week
Save $5.00 [crossed out] $3.00 per week
Be better to parents

Gatsby's father says he found the book by accident. "It just shows you," he explains to Nick, "Jimmy was bound to get ahead. He always had some resolves like this or something."[38]

This notion of self-improvement is woven deeply into the fabric of American culture, beginning with the arrival of the Pilgrims and their Puritan work ethic. It advanced with Benjamin Franklin's famous program of "moral perfection" that he began at age twenty and continued through most of his life. In his autobiography, Franklin explains, "I wish'd to live without committing any fault at any time; I would conquer all that either natural inclination, custom, or company might lead me into. As I knew, or thought I knew, what was right and wrong, I did not see why I might not always do the one and avoid the other."[39] Franklin lists thirteen moral virtues with brief descriptions. First on his list is temperance: "Eat not to dullness; drink not to elevation."[40] Franklin's plan was to work on each virtue, one week at a time, and improve in each area over the course of his life. Born poor and receiving little formal education, yet becoming one of the most respected intellectuals of his time, Franklin is perhaps the best success story for the school of self-improvement.

For the Puritans, virtue could not exist apart from God—specifically, faith in Christ. For Franklin, Christ was not so much a source as an example worthy of emulation, no different from Socrates. By the time we get to Gatsby, God—or religion or faith—is utterly effaced, replaced by the gods of materialism and self. The source, motive, and goal for Gatsby's virtue is himself. Even attainment of Daisy is less about her than it is about him. Indeed, Gatsby does not even seek the real Daisy, but merely a fantasy of her.

Fantasy Not Reality

Gatsby has been obsessed for five years with winning Daisy back. (The fact that she is married does not factor into his thinking. She is not married to one of his friends, after all.) He has read the newspaper faithfully for years in hopes of coming across Daisy's name. Gatsby's lavish home, outrageous parties, and ostentatious lifestyle are all to fulfill the fantasy Gatsby has for their eventual reunion. But Gatsby loves an ideal, not a woman. He loves an idea—winning the prize that to him symbolizes the attainment of his dreams—not flesh and blood. Daisy is for Gatsby like the volumes of books that fill his library shelves: with pages uncut and unread, their value is in what they symbolize, not what they are. Gatsby's vision of Daisy, and of love and life itself, is disconnected from reality. This disconnect began in his youth, when his sense of shame over his "shiftless and unsuccessful" parents inspired a revisioning of himself and his own origins, and "to this conception he was faithful to the end."[41]

Daisy is for Gatsby like the volumes of books that fill his library shelves: with pages uncut and unread, their value is in what they symbolize, not what they are.

Gatsby's faithfulness to this false vision continues through and beyond his faltering reunion with Daisy. His desire has been for something that does not even exist, and he has no taste for what really does exist. It's significant that when they meet for the first time all these years later and she puts her real arm through his, Gatsby cannot enjoy the connection. Instead, he is "absorbed in what he had just said." Not surprisingly, his long-anticipated reunion with Daisy is a devastating letdown. After Daisy leaves, Nick reports,

> As I went over to say good-by I saw that the expression of bewilderment had come back into Gatsby's face, as though a faint doubt had occurred to him as to the quality of his present happiness. Almost five years! There must have been moments even that afternoon when Daisy tumbled short

> of his dreams—not through her own fault, but because of the colossal vitality of his illusion. It had gone beyond her, beyond everything. He had thrown himself into it with a creative passion, adding to it all the time, decking it out with every bright feather that drifted his way.[42]

Daisy, a flat, two-dimensional character, becomes a canvas upon which Gatsby paints the false visions of his imagination. The real presence of Daisy shatters "the colossal significance" of the symbol of her—the green light at the end of her dock, situated across the sound from the mansion Gatsby bought precisely so he could gaze at her dwelling place. That symbol has "now vanished forever." Gatsby's "count of enchanted objects had diminished by one,"[43] for intemperance is "a disease of the imagination."[44]

Like Gatsby, Daisy is materialistic, although she is cut from different fabric. She is as ungrounded in anything substantial or real as Gatsby is. Nick's first sight of Daisy, accompanied by her friend Jordan Baker (soon to be Nick's lover), captures her ethereal fairy nature: "The only completely stationary object in the room was an enormous couch on which two young women were buoyed up as though upon an anchored balloon. They were both in white, and their dresses were rippling and fluttering as if they had just been blown back in after a short flight around the house."[45] Daisy's shallowness culminates in one of the novel's most famous passages, which takes place when Gatsby takes her for the first time on a tour of his magnificent home, purchased and outfitted for the sole purpose of someday winning her back. When Gatsby and Daisy, accompanied by Nick, arrive finally at Gatsby's bedroom, Gatsby throws open two cabinet doors:

His desire has been for something that does not even exist, and he has no taste for what really does exist.

> He took out a pile of shirts and began throwing them, one by one, before us, shirts of sheer linen and thick silk and fine flannel, . . . and the soft rich heap mounted higher—shirts with stripes and scrolls and plaids in coral and apple-green and lavender and faint orange, and monograms of Indian

> blue. Suddenly, with a strained sound, Daisy bent her head into the shirts and began to cry stormily.[46]

Daisy's response is odd for two lovers reunited at last in the bedroom. But it is fitting for someone consumed by materialism: "'They're such beautiful shirts,' she sobbed, her voice muffled in the thick folds. 'It makes me sad because I've never seen such—such beautiful shirts before.'"[47] This image—of Gatsby carelessly throwing his costly shirts into the air and Daisy clutching at them in ecstasy (material rather than spiritual in origin)—is as inevitable as it is startling.

Daisy's response to the shirts can be understood in terms offered by Guy Debord in *Society of the Spectacle.* Consumerism has created a society, Debord argues, in which appearance has replaced both being and having.[48] "The satisfaction which no longer comes from the use of abundant commodities is now sought in the recognition of their value as commodities," Debord explains. Consequently, "the consumer is filled with waves of religious fervor for the sovereign liberty of the commodities."[49] Daisy's ecstatic worship of the shirts reflects a society in which commodities have become god.

The God of Consumerism

This false, modern American god is displayed in the novel as leering over the aptly named "Valley of Ashes" in the form of a billboard bearing the spectacled eyes of Dr. T. J. Eckleburg. Notably, not long before the time in which the novel is set, prior to the rise of consumerist capitalism, such a garish sign would have been scorned as the stuff of "circuses and P. T. Barnum hokum."[50] The symbolic connection of the billboard to God becomes explicit after Daisy accidentally strikes and kills her husband's mistress with Gatsby's car. The dead woman's distraught husband, George Wilson, says to his friend Michaelis, about Daisy,

> "I told her she might fool me but she couldn't fool God. I took her to the window"—with an effort he got up and walked to the rear window and

> leaned with his face pressed against it—"and I said 'God knows what you've been doing, everything you've been doing. You may fool me, but you can't fool God!'"

As he speaks, Wilson is "looking at the eyes of Doctor T. J. Eckleburg."[51] But while the "God" of Gatsby's world sees, he does not act. Therefore, Wilson takes justice into his own hands. Repeating "God sees everything," Wilson draws a false conclusion based on what he himself sees and takes Gatsby's life—and, in the process, his own.

How the Story Is Told

While Henry Fielding's conception of God in *The History of Tom Jones, a Foundling* is reflected by an omniscient and authoritative narrator, the narrator of *The Great Gatsby* embodies a modern worldview that cannot conceive of a God who acts and intervenes in human affairs. The paradox is that even a view of God as impersonal and distant affects the course of human affairs, a paradox reflected in the way that the unreliable, passively observant narrator Nick Carraway changes the course of the story.

Unlike God, Nick does not see everything. Moreover, he cannot even be trusted to report what he does see. For good reporting requires good judgment, and Nick refrains from judging. The novel opens on this very point, with Nick confessing that his father cautioned him against being too quick to criticize others. As a result, Nick is "inclined to reserve all judgments." This "habit" of withholding judgment has made him the confidante of people's "secret griefs," of the sort that were told to him by Jay Gatsby.[52]

Nick assumes the posture of an innocent observer who reserves judgment, but beginning this story in this way cues the reader to withhold trust—for how can trust be given to one who will not judge?

Furthermore, the mere presence of a witness can change the course of events. This idea is illustrated in the *observer effect*, a component of the study of physics, which suggests that the mere act of observing a phenomenon changes that phenomenon. As we've seen, Nick's presence as an observer alters the events of Gatsby's life (and with that, the lives of others). This is just one layer of the effect that the "passive observer" has on Gatsby's life. But another layer is added when Nick returns to the scene, so to speak, years later in order to tell Gatsby's story. Nick becomes a witness to Gatsby's life in two ways: first, in being present during the events of the story, and, second, in testifying to what he has observed.

The narrative demonstrates Nick's active effect on the story—even in his passive way—in a subtle scene at the end of the novel. When Nick returns to the vacant mansion sometime after Gatsby's death, he reports, "On the white steps an obscene word, scrawled by some boy with a piece of brick, stood out clearly in the moonlight, and I erased it, drawing my shoe raspingly along the stone."[53] Nick's act of erasure is a reminder that every telling of every story requires judgments, choices of what to leave in, what to leave out, what best to remember, and what best to forget. In showing us Nick's choice to erase the insult to Gatsby, the novel reminds us that we too are unreliable narrators of our own stories. And therefore the judgments made by our own limited perspectives must be tempered against the all-seeing eyes of God.

"Sydney's Sacrifice"

Chapter three

Justice

A TALE OF TWO CITIES

by Charles Dickens

Do horses run on the rocky crags?
  Does one plow the sea with oxen?
But you have turned justice into poison
  and the fruit of righteousness into bitterness.

—Amos 6:12

One of the most startling things I heard someone say was, "My grandmother was a slave."

The person speaking was a minister and friend, older than me, but not *old*. I did the math quickly in my head and realized that slavery in America is not ancient history after all. It isn't even history. I certainly didn't consider my own grandmother—who was very much alive at the time of this conversation and lived another twenty-five or thirty years more—to be history. I couldn't imagine *my* grandmother being a slave. I recognized how directly and profoundly my life, habits, and worldview had been shaped by her, and how different my own understanding and experience would be, in turn, if her life had been as radically different as the life of a slave. Everything about my own life would be different. I was struck by the truth of William Faulkner's famous words, "The past isn't dead. It's not even past."[1] When we are born into a community, we are shaped by that community's past as much as its present.

Justice and Community

Justice is the morality of the community. The morality of a community shapes individual thinking, values, and behavior. Aristotle calls justice "anything just that tends to produce or preserve happiness and its constituents for the community of a city."[2] In *The Republic,* Plato says that virtue in an individual is "a certain health, beauty, and good condition of a soul."[3] Justice, therefore, can be understood as the virtue of a community, the harmony of all the souls that form it.

But although justice is enacted in community, each community is made up of individuals who together make a society just or unjust. The just society is the one that frees people to do good. In other words, a just society allows all of its members to cultivate the virtue of justice, for even individual ethics "are much affected by the ethos" of the community in which one lives.[4]

The virtue of justice is the habit of desiring and doing what is just.[5] In "As Kingfishers Catch Fire," poet Gerard Manley Hopkins says, simply, "the just man justices."[6] At first glance, these definitions seem circular, saying, in essence, *the just person is just*. Yet it echoes the wisdom of one of the twentieth century's great philosophers, Forrest Gump's mother, who advised her mentally challenged son, "Stupid is as stupid does." Justice is, in this sense, its own measure.

But justice also takes its measure from the relationship of one thing to another. In *On Beauty and Being Just*, Elaine Scarry defines justice as "a symmetry of everyone's relations to each other."[7] Justice is "an absolute good in itself" and is the measure of the other virtues since prudence, courage, and temperance can be virtuous only when oriented toward just ends.[8] All external acts are socially consequential and therefore connected to justice in some way.[9] Indeed, justice is "the whole of virtue," according to Aristotle. The most excellent person, Aristotle says, is the one whose virtue is perfected in relationship to others, and justice is always expressed "in relation to another person."[10] Justice is the mean between selfishness and selflessness. That mean has implications within political, economic, social, and racial realms, just as it has implications for the inner life of the soul. Justice orders a person within herself as well as the lives of people together.[11]

Justice is the mean between selfishness and selflessness.

Two Unjust Cities

Charles Dickens's masterpiece *A Tale of Two Cities* is the terrifying story of what happens to individuals, communities, and nations when injustice reigns. It has been said that *A Tale of Two Cities* is a story without a villain. Some say that history itself is the villain. But there is a villain in the story that is not confined to past events, a villain ever present in human affairs: the vice of excess.

A Tale of Two Cities is a story of extremes and of the havoc wreaked by such extremes, as the famous opening lines suggest: "It was the best of times, it was the worst of times, it was the age of wisdom, it was the age of foolishness, it was the epoch of belief, it was the epoch of incredulity, it was the season of Light, it was the season of Darkness, it was the spring of hope, it was the winter of despair, we had everything before us, we had nothing before us, we were all going direct to Heaven, we were all going direct the other way."[12] In other words, it was an age of polar extremes.

Excess, the novel shows, was both cause and symptom of the perilousness of the times. It was an age of superlatives, of disproportion, of absolutes, and of absolute power. Absolute power by its very nature is unjust,[13] for it lacks the relational proportionality that defines justice. Set in a time so full of injustice, *A Tale of Two Cities* dramatizes the horrible consequences that attend justice too long delayed.

The two cities of the title are London and Paris. Each in its own way is unjust, but the point offered by Dickens the Englishman to his contemporaries, writing a century after the book's events, is that his own country is not immune to those graver injustices perpetrated by a rival country during the previous age. In other words, the novel serves as a warning against injustice.

The daily life of London in 1775, when the novel opens, is riddled with theft and murder; not even the nobility or the mayor are safe. Just as they will in France later in the story, mobs rule here both outside the jails and in. The infamous Newgate prison, rather than being an instrument of justice, is a breeding ground for "debauchery and villainy" and "dire diseases," a place from which "pale travellers set out continually, in carts and coaches, on a violent passage into the other world," many waylaid first at the pillory or the whipping post.[14] But the ultimate punishment—death—is doled out to criminals like burnt porridge in a charity school. It is "a recipe much in vogue," and hundreds of crimes are capital offenses: the forger, the bad-check writer, the purloiner, the horse thief, the counterfeiter—all these were punished by death.[15] The hangman is "ever busy, . . . now stringing up long rows of miscellaneous criminals; now, hanging a housebreaker on Saturday who had been taken on Tuesday; now, burning people in the hand at Newgate by the dozen, and now burning pamphlets at the door of Westminster Hall; to-day, taking the life of an atrocious murderer, and to-morrow of a wretched pilferer who had robbed a farmer's boy of sixpence."[16] Yet such extreme penalties do not even serve as a deterrent to crime. Indeed, "the fact was exactly the reverse."[17]

In between crime and punishment, the court—the place that is supposed both to symbolize and to actually be the seat of justice—offers little hope. Jerry Cruncher, a messenger by day and grave robber by night, learns that one particular day's docket concerns treason and ponders the punishment that will follow:

> "That's quartering," said Jerry. "Barbarous!"
>
> "It is the law," remarked the ancient clerk, turning his surprised spectacles upon him. "It is the law."
>
> "It's hard in the law to spile a man, I think. It's hard enough to kill him, but it's very hard to spile him, sir."
>
> "Not at all," returned the ancient clerk. "Speak well of the law. Take care of your chest and voice, my good friend, and leave the law to take care of itself. I give you that advice."[18]

Here the clerk voices an unquestioning view of the law as always just. But as the story (along with history) proves, the law that is supposed to be just is not always so. Moreover, Cruncher's objection here to "spiling" a man over and above killing him (the term could refer to spoiling his body or spilling his innards—or both—through quartering, which was legal in England until 1870) may not be entirely selfless: Cruncher moonlights as a body snatcher who sells body parts for medical study. The impossibility of pure disinterestedness is why justice is considered the hardest virtue to attain and why Aristotle declared (naively, I think we moderns must say) that the law, not individuals, is justice and that just individuals must obey it.[19] It is also why Augustine, more wisely, says that "a law that is not just does not seem to me to be a law."[20]

Echoing Augustine's famous dictum that an unjust law is no law at all, Martin Luther King Jr. in "Letter from a Birmingham Jail" further defined an unjust law: "How does one determine whether a law is just or unjust? A just law is a man made code that squares with the moral law or the law of God. An unjust law is a code that is out of harmony with the moral law. To put it in the terms of St. Thomas Aquinas [also drawing from Augustine]: An unjust law is a human law that is not rooted in eternal law and natural law. Any law that uplifts human personality is just. Any law that degrades human personality is unjust."[21]

In 1780, Dickens's London court is trying Charles Darnay, a Frenchman, for spying for France. Darnay is an emigrant from France, and the crime he is being tried for—treason—attracts great interest because of the severity of both the crime and its punishment upon a verdict of guilty: "He'll be drawn on a hurdle to be half hanged, and then he'll be taken down and sliced before his own face, and then his inside will be taken out and burnt while he looks on, and then his head will be chopped off, and he'll be cut into quarters," explains one observer eagerly, adding that a guilty verdict is certain.[22] Darnay is innocent of the crime, but the jury is eager for blood. Indeed, many of the spectators have paid for admission. When the justice system becomes a form of entertainment, it surely is unjust. This is as true of the ancient Roman coliseum as it is of twentieth-century American public lynchings and of today's trials by public shaming on social media.

When the justice system becomes a form of entertainment, it surely is unjust.

Darnay is unexpectedly acquitted, however, when his positive identification comes into question because of a man seated in the court who looks just like him. This man, Sydney Carton, years later will save Darnay's life again.

But this is a tale of two cities, not one. The injustices taking place across the English Channel in Paris differ in style but not substance, in degree but not kind. Just as in England, France "entertained herself" with excessive, brutal injustice, such as "sentencing a youth to have his hands cut off, his tongue torn out with pincers, and his body burned alive, because he had not kneeled down in the rain to do honour to a dirty procession of monks which passed within his view, at a distance of some fifty or sixty yards."[23]

While it is likely a fiction that Marie Antoinette said of the starving peasants, "Let them eat cake!" Dickens's own fiction captures the truth of this pervasive and perverse sentiment of the nobility in an exquisite chapter titled, "The Monseigneur in Town." It was supposed to be the role of the noble class to serve as justices of the peace, but this Monseigneur cares nothing about justice:

> Monseigneur had one truly noble idea of general public business, which was, to let everything go on in its own way; of particular public business, Monseigneur had the other truly noble idea that it must all go his way—tend to his own power and pocket. Of his pleasures, general and particular, Monseigneur had the other truly noble idea, that the world was made for them. The text of his order (altered from the original by only a pronoun, which is not much) ran: "The earth and the fulness thereof are mine, saith Monseigneur."[24]

When the Monseigneur arrives in the country, he passes a burial ground where a peasant woman grieving her husband's death stops the carriage. She begs him,

> "Monseigneur, hear me! Monseigneur, hear my petition! My husband died of want; so many die of want; so many more will die of want."
>
> "Again, well? Can I feed them?"
>
> "Monseigneur, the good God knows; but I don't ask it. My petition is, that a morsel of stone or wood, with my husband's name, may be placed over him to show where he lies. Otherwise, the place will be quickly forgotten, it will never be found when I am dead of the same malady, I shall be laid under some other heap of poor grass. Monseigneur, they are so many, they increase so fast, there is so much want."[25]

But the Monseigneur has already driven on.

The nobility allows the wheels of injustice to roll, rather literally, right over the peasants when the villainous Marquis St. Evrémonde strikes and kills a child while speeding his carriage recklessly through town. Stopped by the crowd that feebly attempts to retaliate, his response is utterly inhumane: "'You dogs!' said the Marquis, but smoothly, and with an unchanged front, except as to the spots on his nose: 'I would ride over any of you very willingly, and exterminate you from the earth. If I knew which rascal threw at the carriage, and if that brigand were sufficiently near it, he should be crushed under the wheels.'"[26]

Such cruelty and injustice are so pervasive, so systemic, so expected by the peasants that it is taken as a matter of course, despite their useless outrage. "So cowed was their condition," the narrator explains, "and so long and hard their experience of what such a man could do to them, within the law and beyond it, that not a voice, or a hand, or even an eye was raised. Among the men, not one." Only one—a woman—dares to look the Marquis in the face. "It was not for his dignity to notice it," however, and "his contemptuous eyes passed over her, and over all the other rats; and he leaned back in his seat again, and gave the word 'Go on!'"[27]

Incredibly, the Marquis is even more depraved than this scene reveals. Peel back the layers of injustice, one wrong followed by another and another, and at the center one usually finds the original wound, long forgotten. At the very center of the layers of injustice in *A Tale of Two Cities*—the catalyst from which all its events and relationships emerge—is the brutal and fatal rape of a young peasant woman, perpetrated by the Marquis's brother—the father of Charles Darnay, who is husband to the novel's heroine, Lucie.

A Spiral of Injustice

Making the central event of the novel a brutal rape that occurs years before the story opens is a significant artistic move in a number of ways. First, it is counterintuitive for a work and writer so quintessentially Victorian—an era widely regarded for its prudish and repressed attitude toward sexuality. Despite being veiled by subtle narrative devices, this event forms symbolically and structurally a spiral of injustice. In terms of plot, the rape takes the life first of the victim, then of her husband and her brother; afterward, it destroys the family of the perpetrator; then the victim's sister grows up to take murderous revenge on countless others as part of the counterrevolution.

Furthermore, the fatal rape of a peasant woman by a member of the *ancien regime* is symbolically significant within the context of the French Revolution, as well as within the larger theme of justice as a virtue. For this horrific rape and its consequences illustrate how all injustice works: the injustice of one person against another cannot be contained. Injustice, no matter how seemingly private, always has public consequences. The masses would soon revolt against such depraved excesses and achieve excesses of their own in the Reign of Terror that began in 1793.

The vice that opposes the virtue of justice is anger. Anger in and of itself is not wrong, of course. The Bible tells us to "be angry and do not sin" (Eph. 4:26 ESV), making clear that anger itself is not sin. But excessive anger distorts justice, turning it into vengeance.

A Tale of Two Cities personifies the spirit of vengeance fueling the Terror in the character of Madame Defarge, who, along with her close ally (nicknamed, fittingly, The Vengeance), furiously weaves into her knitting the names of all those destined for execution at the hands of the mob. The mob "stopped at nothing," the story says, "and was a monster much dreaded."[28] Like the fatal overcorrection of a wayward car, the revolutionaries, so long oppressed, prove more unjust than those who had wronged them: "The men were terrible, in the bloody-minded anger with which they looked from windows, caught up what arms they had, and came pouring down into the streets; but, the women were a sight to chill the boldest. From such household occupations as their bare poverty yielded, from their children, from their aged and their sick crouching on the bare ground famished and naked, they ran out with streaming hair, urging one another, and themselves, to madness with the wildest cries and actions."[29]

Injustice, no matter how seemingly private, always has public consequences.

The mobs murder those in power who they have determined—or suspect or imagine or do not even imagine—have committed wrongs against the people. The nobleman Foulon, who has told the starving peasants to eat grass, becomes a particular target of the mob's vengeance. When word comes that they have at last taken him and he is still alive, the crowds echo a vicious refrain: "Give us the blood of Foulon, Give us the head of Foulon, Give us the heart of Foulon, Give us the body and soul of Foulon, Rend Foulon to pieces, and dig him into the ground, that grass may grow from him!"[30]

Dickens's brilliant prose mimics the relentless rhythms of the crowd's cries and the brutal images of the mob possessed by the energy and power that fuel their vengeance, carrying the reader along vicariously within the chaos wreaked by injustice:

> Down, and up, and head foremost on the steps of the building; now, on his knees; now, on his feet; now, on his back; dragged, and struck at, and stifled by the bunches of grass and straw that were thrust into his face by hundreds of hands; torn, bruised, panting, bleeding, yet always entreating and beseeching for mercy; now full of vehement agony of action, with a small clear space about him as the people drew one another back that they might see; now, a log of dead wood drawn through a forest of legs; he was hauled to the nearest street corner where one of the fatal lamps swung . . . the women passionately screeching at him all the time, and the men sternly calling out to have him killed with grass in his mouth. Once, he went aloft, and the rope broke, and they caught him shrieking; twice, he went aloft, and the rope broke, and they caught him shrieking; then, the rope was merciful, and held him, and his head was soon upon a pike, with grass enough in the mouth for all Saint Antoine to dance at the sight of.[31]

The mob's treatment of prisoners defies rhyme and reason. Some arrested are freed only to be capriciously hacked to bits as they leave. One prisoner is released only to be stabbed on his way out, then helped by folks sitting atop the bodies of their murdered victims. It's "an inconsistency as monstrous as anything in this awful nightmare."[32] Over four days, eleven hundred prisoners—which include men and women and children—are killed by the mobs.[33]

Yet this is the crucial point that the narrative makes clear: there "could have been no such Revolution if all laws, forms, and ceremonies, had not first been so monstrously abused, that the suicidal vengeance of the

Revolution was to scatter them all to the winds."[34] It is not mere injustice that brought about the Revolution, but excessive, inhumane, and prolonged injustice. As Martin Luther King Jr. would exclaim a century later, in response to the societal admonition to "wait" longer for justice: "There comes a time when the cup of endurance runs over, and men are no longer willing to be plunged into the abyss of despair."[35]

An Abyss of Despair

The justice system in eighteenth-century France was such an abyss of despair, in fact, that the implementation of the guillotine as a form of execution near the start of the Revolution was considered more humane than former methods, which included hanging, burning, boiling, dismemberment, the breaking wheel, and decapitation by sword. Indeed, the guillotine was viewed as such a "modern" method of execution that it was used in France until 1977. *A Tale of Two Cities* shows, however, that merely implementing a kinder, gentler method to execute an unjust sentence is but a faux mercy.

> "There comes a time when the cup of endurance runs over, and men are no longer willing to be plunged into the abyss of despair."

Dickens indicts his own nation of England, as well, despite its veneer of greater civility. The English mobs that open the novel foreshadow the Terror that comes to France. In England, public trials and executions had become, as noted above, a national form of barbaric entertainment. Not coincidentally, many of the first penal reforms in England, begun just before and during Dickens's lifetime, were led by Christians. Christians were among the first to question widespread application of the death penalty as well as its treatment as a form of public entertainment. Dickens himself contributed to a developing consciousness of the depravity of such excessive punishment and the injustices that cultivated the criminal element in the underclass. Dickens feared that unchecked injustice in nineteenth-century England might re-create what unchecked injustice in France in the previous century had led to, and *A Tale of Two Cities* was his warning call.[36]

The novel's vision exposes the truth that prolonged systemic injustice inevitably bears the bitter fruit of violence. The gothic obsession with blood and violence in *A Tale of Two Cities* sets it apart from Dickens's other work (and is one reason some critics consider it inferior) but is central to its message. The excessive vengeance that feeds the guillotine, for example, takes on such life in the narrative that it is almost a character unto itself:

The novel's vision exposes the truth that prolonged systemic injustice inevitably bears the bitter fruit of violence.

> Along the Paris streets, the death-carts rumble, hollow and harsh. Six tumbrels carry the day's wine to La Guillotine. All the devouring and insatiate Monsters imagined since imagination could record itself, are fused in one realization, Guillotine. And yet there is not in France, with its rich variety of soil and climate, a blade, a leaf, a root, a sprig, a peppercorn, which will grow to maturity under conditions more certain than those that have produced this horror. Crush humanity out of shape once more, under similar hammers, and it will twist itself into the same tortured forms. Sow the same seed of rapacious license and oppression over again, and it will surely yield the same fruit according to its kind.[37]

Here is a picture of injustice unleashed upon the world seemingly without limits. The detail is excessive—but that doesn't make it gratuitous. The excess is the point.

Lighthouses in the Dark

Yet even such excessive injustice cannot extinguish the light of goodness. From such a vast and dark ocean of wrong, bright rays shine forth from small towers of fortitude, lighthouses in the dark.

For example, Miss Pross, the quiet, faithful servant of the heroine, Lucie Manette, shows a sudden burst of fierce loyalty and love when the vengeful Madame Defarge puts Lucie in her sights. The habit of love cultivated by Miss Pross, a prim and proper Englishwoman, primes her for a burst of courage, and "on the instinct of the moment," she fights Madame Defarge with all her strength, "with the vigorous tenacity of love, always so much stronger than hate."[38] During the struggle, Pross shoots and kills Madame Defarge. From the blast, Pross hears "first a great crash, and then a great stillness, and that stillness seems to be fixed and unchangeable, never to be broken any more as long as my life lasts."[39] She will never hear again. But she has saved the life of the innocent Lucie, the brightest light in this dark story, and the "golden thread" who weaves the tale and its people together.[40]

If justice is making right, then seeing people rightly is a form of justice. Lucie sees in Sydney Carton what others cannot, finding him deserving of consideration and respect. "I am sure," she says of Carton in a moment of great foreshadowing, that he "is capable of good things, gentle things, even magnanimous things."[41] Yet even Lucie could not have imagined what Carton was capable of.

Carton blesses Lucie for this "sweet compassion" toward him.[42] Yet love and compassion "cannot substitute for justice."[43] Compassion is individual and voluntary. It also has no cost.[44] Justice, on the other hand, exacts a price. Because the world is broken, making what is wrong right is costly. In other words, justice requires sacrifice. For the sake of Lucie, Carton offers his life as sacrifice to the mob that demands the head of Lucie's husband, Charles Darnay, who is guilty only of being born to those who abused their power—power Darnay has long renounced. Blinded by vengeance, the mob cares little about Darnay's innocence.

Moral philosophers suggest that one way to measure one's own virtue in the realm of justice is to ask, "Do you want your community to be better off with you than without you?"[45] Sydney Carton "concludes that the world—and Lucie—need Charles more than him."[46] In a hint of foreshadowing, he confesses to Lucie, "I am like one who died young." He says with regret, "All my life might have been."[47] Yet, in doing for others but not himself, Carton cannot truly be just. His lack of desire for his own flourishing is a vice.

The Virtuous Mean

Justice avoids both selflessness and selfishness. Only when one attains this virtuous mean can one be just within oneself, and within one's community, for justice is about giving everyone his or her due: oneself, others, and God. "Love your neighbor as yourself," Scripture admonishes (Matt. 22:39). Implicit in this command is the idea that one must love oneself and that one cannot love one's neighbor properly without such love. One cannot love one's neighbor properly if one loves oneself too much—or too little. In an important sense, then, the virtue of justice begins with justice toward the self.

If justice is making right, then seeing people rightly is a form of justice.

On the surface, selflessness seems to be an unmitigated good, especially in an age in which selfishness is rampant. Yet the good of selflessness has limits. Consider the instructions given before every airplane takeoff that in the case of an emergency requiring use of an oxygen mask, anyone wanting to assist others must put a mask on oneself first. Taken to the extreme, selflessness is not *less* of self (which is generally good to a point) but the *erasure* of self (which is not good within any understanding of the intrinsic value of each human being).

Plato says that justice is the proper balancing or proportioning of all parts of the soul.[48] The Christian view of the well-ordered soul identifies how to have all parts of the soul in proper order: by first loving God with all one's heart, soul, strength, and mind. Justice concerns the right ordering of not only the relationships within a community but also the parts of a person's soul.

Sydney Carton is self-effacing to a fault. His selflessness is not in proper proportion with healthy self-regard. He loves himself too little and therefore struggles through most of the story to love others well. An underachieving, drunken lawyer, Carton describes himself as "a disappointed drudge"[49] and "a dissolute dog who has never done any good, and never will."[50] He says, "I care for no man on earth, and no man on earth cares for me."[51] Unable to love well with his life, he can love only with his death.

Of course, none of us is capable of perfect justice, even toward ourselves. Carton moves closer to justice by the story's end, not only because of his heroic act but also because of the self-knowledge he gains in the process. The truth about justice in this world is that it can never set things exactly right. We never will, whether on the personal, the public, or the cosmic scale, be able to bring those delicate scales of justice into perfect balance. And in at least two senses, Carton's sacrifice is not just. First, Charles Darnay's arrest, imprisonment, and punishment were never justifiable in the first place. Even willing payment of an unjust penalty doesn't seem just. Carton's sacrifice is not just because Darnay's death sentence, for which Carton substitutes himself, is not just. Second, it is not just to himself because his selflessness is not purely virtuous.

But it is fair.

Fair Justice

Although the words *just* and *fair* are often used interchangeably, justice usually involves objective, universal standards of judgment, while fairness is often felt subjectively as a sense of right proportion within particular circumstances. In a perfect world, what is just is also fair. In a fallen world, however, justice does not always feel fair. In our fallen humanity we often bristle at the holiness of a God whose justice does not always strike us as fair. The parable of the workers in the vineyard, all of whom are paid the same agreed-upon wage although some worked fewer hours, is a perplexing example of this (Matt. 20:1–16). A sacrifice to the injustice of the Reign of Terror, Carton's death is not just, but it is fair in the sense that he chooses it and does so honorably and nobly. In a world devoid of perfect justice, he serves the one he loves and finds redemption in his sacrifice. But Carton's sacrifice is fair in a more significant way that invokes the other sense of the word *fair,* which means not only "right" but also "beautiful."[52]

Both justice and beauty are the expression of proper proportion.

In aesthetics, the perfect proportion is known as the golden ratio or golden mean. Named after a thirteenth-century mathematician, the Fibonacci numbers quantify the ideal ratio between length and width, a proportion found universally in beautiful faces, buildings, and throughout nature on both cosmic and microcosmic scales. The prevalence and consistency of this ratio offers a startling counter to the subjective (and modern) notion that "beauty is in the eye of the beholder." Beauty arises from the unity of the separate parts. A note that sounds off in one song sounds lovely within the context of another. The Victorian settee that looks garish in a beachside cottage is perfectly suited to a turn-of-the-century mansion. The elegant neck of a giraffe would be absurd on a short-legged creature like a dachshund. Justice, likewise, cannot exist apart from the context of the community of people it serves.

Recall Elaine Scarry's definition above of justice as a symmetry of our relations to each other. Symmetry is a factor of both beauty and justice. And while beauty and justice have objective qualities, they must be observed in order to be appreciated and cultivated. Both require, Scarry says, "constant perceptual acuity," and in this way the perception of beauty can assist in the perception and correction of injustice.[53] "It is as though beautiful things have been placed here and there throughout the world to serve as small wake-up calls to perception, spurring lapsed alertness back to its most acute level. Through its beauty, the world continually recommits us to a rigorous standard of perceptual care."[54] A "rigorous standard of perceptual care" is required to seek and uphold justice as well. Moreover, there is not one way of achieving justice any more than there is one way of being beautiful.

Justice requires a proportionate exchange. Carton's act of self-sacrifice transcends mere equity. In this way, Carton's death, while unjust, is beautiful. Likewise, when Christ took his place on the cross for the sake of humanity and paid the price in blood for the sins of the world, it wasn't fair. But through his sacrifice, we are justified, and that is beautiful.

Justice in this world will ever and always be a matter of correcting, balancing—ever progressing (or regressing), never perfected. The injustice my friend's grandmother experienced in being a slave did not end with her life. That injustice forever shaped her children, and her children's children, including my friend. My friend forgives those injustices. But even forgiveness cannot negate the ripple effects of the past. To pretend otherwise is itself a further injustice.

With the endless injustices and causes that overwhelm us today, it's common for us to set these concerns against one another as though one cause must compete against another: we must choose the cause of women or the poor, of religious liberty or the environment. We often think of justice as parcels of land, and we concern ourselves with the size and distribution of its lots.

But justice is less like finite land and more like the wildflowers that grow there, continually spreading as they bloom and re-seed themselves. Justice—like beauty—is rooted in infinity.

Carton's last words as he approaches Madame Guillotine to rest his neck in her eternal embrace are fitting: "I am the Resurrection and the Life, saith the Lord: he that believeth in me, though he were dead, yet shall he live: and whosoever liveth and believeth in me shall never die." Afterward, those who gazed on the spectacle of injustice said of Carton "that it was the peacefullest man's face ever beheld there."[55]

The story closes by describing the vision Carton sees as he mounts the scaffold to satisfy the bloodthirst and undergo the sacrifice that constitutes the greatest love. It is a vision of the beauty of justice not here but yet to come:

> I see a beautiful city and a brilliant people rising from this abyss, and, in their struggles to be truly free, in their triumphs and defeats, through long years to come, I see the evil of this time and of the previous time of which this is the natural birth, gradually making expiation for itself and wearing out. I see the lives for which I lay down my life, peaceful, useful, prosperous and happy. . . . It is a far, far better thing that I do, than I have ever done; it is a far, far better rest that I go to than I have ever known.[56]

"Courageous Jim"

Chapter Four

Courage

THE ADVENTURES OF HUCKLEBERRY FINN

by Mark Twain

Have I not commanded you? Be strong and courageous.
Do not be afraid; do not be discouraged, for the Lord
your God will be with you wherever you go.

—Joshua 1:9

Brave is a word that gets thrown around a lot these days. Pretty much anyone—particularly a woman, it seems—who tells a personal story, changes a view, or bucks a trend (which is itself a trend) is likely to earn the accolade *brave*. Although *bravery* and *courage* are often used synonymously today, the history of the word *brave* has some interesting differences from *courage*. The older meanings of *brave* include some that are far from virtuous: "cutthroat," "villain," "crooked," and "depraved."[1] The current meaning of *brave* is closely allied to the word *bold*, which isn't attached to virtue or vice. Boldness can be bad just as it can be good. In a culture as fragmented as ours, nearly anyone who takes a stand on something can find support somewhere. Right or wrong, anyone who is bold will be considered brave by someone.

Virtuous courage, in contrast, is more than boldness for boldness's sake. Courage is measured not by the risk it entails but by the good it preserves.

The virtue of courage is exemplified in the 2015 news story of three passengers on a high-speed train bound for Paris who subdued a rifle-wielding terrorist on the train just before he attacked. A later interview with one of the heroes, a US National Guardsman, hints that such courage wasn't accidental but rather the result of habits ingrained by military training. "In the beginning it was mostly gut instinct, survival," he explained. "Our training kicked in after the struggle."[2]

Courage is measured not by the risk it entails but by the good it preserves.

The person who is virtuously courageous displays not merely a single act of courage but the habit of courage. Courage—or fortitude, as it is often called—is defined most succinctly by moral philosophers and theologians as the habit that enables a person to face difficulties well.[3] This is a seemingly simple definition, but much is packed into those three terms. What does it mean to "face" something? What makes something "difficult"?

And what does it mean to face a difficulty "well"? Understanding how the virtue of courage is tied to these components points to the difference between it and mere bravery.

Courage and the Heart

The word *courage* comes from the same root word that means "heart." To be encouraged is to be heartened or made stronger. When we exhort a person to "take heart," we mean for her to stand strong and be of good courage. It is noteworthy, too, that we use the word *heart* to signify our desires and passions. When someone says she has "a heart for the poor," for example, it means she has a passion for the good of poor people. When the Bible says, "Where your treasure is, there your heart will be also" (Matt. 6:21), the word *heart,* likewise, suggests passion and desire.

It might seem hard at first to see the connection between courage and desire, but courage, ultimately, demonstrates that one's desires have been rightly ordered to put first things first—even to the point of laying down one's life for something of even greater value. The person who enters a burning building to rescue a child inside values that child's life more than his own. We can see similarly proper ordering even with more mundane acts of courage. A person's great desire to avoid fumbling for words in front of people might be surpassed by her love for the newlywed couple to whom she wishes to offer a toast. One of the most courageous people I know simply got herself out of bed and to work every day (well, almost every day) after her new marriage came to a devastating end, and she would have preferred simply to die rather than go on from day to day. Courage requires putting a greater good before a lesser good. Courage is getting your heart in the right place at the right time despite the obstacles.

Huckleberry Finn is a boy who is all heart. And *Huckleberry Finn* is the story of that boy getting his heart in the right place as he learns to rightly order his desires.

Huck doesn't start out courageous. In fact, poor Huck begins his story as a forlorn, neglected little fellow, a bit of a pushover to his strong-willed pal Tom Sawyer. When the novel opens, Huck has spent much of his short and unfortunate life running from the varied troubles that ceaselessly dog him. Having known only hardship, Huck has no sense of proportion and runs as determinedly from the Widow Douglas's attempts at "sivilizing" him as from the brutal "lickings" he receives at the hands of his drunken and abusive father.[4]

But by the story's end, Huck finds his courage, albeit accidentally, through circumstances that come partly from his own doing and partly from sheer bad luck. In depicting this attainment of virtue through a combination of consequence and coincidence, *Huckleberry Finn* reflects the way life falls out for most of us most of the time: some choices we face are the result of our own doings, others completely outside of our control, most some combination of the two. How much nicer it would be not to face difficulties at all. Given the impossibility of that, the next best thing is to face hard circumstances with the virtue of courage.

Courage requires putting a greater good before a lesser good.

We are introduced to Huck's boyish heart early in the story in a humorous passage that pokes fun at the empty religiosity of Huck's society (a frequent target of Mark Twain's satire). The pharisaical Miss Watson tries to impart religion to Huck in various ways, among them the practice of prayer. Her lessons suggest to Huck (as similar lessons have suggested to many people across the ages) that the purpose of prayer is to get us the things we want. Miss Watson, Huck says, "told me to pray every day, and whatever I asked for I would get it." To his dismay, Huck discovers "it warn't so." Still, Huck doesn't give up, but keeps trying to make prayer work. "Once I got a fish-line, but no hooks. It warn't any good to me without hooks. I tried for the hooks three or four times, but somehow I couldn't make it work," he laments. Finally, he concludes that "if a body can get anything they pray for, why don't Deacon Winn get back the money he lost on pork? Why can't the widow get back her silver snuffbox that was stole? Why can't Miss Watson fat up? No, says I to my self, there ain't nothing in it."[5] It's an amusing picture. But it's also one that resonates for most of us if we're honest. There's a little bit of the prosperity gospel in all of American Christianity, and this has been true ever since the country was founded upon the very idea of that pursuit of happiness we call the American Dream.[6]

The Work of Prayer

After Huck has run away down the river, he concedes that perhaps prayer does work, if only for others and not for him. At this point, Huck has grown terribly hungry, and he remembers that it's customary for searchers to float bread loaded with quicksilver to locate a drowned body (which he is presumed to be). When he soon enough locates some of the bread (and fine-quality bread at that) and eats his fill, it occurs to Huck, "The widow or the parson or somebody prayed that this bread would find me, and here it has gone and done it. So there ain't no doubt but there is something in that thing—that is, there's something in it when a body like the widow or the parson prays, but it don't work for me, and I reckon it don't work for only just the right kind."[7]

Yet despite his grudging admission, Huck still doesn't see that prayer isn't about changing one's circumstance but about changing one's heart. The Widow Douglas had attempted to explain this to Huck after he complained to her that his prayers weren't working. She told him then that "the thing a body could get by praying for it was 'spiritual gifts.'" Huck recalls her explaining to him that "I must help other people, and do everything I could for other people, and look out for them all the time, and never think about myself."[8] In other words, his desire—his heart or courage—must be to put others before himself. Such a thing seems impossible to young Huck. But this effect of prayer is fulfilled by the end of the story.

No Courage in a Mob

The novel's most explicit passage about courage occurs in an abrupt and startling scene that, on the surface, appears to be just one more in a series of adventures with an endless stream of characters briefly introduced into the story and never heard from again. Yet the seriousness of the scene contrasts so sharply with the comedy that characterizes the rest of the story that it stands out in significance.

While traveling with two con men that Huck and Jim (Miss Watson's escaped slave) have, unfortunately, fallen in with, the group stops in a rough-and-tumble town. There a drunken vagabond randomly insults one of the townspeople, and the insulted man simply and suddenly shoots the drunk dead. When the townspeople decide to take justice into their own hands and descend upon the home of the murderer, he emerges from his house, eyes the mob slowly, and issues a startlingly serious and eloquent speech. "The idea of *you* lynching anybody!" he begins. "It's amusing." He continues,

> The idea of you thinking you had pluck enough to lynch a *man*! Because you're brave enough to tar and feather poor friendless cast-out women that come along here, did that make you think you had grit enough to lay your hands on a *man*? Why, a *man's* safe in the hands of ten thousand of your kind—as long as it's daytime and you're not behind him. . . . The average man's a coward. . . . Your newspapers call you a brave people so much that you think you *are* braver than any other people—whereas you're just *as* brave, and no braver. Why don't your juries hang murderers? Because they're afraid the man's friends will shoot them in the back, in the dark—and it's just what they *would* do. So they always acquit; and then a *man* goes in the night, with a hundred masked cowards at his back and lynches the rascal. Your mistake is, that you didn't bring a man with you; that's one mistake, and the other is that you didn't come in the dark and fetch your masks. . . .
>
> You didn't want to come. The average man don't like trouble and danger. *You* don't like trouble and danger. But . . . you're afraid to back down—afraid you'll be found out to be what you are—*cowards*—and so you raise a yell, and hang yourselves on to that half-a-man's coat-tail, and come raging up here, swearing what big things you're going to do. The pitifulest thing out is a mob; that's what an army is a mob; they don't fight with courage that's born in them, but with courage that's borrowed

from their mass, and from their officers. But a mob without any *man* at the head of it is *beneath* pitifulness.[9]

An essential ingredient of courage emerges from this lengthy speech (much shortened here), which is given, ironically, by a cold-blooded murderer. He sees through the outward gall of the men who confront him and sees into their inner cowardice, a cowardice inherent in any mob. The false bravery of a mob doesn't constitute courage because the nature of a mob is one that reduces risk for the individuals that form it. Their "courage" is "borrowed from their mass." No risk means no difficulty. And no difficulty means no courage because, for an act to be truly courageous, it must entail a known risk or potential loss.[10]

I am writing this chapter, coincidentally, one day after a small mob—fifty members of the Ku Klux Klan—held a demonstration not an hour from my home. Wearing the exhausted robes and depleted sentiments of a barbaric past, the mob ranted and raved for forty-five minutes within the confines of a fenced-off area, under police protection, surrounded by a thousand counterprotesters and swarms of cameras and journalists. (Six weeks later, a larger mob returned, and by the time they were dispersed, one of them had driven his car into the crowd of counterprotesters, killing one and injuring many others.)

In contrast to this scene of mob cowardice, two years before, a lone woman wearing climbing gear and a helmet scaled a thirty-foot flagpole at her state capitol and carried down the flag symbolizing the state's racist past. Upon returning to the ground, the courageous Bree Newsome surrendered—willingly, head held high—to the authorities waiting to arrest her.

Courage exists only in relationship to something other than itself. Courage cannot "trust itself"[11] but must refer to some outside, objective standard of goodness. A brave act must be for a noble end in order to constitute the virtue of courage. Aristotle says that "it is for the sake of what is noble that the courageous person stands his ground."[12] An act of daring committed for an ignoble purpose may be bold, but it's not truly courageous. It may, in fact, be worse. Ambrose says that "fortitude without justice is the source of wickedness."[13] Such acts cannot be considered virtuous and therefore are not acts of courage. Courage must always be connected to a just end.

Courage Allied to Justice

The shenanigans of the imposter Duke and King, the two con men that take up with Huck and Jim on the river, prove the wisdom of the ancients in linking courage to justice. The imposters display ample boldness as they pretend to be European royalty, Shakespearean actors, and long-lost heirs to a recently executed will. But gall is not the same as courage. Men who swindle, cheat, and steal their way through life, no matter how brazenly, are far from virtuous, and therefore do not have virtuous courage. Their absurd and immoral antics show perfectly how chutzpah unconnected to justice results only in evil: in this case, the sale of Jim back into captivity.

Because courage is always connected to justice, and because justice is judged by reason, philosophers refer to courage as "a work of reason."[14] Reason is part of knowing what constitutes the good. Taking a risk isn't virtuous if done merely out of inclination without intending some good. Not only is the ability to reason necessary in establishing what is just, but it is also the faculty that produces fear in a dangerous situation. Reason recognizes and acknowledges risk. To ignore or overlook potential harm is unreasonable, mere recklessness or foolishness. This is why courage, as the famous aphorism says, does not mean an absence of fear. In fact, if courage entails facing difficulties well, then the presence of fear adds to the difficulty. As Starbuck in *Moby-Dick* tells his ship's crew, "I will have no man in my boat who is not afraid of a whale."[15]

Thus not all boldness can be counted as the virtue of courage. A toddler who plunges into traffic after a wayward ball, unaware of the danger, isn't displaying courage. But the man who gasps and races into the street to push the child away from an oncoming vehicle is. Fear comes from the awareness of a vulnerability or potential loss. Aristotle puts it this way: "So the courageous person is the one who endures and fears—and likewise is confident about—the right things, for the right reason, in the right way, and at the right time; for the courageous person feels and acts in accordance with the merits of the case, and as reason requires."[16] One must be vulnerable to suffering some kind of injury in order to be considered courageous.[17] If facing difficulty were the only thing required of courage, then all a would-be hero would have to do is create obstacles to overcome, and voilà!—courage would be born. This is exactly what the lovable but foolish Tom Sawyer does in "helping" Huck release the captive Jim.

Freeing Jim from the cabin where he is imprisoned certainly requires risk on the part of the two boys. But rather than minimize the risk, Tom, his head full of ludicrous tales from his steady diet of pulp fiction, does all he can to increase it, thereby to increase the sense of adventure. When Huck proposes slipping off with the keys to unlock Jim after everyone in the house has gone to sleep, Tom protests that while that plan would work, "it's too blame' simple; there ain't nothing *to* it. What's the good of a plan that ain't no more trouble than that?" Instead Tom proposes a plan that would, Huck says, "make Jim just as free a man as mine would, and maybe get us all killed besides."[18] Tom's plan involves the staples of the most sensational stories a boy might read: saws, trenches, rope ladders, notes written in blood, and flowers watered with tears. "You got to invent *all* the difficulties," Tom explains.[19] Such comedy is what makes the tales of Huck and Tom delightful and entertaining, as well as instructive.

Lest it create other and future dangers, courage must confront evil with moderation, "restraining fear and moderating acts of daring."[20] Moderation is exactly what Tom lacks. The necessity of moderation for true courage is borne out by the story. While the boys do manage, barely, to free Jim and run away from his captor, Tom's romantic insistence on increasing the level of adventure—and therefore the risk—brings its natural consequences when Tom is shot in the leg during their escape. Courage can be excellent only as it is "'informed' by prudence."[21] The truly courageous person "does not suffer injury for its own sake."[22] Courage "has nothing to do with a purely vital, blind, exuberant daredevil spirit." The person "who recklessly and indiscriminately courts any kind of danger is not for that reason brave; all he proves is that . . . he considers all manner of things more valuable than the personal intactness he risks for their sake."[23]

It all ends well for Huck, Jim, and Tom, despite Tom's bravado, which turns out to be—like the Duke and King's staging of Shakespeare—merely bad acting. Only after risking his friends' lives as well as his own does Tom finally admit what he has known all along: Jim has been a free man all this time. Miss Watson, who had died two months before, set him free in her will.

> Lest it create other and future dangers, courage must confront evil with moderation.

However, before all this is revealed, things are well on their way to going wrong. And in the midst of the near disaster, Jim shows himself to be the most courageous character in the book, facing difficulty well, with both prudence and moderation in pursuit of the good.

The Courage of the Runaway Slave

Jim's kindness and loyalty to Huck are on display from the story's beginning, even when so much is at stake for Jim as he seeks freedom for the sake of his family. Jim exhibits the virtue of courage throughout, but the fortitude he shows at the end of the story illustrates particularly well one of the essential qualities of courage: endurance.

Some readers interpret Jim's passivity through most of the story as the portrayal of a stereotypical "Uncle Tom." He endures the corrupt Duke and Dauphin, who commandeer the raft and put both Huck and Jim in harm's way. He submits to Tom's quixotic plans for his escape. Of course, Jim doesn't have much other choice in these situations. So he endures. Such endurance is necessary for courage: "Enduring comprises a strong activity of the soul, namely a vigorous grasping and clinging to the good; and only from this stout-hearted activity can the strength to support the physical and spiritual suffering of injury and death be nourished."[24]

But upon Tom's being shot during Jim's escape, Jim emerges out of hiding in order to save him—believing that this will surely mean giving up his freedom. Recognizing the risk and facing it for a greater good—a boy's life rather than his own freedom—Jim embodies the virtue of courage. The character who has the least power in the book (a runaway slave had even less authority than a poor, runaway child) exercises more power than any other character in the story. And more courage.

Jim's courage is rooted in both reason and conscience. Reason can lead to the wrong decision in one of two ways. Our reason can be flawed, leading us to think we are choosing rightly. But we can also know what the right thing to do is and choose wrong anyway.

Deciding whether one is acting rightly or wrongly is the domain of conscience. Conscience (which literally means "with knowledge") is the application of knowledge or reason.[25] There are two elements of conscience, one that acts as guide toward right conduct, the other that judges the action undertaken.[26] In this way, conscience is similar to prudence. Based on reason and a well-developed conscience, Jim chooses rightly and courageously.

Sometimes, from lack of knowledge or experience or from faulty teaching, what is right or wrong in a given situation is difficult to discern. This is clearly the situation Huck is in. It's what makes Huck an unreliable narrator (and it is, of course, the means of Twain's comedic and satiric approach). The entire story of *Huckleberry Finn* centers on the difficulty Huck faces in resolving to do, and then carry out, the right thing in helping his friend Jim to freedom.

Courage and the Malformed Conscience

The problem for Huck—and all of us—is that his conscience is not an entirely reliable guide. In fact, one main target of Twain's satire in the novel is the conscience that is malformed by a corrupt culture. Huck harbors distorted views of right and wrong, ones imparted to him by his flawed society. The progress he undergoes that corrects the wrong lessons his culture has taught him is the essence of *Huckleberry Finn*. We see his deformed conscience at work throughout the novel, as well as Huck's struggle to reform it. Taught that slavery is good, Huck's conscience reasons from this starting point and ends up in all the wrong places.

Huck's sense of right and wrong is so distorted that he can't even understand why Jim himself would want to be free. Huck is baffled that such a good fellow like Jim would want to do something so "wrong" as run away from his "rightful" owner. Huck has been raised in a society that taught him that slaves are not human, slavery is good, slaves are the property of their owners, and depriving someone of property is wrong.

Huck, like many in the antebellum South, developed a conscience with a distorted sense of right and wrong. In *Introducing Moral Theology*, William Mattison uses slavery as an example to show how the conscience can be malformed by social norms such that a slaveholder in eighteenth-century America could "genuinely" believe "in his heart of hearts" that owning slaves was "a virtuous act."[27] Mattison explains, "One can follow one's conscience, and in doing so honestly think in one's heart of hearts one is acting well, and yet be acting wrongly," as in the case of the "erroneous conscience" of the slaveholder.[28] Such thinking demonstrates the seared conscience the Bible talks about in 1 Timothy 4:1–2, a conscience rendered insensitive by abandoning scriptural teaching for too long. Both individuals and societies can abandon biblical principles. When society does, then it plays a significant role in searing the consciences of individuals within it with unscriptural teachings and false values. Every society has its own blind spots, of course. It is possible, as we see in Huck's case and in many others throughout history, to veil with human customs and morality what God has established in human nature and natural law. To expose the lies that hide the moral truth revealed by nature and the God of nature requires effort, trauma, or some sudden epiphany. Or a great novelist.

When Huck decides to help Jim escape, he does so believing it is "wrong" to do so. He tells Tom, "I know what you'll say. You'll say it's dirty, low-down business; but what if it is? I'm low down; and I'm a-going to steal him, and I want you keep mum and not let on. Will you?"[29] When Tom agrees to help him, Huck says that Tom, like Jim, "fell considerable in my estimation." He goes on:

> Here was a boy that was respectable and well brung up; and had a character to lose; and folks at home that had characters; and he was bright and not leather-headed; and knowing and not ignorant; and not mean, but kind; and yet here he was, without any more pride, or rightness, or feeling, than to stoop to this business, and make himself a shame, and his family a shame, before everybody. I *couldn't* understand it no way at all. It was outrageous, and I knowed I ought to just up and tell him so; and so be his true friend, and let him quit the thing right where he was and save himself.[30]

Huck struggles to reconcile Jim's humanity with the false teaching of his society. When he hears Jim express love and longing for his family, Huck doesn't know what to make of it. "I do believe he cared just as much for his people as white folks does for their'n," he marvels. Then he concludes, "It don't seem natural, but I reckon it's so."[31] Huck listens to Jim's plans, once he's freed, to save money in order to buy the freedom of his wife and children—or steal them away. Because his moral view is upside down, Huck is horrified. "It most froze me to hear such talk," he says. Jim is "lowered" in Huck's eyes, and Huck feels guilty for assisting in such a crime. "My conscience got to stirring me up hotter than ever," Huck says as he is rowing Jim to freedom, "until at last I says to it, 'Let up on me—it ain't too late yet—I'll paddle ashore at the first light and tell.'" His malformed conscience is eased by his decision: "I felt easy and happy and light as a feather right off. All my troubles was gone."[32]

Moral philosophers explain that the ignorance that can misinform one's conscience is of two kinds: vincible and invincible. Vincible ignorance is avoidable if one is duly attentive. Invincible ignorance occurs when a person could not have known better. The difference in the two is in acting in good faith or not.[33] These two kinds of ignorance illuminate the fact that it is possible to do "things we sincerely think are good, but which actually corrupt us, others, and society as a whole."[34]

Huck's is an invincible ignorance. He is, after all, a child and therefore lacks much moral culpability. Not only that, but he is a child who has been taught by his society and those in authority over him that slavery is right. Yet despite the malformation of his conscience, the law of God is written on his heart, and that law grapples throughout the story with the false ideas imparted to him by his society.

After two armed men come upon him and Jim on the raft, Huck instinctively lies to protect Jim. Afterward, believing he was wrong to do so, Huck becomes exasperated. Lacking a coherent moral apparatus that can explain why his conscience bothers him so, Huck settles for a pragmatic ethics:

> I knowed very well I had done wrong, and I see it warn't no use for me to try to learn to do right; a body that don't get *started* right when he's little ain't got no show—when the pinch comes there ain't nothing to back him up and keep him to his work, and so he gets beat. Then I thought a minute, and says to myself, hold on; s'pose you'd a done right and give Jim up, would you felt better than what you do now? No, says I, I'd feel bad—I'd feel just the same way I do now. Well, then, says I, what's the use you learning to do right when it's troublesome to do right and ain't no trouble to do wrong, and the wages is just the same? I was stuck. I couldn't answer that. So I reckoned I wouldn't bother no more about it, but after this always do whichever come handiest at the time.[35]

But Huck's conscience is more developed than he realizes, and he continues to wrestle with it as he tries to convince himself to do the "right" thing by returning Jim to his owner, Miss Watson. Huck's wavering back and forth between what his society has taught him is right and what his godly conscience tells him is wrong forms a considerable part of the narrative.

Finally, he thinks back to the lessons on prayer that Miss Watson and the Widow Douglas taught him. He remembers that prayer has never worked for him but thinks that perhaps if he does the "right" thing by writing the letter that reveals Jim's whereabouts, God will hear and answer his prayers. As soon as he writes the letter, Huck says, "I knowed I could pray now."[36]

But before he begins to pray, Huck's mind is flooded with memories of his and Jim's time together on the river, of Jim's kindness and care for him, and of how Jim called him the best friend he'd ever had. Then, Huck looks at the letter: "I took it up, and held it in my hand. I was a-trembling, because I'd got to decide, forever, betwixt two things, and I knowed it. I studied a minute, sort of holding my breath, and then says to myself: 'All right, then, I'll *go* to hell'—and tore it up." Upon condemning himself to hell, Huck reflects on the seriousness of his decision, which only deepens his commitment to it.

> It was awful thoughts and awful words, but they was said. And I let them stay said; and never thought no more about reforming. I shoved the whole thing out of my head, and said I would take up wickedness again, which was in my line, being brung up to it, and the other warn't. And for a starter I would go to work and steal Jim out of slavery again; and if I could think up anything worse, I would do that, too; because as long as I was in, and in for good, I might as well go the whole hog.[37]

Huck is mistaken in his belief that he will go to hell for helping Jim escape, of course, but he does not know that. He faces (he thinks) the greatest danger a person will ever face—eternal damnation of the soul—and chooses the well-being of another over his own. When Huck hears the call of God's law on his heart, he mistakes it, ironically, for temptation to do wrong. His decision to help Jim run away is not, in his mind, an act of nobility directed toward justice. But this is the great irony of Twain's satire: we know that it is. And despite Huck's erroneous belief that his intention is unjust, Huck shows courage in his willingness to sacrifice his very soul to obtain Jim's freedom.

Knowingly facing risk or danger is necessary for an act to be courageous.[38] Based on the knowledge Huck has (false though it may be), Huck's decision is courageous. His courage is echoed by the real-life words written many years later by a real-life martyr, Dietrich Bonhoeffer: "When a man takes guilt upon himself in responsibility, he imputes his guilt to himself and no one else. He answers for it. . . . Before other men he is justified by dire necessity; before himself he is acquitted by his conscience, but before God he hopes only for grace."[39]

In our highly individualistic age, we think of things like conscience and courage in mainly individual terms. In its individualism and its experientialism, Huck's brand of courage is that particularly modern kind described by Charles Taylor as the "quest for authenticity."[40] Huck's courage is in overcoming a malformed conscience in order to do what reason and nature confirm is transcendentally and eternally good and right.

But the cultivation and expression of virtue (and vice) and the formation of conscience is not merely an individual act but also a communal one. In addition to shaping individual experience and character, great literature has a role in forming the communal conscience and public virtue. We can understand a great deal about a culture—its strengths, its weaknesses, its blind spots, and its struggles—when we examine the literature that it not only produces but reveres.

Huck's transformation from ne'er-do-well into a boy whose developing fortitude drives him to stand against a great wrong supported by his society has made Huck Finn one of the most paradigmatic characters in all of American literature. In *The Republic of Imagination: America in Three Books,* Azar Nafisi says American individualism "at its best" is exemplified in Huck's "quiet and unobtrusive moral strength."[41]

Moral strength is one kind of courage. Perhaps it's the foundation of all courage.

Part Two

The Theological Virtues

"Just a Formality"

CHAPTER FIVE

Faith

SILENCE

by Shusaku Endo

Now faith is confidence in what we hope for
and assurance about what we do not see.

—Hebrews 11:1

Some years ago, when my husband and I were members of a little independent Bible church in the countryside, a famous revivalist came to preach. He gave what I later learned was his most well-known sermon: a come-to-Jesus bidding drawn from the parable of the wheat and the tares found in Matthew 13:24–30. In the parable, Jesus tells of a farmer who allows good seed that has been mixed with bad to be sown and to grow together until the harvest. When that time comes, the wheat grown from the good seed is gathered in the barn, but the tares grown from the bad seed are bundled up and burned.

The preacher's sermon spurred some, fearing that they were really tares and not wheat, to the altar at the sermon's close. Among them was a young married couple who had recently joined the church after professions of faith and baptism. "Are we truly wheat?" my friends wondered. "Or are we just bad seed mixed in with good?" After all, the preacher had warned, "Not everyone who says to me, 'Lord, Lord,' will enter the kingdom of heaven." Even having to ask, my friends thought, must be evidence that they were not truly saved. So they went forward during the altar call that day to make another profession of faith and be saved—again.

Later these young Christians learned, from me and from others, that most believers have fleeting moments (or hours or days or years) of doubt, and that the inevitable self-examination that results is not only normal but can be good and healthy. While I don't think hellfire and brimstone sermons are the best way to achieve it, such scrutiny can be evidence of a living faith—one that is active, growing, and bearing fruit. In contrast, a faith that never feels challenged is most likely dead.

What Is Faith?

What is faith? We use the word in so many ways. We can have faith in a person or an institution. The law might consider a transaction to be one made "in good faith." We describe our level of self-confidence as the amount of faith we have in ourselves. But faith as a virtue has a particular meaning, one expressed in the Bible when it explains that faith comes from the grace of God, not from human works (Eph. 2:8–9). Faith is the "instrument" that brings us to the Christ who saves us.[1]

Faith, along with hope and love, is a theological virtue. The theological virtues differ from the cardinal virtues because they are not attained by human power but come from God. Conferred by God, these virtues provide "an ennobling of man's nature" beyond natural human ability,[2] "something essentially inhuman."[3] They are called theological virtues because their object is God, they assist us in seeking and finding God, and they come to us by God's grace alone.[4] The theological virtues differ in their origin, but like the other virtues, they can become excellent through practice. Thus faith, "over time through the hard work of habituation,"[5] can become a "consistent and enduring quality of one's character."[6]

A faith that never feels challenged is most likely dead.

The excellence of one's faith can be measured a number of ways: by the strength of one's conviction, by the response to that conviction, and by the actual trust one places in the object of faith.[7] Similarly, a colleague who is a New Testament scholar describes faith as having three primary elements: belief (cognitive), trust (relational), and fidelity (obedience).[8] Consider, for example, the faith a child has in a parent: the child may believe that she should trust her parents, and she may obey them, but she may do so without trusting them. On the other hand, a child could believe in and trust her parents—and willfully disobey anyway. Some doubts cannot be expressed apart from faith in God. "Thus, rather than having faith in faith itself, as a point of certainty that relies on our volition only, true faith is a childlike trust in God, who allows his children to question him as they might question their earthly parent, and to do so in the certainty of the relational knowledge and trust of the Father."[9]

A Disorienting and Devastating Picture of Faith

Few works of modern literature grapple as provocatively and deeply with the virtue of faith as Shusaku Endo's novel *Silence*. Chosen by HarperCollins as one of the "100 Best Spiritual Books of the Century,"[10] *Silence* wrestles with hard, uncomfortable questions about the nature and limits of personal faith, as well as the ways cultural conditions can foster or discourage faith.

To be sure, the picture of faith in *Silence* is disorienting and devastating. The novel centers on a test of faith that is unimaginable for most Christians today, whose Christianity is marked by a Western triumphalism that dramatically differs from the defeat and defeatism of the Christian experience in seventeenth-century Japan. Yet this strange and troubling portrayal offers the opportunity to examine the true nature of the virtue of faith—the true wheat—apart from the limitations of both personal and cultural experience. *Silence* asks a question that is difficult for many readers to answer with certainty: Is the faith of its main character, Father Rodrigues, a saving faith that endures to the end?

But the purpose in reading this novel—or any novel—is not to find definitive answers about the characters. It is rather to ask definitive questions about ourselves. To read about an experience of faith as it falters is an opportunity to seek resolution not in the work of fiction but in the work of our own faith.

Historical background helpful to understanding the story, a fictionalized account of actual persons and historical events, is provided in the translator's preface to the English language version of *Silence*. The preface explains that Christianity was brought to Japan by Jesuits in the sixteenth century during a time when Japan had undergone destabilization and decentralization by war. However, the initial flourishing of Christianity ended early in the next century with changes in Japan's trade relationships with other countries. Japanese leaders came to distrust the foreign missionaries and, consequently, to persecute Japanese Christians with horrific methods of torture and execution aimed, not only at killing the victims, but at wiping the faith from the land entirely. One favored technique was forcing Christians to trample on a *fumie*, an image of Christ or Mary carved into a flat piece of stone or wood. Japan did not succeed in eradicating Christianity, however, despite killing five to six thousand Christians during this period. *Silence* is rooted in these historical events and centers on the fictional character of Sebastian Rodrigues, who is based on an actual person, Giuseppe Chiara. Chiara was one of a group of missionaries who came to Japan in the wake of reports that his mentor, the Portuguese Jesuit priest Christovao Ferreira (both a historical person and a character in the novel), had apostatized following renewed persecutions against Christians. While most of the details are imaginatively filled in by the novelist, the major events depicted—the persecution, torture, and killing of Christians, as well as the fall of these two priests—are factual.

Father Rodrigues arrives in Japan an earnest but proud man. He is proud of his education and office and proud of his faith and that of the former mentor he has come here to find. In contrast, the Japanese Christians, humble, persecuted, poor, and hidden in remote villages, are joyous to have priests among them at last, to teach them and to administer the sacraments to them. Rodrigues's disdain for them is clear when, while baptizing one of the children, he reflects, "This child also would grow up like its parents and grandparents to eke out a miserable existence face to face with the black sea in this cramped and desolate land; it, too, would live like a beast, and like a beast it would die. But Christ did not die for the good and beautiful. It is easy enough to die for the good and beautiful; the hard thing is to die for the miserable and corrupt—this is the realization that came home to me acutely at that time."[11]

"Christ did not die for the good and beautiful."

Rodrigues, and perhaps the cursory reader, might think these thoughts are noble and compassionate. But, in truth, they are at base condescension, the outworking of inner spiritual and cultural pride. Father Rodrigues's spiritual arrogance is seen again later in an important moment of irony and foreshadowing when some of the villagers ask him what they should do if authorities try to force them to trample the *fumie*. He unhesitatingly, almost dismissively, advises them, "Trample! Trample!"[12]—as if these humble peasants are not capable of the inner torment he will eventually undergo himself in facing the same dilemma.

The climax of the novel finds Father Rodrigues himself facing the decision of whether to comply with the order to trample. The stakes are impossibly high: before being brought to the *fumie,* he hears the moans of the Christian villagers undergoing unspeakable torture. The authorities tell him that if only he will trample, their torture will end. It is one thing to face the temptation to deny Christ to save yourself from suffering. It is another thing altogether to face this temptation in order to end the suffering of others.

Just a Formality

Surrounded by Japanese authorities, Rodrigues looks at the *fumie* in the dirt at his feet. It is "a simple copper medal fixed on to a gray plank of dirty wood" that bears "the ugly face of Christ, crowned with thorns and the thin, outstretched arms."[13] It is not the beautiful face of Christ he has imagined in his mind over and over to sustain him while here in this godforsaken land. The gentle goading of the Japanese officials echoes Satan's temptations of Christ in the wilderness (Luke 4:1–13). "'It is only a formality. What do formalities matter?' The interpreter urges him on excitedly. 'Only go through with the exterior form of trampling.'"[14] The torturer's words belie, of course, his knowledge of the power of a symbolic act. Nothing that is truly "just a formality" would be so urgently insisted upon.

We easily fool ourselves about the meaninglessness of such "formalities" or mere "symbols." People who resist getting married by insisting that formal marriage is "just a piece of paper" ironically demonstrate just how important that paper is in their very desire to avoid it. Similarly, our nation is currently divided over symbolic postures toward the American flag as well as the place monuments to evil deeds should have within the public square. Such controversies attest to the fact that cloth and stone are more than mere materials, that symbols have power. I once considered adopting an orphan from a Muslim country I had visited several times. The government of this country required without exception that adoptive parents affirm the declaration, "There is no God but Allah, and Muhammad is his messenger." The government, and even some Christian friends, insisted that it was "just a formality." Yet, if it were, why would it be so necessary? Despite seeing and holding little children without families or homes, I was convicted that to affirm something I don't believe, even for such a good reason, would be to have too little faith—in the power both of God and of symbols.

Rodrigues, urged on by the officials who torment him with the promise of releasing the others from their ongoing torture if only he will comply, finally "raises his foot."

> In it he feels a dull, heavy pain. This is no mere formality. He will now trample on what he has considered the most beautiful thing in his life, on what he has believed most pure, on what is filled with the ideals and the dreams of man. How his foot aches! And then the Christ in bronze speaks to the priest: "Trample! Trample! I more than anyone know of the pain in your foot. Trample! It was to be trampled on by men that I was born into this world. It was to share men's pain that I carried my cross."[15]

He tramples.

Whether Rodrigues's act of trampling is truly a denunciation of Christ—the blasphemy of the Holy Spirit that would indicate an unredeemed state—is the most controversial and vexing question of the novel. The complexity of the story allows for a range of conclusions, and readers and critics have weighed in accordingly. Regardless of other ambiguities, however, the lines that follow this part of the text are unambiguous: "The priest placed his foot on the *fumie*. Dawn broke. And far in the distance the cock crew."[16] The cock crowing is a clear signal that Rodrigues has, like Peter, betrayed Christ.

Rodrigues spends the years of his life following his apostasy assimilated into Japanese culture, employed by the Japanese government to identify Christian contraband smuggled into the country, and eventually taking a Japanese wife and name at the orders of the government. The teasing of the neighborhood children who call out to him, "Apostate Paul! Apostate Paul!" echoes the guilt that dogs him the rest of his days. On the surface, Rodrigues seems to have taken the same path as his mentor, Father Ferreira, who also has taken a Japanese name and wife and is writing a book that he claims will unmask the deceit of Christianity.

However, despite Rodrigues's forced assimilation into Japanese culture and the hiddenness of his faith, evidence remains that he still believes. For while Rodrigues's faith may be hidden, that does not mean, necessarily, that it is not living. In fact, some readers think that the moment of Rodrigues's seeming apostasy is actually the moment of his true conversion. Such an interpretation is supported by Rodrigues's transformation after this crisis point from a position of arrogance, self-reliance, and imperialism to a posture of brokenness, submission, and humility. The virtue of faith, if God has given it, might be diminished by lack of exercise and nourishment like any other virtue, but that decrease does not mean that one never had it or that it has been lost. This question is the merit of the self-examination that the parable of the wheat and the tares elicits.

Some time later, as "the last priest in this land,"[17] Rodrigues is sought out in secret by fellow apostate Kichijiro in order to hear his confession. Kichijiro, who has been dogging Rodrigues throughout the narrative, apostatized years before Rodrigues's arrival in Japan, after the government murdered his family. Since then he has been caught in an endless cycle of betrayal and confession, futilely trying to escape the weight of his perpetual fear and shame. Kichijiro is Rodrigues's doppelganger, a double who shadows him and whose needling presence offers a check on Rodrigues's spiritual pride, although that check is ignored. Kichijiro reflects Rodrigues's own guilt—as well as his continued clinging to faith despite his faltering. Both men embody the Japanese Christians that the author of *Silence* considered to be (along with himself) "children of failed faith" who, "unable to completely walk away from their faith," thus "lived with utter shame, regret and the dark pain of their past constantly."[18] Kichijiro now wants to give his confession once more. His request of Rodrigues prompts Rodrigues to grapple with God in an internal dialogue.

"Lord, I resented your silence," he confesses.

He receives from God the response, “I was not silent. I suffered beside you.”[19]

After administering the sacrament to Kichijiro, Rodrigues acknowledges to himself that “his fellow priests would condemn his act as sacrilege,” since he is no longer considered to be within the church. But, Rodrigues thinks, “even if he was betraying them, he was not betraying his Lord. He loved him now in a different way from before. Everything that had taken place until now had been necessary to bring him to this love.”[20] These lines capture the perhaps irresolvable interpretive question about the nature of Rodrigues’s faith. Does his expression of love for God evidence his faith? Can a person who keeps his faith hidden because of persecution have what is truly a saving faith?

A Hidden Faith?

The responses of Christian readers to the questions *Silence* raises follow predictable lines. Progressive Christians praise the novel’s ambiguity, the idea that Jesus would approve of denying him, and the way “love wins” in the lines quoted above. For example, Father James Martin, a liberal Catholic priest, says Rodrigues’s apostasy is allowable “because Christ asks him to” trample on the *fumie*. Martin praises the story’s emphasis on the role of individual conscience over rules and its emphasis on “‘discernment’ for people facing complicated situations, where a black-and-white approach seems inadequate.”[21] In contrast, some theologically conservative readers see the novel as celebrating, or at least justifying, apostasy and suggesting that one can have an internal faith that is not evidenced by outward behavior. Even more serious a concern for such readers is that the novel lends weight to contemporary ideologies that, as one critic puts it, “seek to absolutize the ‘dictatorship of relativism’ by making effective public adherence to the Christian tradition seem ‘selfish’ and finally futile.”[22]

Ironically, both types of readers are reading the novel in the same way: as a literal exposition of Christian doctrine with which they accordingly either agree or disagree. But *Silence* is a work of literary art and should be read as such. Endo himself insisted it was not a work of theology.[23] It is fiction, a novel, and even a particular kind of novel. Reading virtuously, reading faithfully, depends greatly on accepting a text on its own terms and attending to *how* it is told as much as, if not more than, *what* it tells.

The narrative structure offers the most significant cue for how to read *Silence*. It begins with a prologue by a third-person narrator. Then the first half of the book shifts to first-person narration in the form of letters written by Rodrigues. But once Rodrigues is captured—betrayed by the Judas-like Kichijiro—the narrative point of view shifts back to the third person. The last chapter of the novel introduces a new narrative style in the form of diary extracts from a clerk with a Dutch merchant, followed by an appendix consisting of diary entries from an officer assigned to Rodrigues's residence, concluding with the officer's report of Rodrigues's death and his Buddhist burial.

These narrative points of view taken together and in order effect a movement that begins at a distance from Rodrigues and his experience of faith, then moves closer, then moves away again, and then, finally, moves even further away. This movement significantly shapes the reader's experience of the story, not only in terms of shifting proximity to Rodrigues, but also in offering various angles of his life and faith. This interplay of subjective and objective, as well as limited and omniscient points of view, complicates the reader's experience and suggests implications and applications of the story's content beyond the pages of the book—in a way similar to how a parable works.

The truth a parable expresses is not found in a straightforward or literal reading. In fact, the Greek original of the word *parable* means to "throw beside." A parable is not an allegory (a form to be discussed in chap. 9), because a parable does not have a one-to-one correspondence of symbolic meaning as an allegory does. Whatever spiritual truth is gleaned from a parable, as in *Silence* or in Jesus's story of the wheat and the tares, is less absolute. Like a parable, *Silence* raises questions even as it offers possible answers.

Endo was himself Japanese and wrote the novel in Japanese, yet even his original Japanese audience—modern, secular, skeptical—found the subject matter strange. After all, Christians make up just 1 percent of the Japanese population today. In his insightful examination of *Silence,* Japanese artist and Christian Makoto Fujimura likens Endo's approach to the Christian faith within his own cultural context to that of Flannery O'Connor within hers: both authors were writing to a hostile culture in which Christ was either haunting or hidden.[24]

Accordingly, *Silence* uses emblematic, "deeply layered, conflicted language" that is more likely to convey to "a cynical and faithless world" something of the power of a faith it no longer believes in,[25] Fujimura explains. Similarly, the "weak, sometimes failed characters" of *Silence* "expose our true selves" to careful readers able to see how we can be like them.[26] Indeed the novel sets a trap for readers by inviting us first "to judge Kichijiro in the same way that Father Rodrigues does"[27] and then to indict Father Rodrigues too.

Endo had harsh words for readers quick to judge the failure of Rodrigues: "How can anyone who has never experienced the horrific tortures of the Christian persecution era have any right to say anything about the depth or shallowness of the believers then? . . . First, that person has no imagination. It shows not the shallow faith of those who end up apostatizing, but it reveals the lack of compassion in the ones making such a judgment."[28] Too often, in our tendency to make heroes out of faith leaders, "we fall into a false dichotomy of seeing faith only in terms of victory or failure, which leads us to dismiss and discard the weak,"[29] Fujimura points out. This seems particularly true within modern American evangelicalism.

An Old Story for Modern Times

Silence is based on history several centuries old, but the story is reframed in terms that address modern questions, including the very modern concern of "individual uncertainty over broader historical or social issues."[30] As one critic observes (in objection not praise), Rodrigues's plight, although set in seventeenth-century Japan, reflects the condition of belief in the Western culture of the twentieth century. "A lot has happened in three hundred years," this reviewer points out. "As secularization has advanced and man has had to learn to live without God, his solution for the most part has been to draw closer to other people, in unprecedented, ultimately untenable ways." One of these ways, which the novel shows by placing Rodrigues in the position of having the power to end or continue the torture of other Christians, is that "man attributes too much agency to himself."[31] And certainly, we can see the same attribution of too much agency in ourselves within modern church culture when we base the knowledge of our salvation on fleeting feelings and consequently find ourselves going forward to the altar to receive salvation again and again.

But this incompatibility between the seventeenth-century setting of *Silence* and its twentieth-century questions is less a weakness than an indication of the novel's affinity with the tragic mode. Ancient tragedies were, like *Silence*, retellings of history. In their treatment of the Oedipus myth, for example, both Homer and Sophocles took a story from history and retold it "in such a way that it raises and reflects issues of contemporary concern, issues that are within the day-to-day experience of his audience."[32] Additionally, tragedies deal in the mythical and religious, not the realistic. Although a pre-Christian literary form, ancient tragedies were deeply rooted in religious worship and expressive of religious beliefs. "Commonly regarded as the highest form of literature, [ancient tragedy] deals with the problem of pain and evil, the incongruity of the way things are and the vision of them as they should be."[33] *Silence* shares all this in common with ancient tragedy.

We can see the same attribution of too much agency in ourselves within modern church culture when we base the knowledge of our salvation on fleeting feelings and consequently find ourselves going forward to the altar to receive salvation again and again.

Silence reinvents the historical account in order to address contemporary questions and concerns. The historical figure the character of Rodrigues is based on did apostatize, but it was after he underwent the pit torture himself, not in order to save others from torture.[34] One critic objects to this anachronism, saying that Endo's decision to have Rodrigues apostatize in order to save others rather than himself from torture "turns on an act of emotional blackmail. . . . If it is always and everywhere difficult for human beings to hold in their minds seemingly contradictory tenets of Christianity, *Silence* makes the task feel impossible. Mercy is pitted against truth, love of neighbor against allegiance to God."[35] But such an impossibility, an irresolvable dilemma, is the heart of tragedy and of *Silence*.

Consider the tragedy of Oedipus. Told in a prophecy that he would murder his father and marry his mother, Oedipus runs away to avoid his fate—and in running away ends up unwittingly fulfilling it. Sigmund Freud, who drew upon the Oedipal story in developing his psychoanalytical theory, explained, "Its tragic effect depends on the conflict between the all-powerful will of the gods and the vain efforts of human beings threatened with disaster; resignation to divine will, and the perception of one's own impotence is the lesson which the deeply moved spectator is supposed to learn from the tragedy."[36] This impossibility arouses in the viewer or reader fear and pity: fear of the gods and pity for human suffering. Literature, Aristotle says in *Poetics*, cultivates virtue in arousing such emotions and then purging them through a catharsis brought about by the plot's just resolution.[37]

Like *Oedipus Rex*, *Silence* offers in Rodrigues a lofty figure who falls through a combination of his own flaw and forces beyond his control. We experience with the characters, through various perspectives, the terrors of torture and martyrdom and fear in being faced with the temptation to deny Christ.

However, where the modern novel *Silence* departs from classical tragedy is in its lack of complete catharsis. Its ambiguity prevents catharsis in the classical sense. If Oedipus's self-blinding and self-exile as a result of his unwitting acts of patricide and incest end the drama with a bang, Rodrigues's death in old age as a hidden Christian working for the Japanese government ends with a whimper. *Silence* is not a classical tragedy; its tragedy is very much in the modern mode.

Silence shares more in common with Christian tragedy. In classical tragedy, closure is contained within the text. Christian tragedy, on the other hand, looks outward, upward, and beyond for redemption. Following a dormant period for drama, the Middle Ages saw a rebirth of tragedy. Since then "Christian life and thought have been the matrix out of which tragedy was reborn. It takes account of the Redemption, the absence of which characterized, in part, pagan tragedy. The tragic event in human life is no longer the final word." Christian tragedy differs from classical tragedy in its emphasis on "the next world's destiny being determined in the present one," thus making it "infinitely more intense and serious than any other mode of tragedy."[38]

Understanding *Silence* as myth more than realism, as parable more than doctrine, requires a different response from the reader than merely determining the theological category of Rodrigues's solution to his irresolvable dilemma. The literary qualities of *Silence* that go beyond mere realism test "one's imaginative ability to move beyond the obvious,"[39] which is helpful in exercising faith because "an unimaginative perspective limits one's faith in the mystery of God."[40] Indeed, "*Silence* works as a powerful antidote to the modernist reductionism that entirely rejects doubt—as if we, in our limited minds and knowledge, can know everything God and the universe offer to us."[41]

A Test of Faith

In *Silence,* the unique particularities surrounding one man's faith and the testing of that faith provide a strangeness that allows readers to view through a different lens what the virtue of faith looks like as it is being practiced well (or not).

What does it mean to practice faith well? While our works cannot save us, our habits can strengthen our faith. Martin Luther cautioned, "Do not think lightly of faith. It is a work that is of all works the most excellent and most difficult."[42] An understanding of faith as not only a gift that is received but also a virtue that is exercised will emphasize any single moment less and the accumulation of moments more. Fortunately, the Bible gives a clear recipe for building on the foundation of faith, which can only strengthen faith itself: "Giving all diligence, add to your faith virtue, to virtue knowledge, to knowledge self-control, to self-control perseverance, to perseverance godliness, to godliness brotherly kindness, and to brotherly kindness love. For if these things are yours and abound, you will be neither barren nor unfruitful in the knowledge of our Lord Jesus Christ" (2 Pet. 1:5–8 NKJV).

Christian tragedy looks outward, upward, and beyond for redemption.

Rodrigues's former mentor, Ferreira, in trying to convince Rodrigues to abandon the faith as he himself has, tells him that all their efforts to bring Christianity to the Japanese culture were in vain because Japanese culture rendered its people incapable of understanding the faith. Understandably, Rodrigues is discouraged and demoralized. Could this be true?

Of course it is. It is true of all of us. Sometimes our faith is great. Sometimes it is small. There are times for most believers when they wonder if it is there at all. But faith tests true (or not) over time. We can grow in faith only when we recognize that our faith is imperfect.[43] Our faith is perfected only in Christ, not in ourselves or our understanding: "We may speak of the virtue of faith but only if we finish it by saying 'is Christ.' He must be the virtue of faith because he is the object of faith. There is nothing intrinsic to faith that makes it powerful. . . . It isn't even the act of believing itself. Christ and nothing else is the virtue of faith."[44] This is why faith is "the virtue whereby, paradoxically, we excel in our dependence upon God."[45]

"Carry the Fire"

Chapter six

Hope

THE ROAD

by Cormac McCarthy

Not only so, but we also glory in our sufferings,
because we know that suffering produces perseverance;
perseverance, character; and character, hope.

—Romans 5:3–4

Nothing is more hopeless than an apocalypse. Or so it might seem. In its original sense, *apocalypse* means "revelation." The word later came to be associated with an end-of-the-world cataclysmic event because of the link John's Revelation in the Bible makes between revelation and the end of this world.[1] The utter destruction of the world as we know it, and with it the "dismantling of perceived realities,"[2] can, paradoxically, point us to hope. In revealing our present condition, traditional, religious apocalyptic literature directs our future hope. In a religiously based apocalypse, "the suffering and pain we encounter in this life gains meaning" and "hope is restored."[3]

But what about a secular apocalypse such as Cormac McCarthy's novel *The Road*, which depicts a world devoid of religion and nearly all reference to God? Modern apocalyptic literature, which is largely secular apocalyptic literature, demonstrates the truth about the modern condition: because we have replaced God with ourselves as the source of meaning and the center of the universe, "all we see on the horizon is our end."[4]

Apocalyptic stories, whether in the form of novels, film, or television, have experienced a resurgence in recent years. On the publication of *The Road* in 2006, one news story explained the rise of this genre: "The world feels more precariously perched on the lip of the abyss than ever, and facing those fears through fiction helps us deal with it. These stories are cathartic as well as cautionary. But they also reaffirm why we struggle to keep our world together in the first place. By imagining what it's like to lose everything, we can value what we have."[5] Of course, "what we have" is, too often, not enough. *The Road*, perhaps accidentally, reveals this very thing, even as a secular apocalypse.

To be human is to be "in the state of being on the way,"[6] which is a kind of hope. From Homer's *Odyssey* to Dante's *Divine Comedy* to Chaucer's *Canterbury Tales* to Bunyan's *Pilgrim's Progress*, the journey is one of the oldest and most prevalent motifs in literature. Hope has been called "the virtue of the wayfarer,"[7] and *The Road* is the simple, but harrowing, story of a father and son who are wayfarers in a postapocalyptic world bereft of nearly all life. Few people remain, and because some of those who have survived are evil to the point of cannibalism, strangers the two chance upon cannot be easily trusted. Most land is burned and covered with gray ash from some unnamed catastrophic event. Food, shelter, and supplies are difficult to come by. Their journey participates in the accumulated symbolism of all the journeys throughout the canon of literature, much of it profoundly religious. Indeed, early in the story, the father and son are likened to "pilgrims in a fable."[8] Later in the story they are said to be "like mendicant friars sent forth to find their keep."[9]

Even the form of the book—a continuous narrative with no chapters, only occasional and sporadic breaks—reflects the meandering shape of a journey whose end is unknown. The sparse, minimalist prose, lacking even much punctuation, mimics the stark reality of the story's world. The father and son are never even named, called by the narrator simply "the man" and "the boy" (although the boy calls his father "Papa").

Such a place seems unlikely to cultivate hope. But sometimes in circumstances that seem most hopeless, hope is by necessity strengthened. Reading the story is itself an exercise in hope, similar to what one might experience reading any book of good repute, to be sure, but heightened even more by the lack of structural and narrative touchstones readers expect in modern-day novels.

The four conditions of hope are that it regards something *good* in the *future* that is *difficult* but *possible* to obtain.

Indeed, literary reading—reading that makes on the reader more demands of time, attention, and thought than casual reading—requires the same conditions that Aquinas finds in hope. The four conditions of hope are that it regards something *good* in the *future* that is *difficult* but *possible* to obtain. The practice of hope, Aquinas says, is "a certain stretching out of the appetite towards good."[10]

This notion of stretching out the appetite is evocative. First, to be human is to have natural appetites and, as seen in chapter 2, necessitates the virtue of temperance. For, while the existence of those appetites is a given, the form and direction they take is not necessarily so. These appetites express what James K. A. Smith calls our "bodily orientation to the world," and that orientation is shaped by our practices and our loves.[11] The journey of the man and the boy in *The Road* is excruciatingly bodily. Second, the word *stretch* (notice its bodily meaning) implies a degree of discipline and sacrifice that is missing when hope is used synonymously with a word like *wish*. To wish is not to hope. A wish is not a virtue. Hope is.

Hope as Passion and Hope as Virtue

To say that hope is a virtue does not paint the full picture, though. Aquinas identifies two kinds of hope, and the difference between them (as well as their relatedness) illuminates my reading of *The Road*.

The first sort of hope is one common to all human experience. It's a sense of anticipation for a future outcome: "I hope it snows tomorrow" or "I hope to be in France next summer" or "I hope I do well on this exam." Such hope is a natural passion, one that even animals exhibit, as when, Aquinas points out, a dog chases a hawk or hare.[12] "In its basic form," Aquinas explains, "human hope does not differ essentially from animal hope."[13] In both human beings and in animals this natural hope arises either out of experience or by teaching and persuasion.[14]

But the hope that is a theological virtue, the hope spoken of in the Bible that is regarded as akin to faith and love (1 Cor. 13:13), is not a natural passion but a supernatural gift conferred by God. This virtue of hope cannot be understood apart from God. It is supernatural in both origin and sustenance, the gift of grace, not the result of mere human effort, although the Christian's careful cultivation of hope may, like the exercise of all virtues, bring about its increase. Theological hope "is a steadfast turning toward the true fulfillment of man's nature, that is, toward good, only when it has its source in the reality of grace in man and is directed toward supernatural happiness in God."[15] As with all spiritual gifts, its source can be nourished or quenched.[16] Thus, while it originates in God, theological hope is a "habit of the will."[17]

Both the natural passion of hope and the theological virtue of hope share the same object: "the future good that is difficult but possible to attain."[18] So while both God and theological hope are nearly absent from *The Road*, this object is ever present.

The man and the boy are the embodiment of natural hope. But we see hopelessness early in the story when it is revealed that at some point before the narrative begins the boy's mother took her own life. She feared (reasonably) that she and the boy would be caught, raped, killed, and eaten by the marauders. She told the man, "As for me my only hope is for eternal nothingness and I hope it with all my heart."[19] She stole away one night, leaving him and the boy in order to die, at her own hands, "alone somewhere in the dark."[20] She was, in truth, hopeless.

Two Kinds of Hopelessness

There are two kinds of hopelessness: presumption and despair. Presumption (or false hope) assumes that one's hope will be fulfilled; despair anticipates that one's hope will never be fulfilled. Both presumption and despair "are in conflict with the truth of reality."[21] Both "destroy the pilgrim character of human existence."[22] We can presume or despair in many areas of life, whether about our jobs, our relationships, or our future. I have observed anecdotally that despair is often rooted in unrealistic expectations or idealism, the kind of thinking that inevitably brings disappointment. People quit relationships, jobs, and churches over unmet expectations, often expectations that were never fair or realistic in the first place. In *The Road*, one way the man is able to keep up his hope, despite his natural moments of despair, is by being realistic. Of course, a realistic outlook in a postapocalyptic world is pretty dim. But the human spirit is amazingly resilient and adaptable. All across the world and history, people live, or have lived, with joy in conditions that other people find unimaginable.

Within a theological context, the vices of despair and presumption concern our posture toward God's ability and willingness to forgive sin. To presume forgiveness is a sin against God in his justice.[23] Aquinas says, however, that the sin of presumption is "less grave than despair"[24] because to despair is a sin against God in his goodness and mercy.[25]

Of course, we need not turn to apocalyptic literature to encounter grave despair. Not only is despair a vice in itself, but it can lead to further wrongs, such as choosing the pragmatism of quick fixes rather than sticking to the principle of faithfulness over the long term. I think, for example, of the despair that has characterized the political landscape of America of late, particularly within some parts of the Christian community. Despair has encouraged some to place more faith in political leaders than in biblical principles. In turn, some Christians, disillusioned over what other believers have said or done, have chosen to disavow their family of faith, giving in to despair. To despair over politics—regardless of which side of the political divide one lands on—as many Christians have done in the current apocalyptic political climate, is to forget that we are but wayfarers in this land. Choosing hope—whether amid the annihilation of the world or merely a political breakdown—is virtuous.

> Choosing hope is virtuous.

In *The Road*, the boy's mother despairs. His father, rather than despairing over his failure to save the woman, steels his determination to save the boy and chooses hope. The "child [becomes] his warrant,"[26] his prompt, demonstrating Aquinas's observation that hope gives birth to love and activity.[27]

> In so far, then, as hope regards the good we hope to get, it is caused by love: since we do not hope save for that which we desire and love. But in so far as hope regards one through whom something becomes possible to us, love is caused by hope, and not vice versa. Because by the very fact that we hope that good will accrue to us through someone, we are moved towards him as to our own good; and thus we begin to love him. Whereas from the fact that we love someone we do not hope in him,

> except accidentally, that is, in so far as we think that he returns our love. Wherefore the fact of being loved by another makes us hope in him; but our love for him is caused by the hope we have in him.[28]

What else but love, the fruit of hope, could fuel the fire of such an arduous action as survival in a postapocalyptic world?

A Story of Love

Indeed, before it is a story of hope, *The Road* is a story of love: the love of a father for a son. Love contributes to the attainment of a difficult object, Aquinas explains, because "it happens sometimes that what is difficult becomes possible to us, not through ourselves but through others; hence it is that hope regards also that by which something becomes possible to us."[29]

Hope is characterized by "quiet confidence,"[30] a quality the man embodies throughout the story. When the novel opens, the two have already set out toward a warmer clime and the sea, not knowing what might lie before them there or anywhere else. After one brush with danger, the man gently reassures the boy, "I know you thought we were going to die. . . . But we didnt."[31] They travel for months along burned-out highways, sleeping in woods or abandoned homes, carrying whatever stores they can find in an old shopping cart. They seem to be alone in the world. Yet, the man promises the boy, "There are people. There are people and we'll find them. You'll see."[32]

And there are people, they soon see. But they are not necessarily good people.

As in most postapocalyptic worlds, there are only "good guys" and "bad guys." The man tells the boy they have to be vigilant, especially if they hope to find more of "the good guys." But the bad guys are very, very bad. In order to survive, they eat people. And worse. The man and the boy are among the good. The father reassures the boy of this as often as he warns him of the other.

> We're going to be okay, arent we Papa?
> Yes. We are.
> And nothing bad is going to happen to us.
> That's right.
> Because we're carrying the fire.
> Yes. Because we're carrying the fire.[33]

The man never tells the boy (nor does the narrator tell the reader) what "carrying the fire" means. It needs no explanation.

The fire they are carrying is what makes them good guys. It entails hope. "This is what the good guys do," the father tells the boy. "They keep trying. They dont give up."[34] Hope is "a desire for something good in the future," as well as "the thing in the future that we desire" and "the basis or reason for thinking that our desire may indeed be fulfilled."[35] Because hope is oriented toward the future, it is, in a certain way, "the basis of morality,"[36] since moral choices incur future consequences. The direness of the pair's situation transforms decisions that would be otherwise ordinary or inconsequential into profoundly moral ones, beginning with the decision to embark on the road.

When the boy asks, "Are we going to die?" the man answers, "Sometime. Not now."[37] But as they continue to struggle to find food, take shelter, fight illness, and avoid the bad guys, the boy continues to be afraid. The man tells the boy, "Dont lose heart. . . . We'll be all right."[38] When the boy is scared because of his dreams, the man exhorts him not to give in to fears and not to give up. "I wont let you," he says.[39] Over and over, the man tells the boy, "It will be okay." The boy begins to echo the man's word, saying, "It's okay."[40]

So, as they journey, the boy grows and matures. When his father admonishes him to stop crying, he says, "I'm trying." And he is trying. When his father tells him that he (the boy) is not the one who has to worry about everything, the boy tells him, "Yes I am. . . . I am the one."[41] The man is surprised when the boy asks, "What are our long term goals?" and asks him where he heard the phrase. Finally, the boy remembers: "You said it. . . . A long time ago."[42]

Against All Hopes

Despite the hope that prevails, the man does, understandably, slip into moments of "numbness" and "dull despair."[43] Despair "responds to the difficulty of the good by pulling back or falling off,"[44] and this is the temptation the man fights against every day, every hour. "There were few nights lying in the dark that he did not envy the dead," the story says.[45] "What he could bear in the waking world he could not by night and he sat awake" in fear.[46] The man senses the "world shrinking," the "names of things slowly following those things into oblivion" as his grasp on the former world fades: "Colors. The names of birds. Things to eat. Finally the names of things one believed to be true. More fragile than he would have thought. How much was gone already? The sacred idiom shorn of its referents and so of its reality."[47] One day, after the man's leg is pierced by an enemy's arrow, the boy asks him, "What's the bravest thing you ever did?" The man answers, "Getting up this morning."[48]

Despite his assurances to the boy that they will not die, the man is convinced at one point that "death was finally upon them" and considers ceasing their journey in order to find a place to hide and die.[49] But they press on. After they later stumble upon an underground bunker filled with food and supplies, where they get cleaned, rested, and refreshed, the man recognizes the fault in his despair. "He'd been ready to die and now he wasnt going to and he had to think about that."[50]

Hope is not the same as oblivion or naiveté. Hope requires reckoning with the world as it is, with reality. The man does this. When the boy asks the man if crows still exist, the man tells him it's unlikely. And when the boy realizes that they have narrowly escaped being cannibalized, his father does not deny this horrific truth, as well as the fact that they couldn't help other soon-to-be victims because then they'd be eaten too. Being reasonable is one of the man's most prominent characteristics. He remains watchful all the time on the road. When the boy asks if he's scared, he says, "Well. I suppose you have to be scared enough to be on the lookout in the first place. To be cautious. Watchful."[51]

Watchfulness is part of hope. Watchfulness counters both despair and sloth, which is the "beginning and root of despair" and inhibits "courage for the great things."[52] Sloth is considered a capital sin because it prevents a person from becoming what God wants her to be and who she truly is.[53]

One counter to sloth is magnanimity, greatness of soul. Despair cannot be conquered by effort alone but must be accompanied by a "clear-sighted magnanimity that courageously expects and has confidence in the greatness of its nature."[54] Magnanimity perfects natural hope.[55] Like all virtues, magnanimity is acquired and is a habit to be cultivated. Its object is "the doing of great things."[56] The man in *The Road* exemplifies well how "the magnanimous [person] aspires to greatness, and so pushes through difficulty towards a great good."[57] Keeping himself and the boy alive is the great thing the man hopes to obtain. But as a counterbalance, the virtue of magnanimity must also be accompanied by humility. Magnanimity "requires humility, so that it truthfully estimates its own possibilities, rather than exaggerate them."[58] Hope is thus bordered on one extreme by magnanimity and on the other by humility. Magnanimity points to possibility while humility recognizes limitations.[59] Hope is inherently humble.

Hope requires reckoning with the world as it is, with reality.

Hope as Pursuit of the Good

Pursuing the great good allows—or perhaps requires—appreciation of the other goods along the way. Both magnanimity and humility assist this. For even in a postapocalyptic world, goodness can be found. These moments of goodness are what turn an otherwise horrifying story into a work of beauty and power. The story is filled with—to use George Saunders's phrase—"drops of goodness."[60]

Even the word *good* appears over and over in the story. *Good* is such a wonderful word. A good word.

Some years ago, I noticed amid the grading of many papers (the plight of every English professor) how often the positive feedback I wrote on my students' work consisted simply of the comment "good." I contemplated varying that word with others. But then I realized that *good* is the best word. (It is certainly easy to write!) Once in a while, the word *excellent* might be warranted. But not often. We live in a society so obsessed with "the best" that *good* is seldom good enough. But good *is* good. It is very good. It is the way God characterized his own creation in Genesis.

Paradoxically, the bleak world of *The Road* is an affirmation, even a celebration, of what is good, all the more marvelous in a world with so little good seemingly left in it. Goodness, Vladimir Nabokov says in *Lectures on Literature*, "is something that is irrationally concrete."[61] The "supremacy of the detail over the general, of the part that is more alive than the whole," is the basis, Nabokov says, for the "irrational" belief, against all contrary facts, in the goodness of man.[62] And the "capacity to wonder at trifles—no matter the imminent peril," Nabokov explains, is how "we know the world to be good."[63]

We live in a society so obsessed with "the best" that *good* is seldom good enough. But good *is* good. It is very good.

One of the most poignant scenes in *The Road* bears this out. Early in their journey, the man and the boy search for food in an abandoned supermarket. When the man retrieves a can of Coke from a toppled machine, he gives it to the boy, who has never seen such a thing.

> What is it, Papa?
> It's a treat. For you.
> What is it?
> Here. Sit down.

The man opens the can and hands it, fizzing, to the boy, who drinks it. "It's really good," he says.

Yes. It is.
You have some, Papa.
I want you to drink it.
You have some.

The man takes the can, drinks a little, and hands it back to the boy, insisting he drink it as they sit awhile.[64] Later, when the man and boy come across a refreshing waterfall where the boy can wash and swim too, the man encourages him: "You're doing good, the man said. You're doing good."[65] After finding some mushrooms in the woods they can eat, the boy asks if they are good. His father tells him to take a bite. "These are pretty good," the boy says. When they make camp, the boy says, "This is a good place Papa."[66] The boy is concerned about a little boy he glimpsed on their travels. He asks his father who will find the boy if he is lost. "Goodness will find the little boy. It always has. It will again."[67] The man constantly assures the boy that they are "the good guys." And "we always will be."[68] Even though they are starving, they will not become like the cannibals they have run from. "No matter what," the man reassures the worried boy. "Because we're the good guys."[69]

Natural Hope as a Bridge to Theological Hope

The hope seen in *The Road* is ultimately merely human hope, the natural passion that Aquinas says we share with the animals: the arduous pursuit of some good. Yet, while the passion of hope and the theological virtue of hope differ in both source and kind, they are not entirely unconnected.

Theological hope is an implicit surrender to the help of another—God—in obtaining a good. Theological hope requires a similar recognition of one's own limitations as required by the natural passion of hope. The magnanimous seek greatness that is within their power based on a rational assessment of what is and is not within that power.[70] The presumptuous, on the other hand, "habitually regard ourselves as capable of attaining through our own powers things that in fact are impossible without help from others. Untruthfully exaggerating our own capacities . . . we render ourselves unlikely (if not unable) to lean on the help of God."[71] Theological hope requires humility in the same way that the natural passion does. Having natural hope, philosopher Robert Miner explains, can prepare one for the supernatural hope that comes from God:

Theological hope is an implicit surrender to the help of another—God—in obtaining a good.

> Why should we suppose that persons who lack the habit of aiming for the arduous good in earthly matters are nonetheless well prepared to attempt the most difficult of goods? There may be no logical impossibility. God *can* infuse the virtue of hope even in souls that have no prior discipline in aiming for the difficult good. But in the usual order of things, . . . things do not happen in this manner. Souls indifferent to the achievement of human things cannot be expected to exert themselves in divine things.[72]

Miner goes on to observe, "Those with flat souls will often be unable to discern goods beyond the most obvious of bodily pleasures." Such people "perceive spiritual goods as tasteless or insignificant," leaving "no room in the soul" for the virtuous hope that comes only from God.[73]

Moreover, as N. T. Wright explains in *Surprised by Hope*, the theological virtue of hope is manifested not merely in eternity, but in the implications of eternity for present realities[74]—in other words, here and now in the relationship of the transcendent to the immanent. Only in the immanent can we as embodied creatures encounter transcendence. Transcendence meets human needs, one moral philosopher argues, only when understood "as a person—as a Thou."[75] Modern secular apocalypses—those that reveal a *telos*, or end, apart from the transcendent meaning and purpose—express even so a yearning "for Revelation—to make the deep pain and difficulties of our lives meaningful and finished."[76] In the absence of a "Thou," the best a secular apocalypse can offer is a "thou."

Once, while the boy is sleeping, the man watches over him, reflecting, "All things of grace and beauty such that one holds them to one's heart have a common provenance in pain. Their birth in grief and ashes. So, he whispered to the sleeping boy. I have you."[77]

Because transcendence requires "revelation and faith,"[78] the desire for transcendence is, whether recognized as such or not, ultimately the desire for God. Despite the absence in *The Road* of religious faith—and, seemingly, God—something of transcendence is omnipresent nevertheless. Indeed, transcendence is the fuel, the fire itself, for the whole story and its entire journey. The world of the modern secular apocalypse offers something like the imaginary catastrophe Alasdair MacIntyre describes in the opening of *After Virtue*, one whose destruction leaves survivors trying to reassemble fragments of knowledge absent the traditions and structures that once gave the now decontextualized terms and facts coherence. In place of a "conceptual scheme" are only echoes of transcendence.[79] Such an echo is seen in *The Road* during a snowfall. The boy catches a flake in his hand and watches "it expire there like the last host of christendom."[80]

The hope the man has had all along—his hope in the boy and in the "fire" they carry—points to something more than natural hope, more than the hope of Aquinas's dog in pursuit of the hare. The man's hope allows him to succeed in the quest to reach the warmer clime and the sea. By the time he and the boy arrive there, the world as it is has taken its toll on the man. The illness that has been slowly overtaking him along the journey settles in. Knowing his life will soon end, the man passes on his natural hope to the boy. "You need to go on, he said. I cant go with you. You need to keep going. You dont know what might be down the road. We were always lucky. You'll be lucky again. You'll see. Just go. It's all right." But when the boy insists he can't continue without his father, the man tells him,

> You have to carry the fire.
> I dont know how to.
> Yes you do.
> Is it real? The fire?
> Yes it is.

> Where is it? I dont know where it is.
> Yes you do. It's inside you. It was always there. I can see it.[81]

The man poignantly places his hopes for transcendence entirely in his son, declaring that "if he is not the word of God God never spoke."[82] Yet, even in his error in placing his hopes in the created rather than the Creator, the man seeks the sacred, and in so doing recognizes in his son the image of God: "He sat beside him and stroked his pale and tangled hair. Golden chalice, good to house a god. Please dont tell me how the story ends."[83]

Hope is, like all virtues, a practice. It is autobiographical, the story of the one who possesses it, "stretching [that story] forward to its best possible ending."[84] Like the unity and direction of a good narrative—or a pilgrimage—hope leads one to consider oneself within the context of one's story, stretching it forward to its best possible ending. The man in possession of merely the hope that is a natural passion does not see the hope that comes only from God: participation in the new heaven and the new earth.

Neither *The Road* nor the man demonstrate theological hope directly. But in hinting at something beyond mere animal passion, at something transcendent, the work points toward a hope that surpasses even the best human pursuits.

The Myth of Progress

In *A Secular Age*, Charles Taylor describes three senses of transcendence, three ways of reaching beyond the flatness of the here and now: through belief in God or some higher power, through the extension of natural or mortal life, and through *agape* love.[85] Clearly, the man in *The Road* achieves at least this last kind of transcendence.

The man also resists secularity as Taylor defines it. One quality of secularity, according to Taylor, is that human flourishing becomes the highest good.[86] Although a pilgrimage—whether literal religious travel or metaphorical spiritual journey—involves both linearity and change, it differs subtly but significantly from the modern idea of progress, the foundation for the secular notion of human flourishing. Postapocalyptic stories confront the myth of progress. Progress is not the same as hope. The modern idea of progress is founded on a belief in the perfectibility—or at least the unbounded improvability—of humankind. Progress is an Enlightenment idea, grounded in the obvious and measurable progress of science but erroneously applied to the human condition. This explains why the science that informs medicine improves over the ages but our poetry does not. Although human manners and morals shift and change, and human cultures exchange one systemic sin for another, human nature does not change, let alone progress. "Ironically, by affirming human powers, modern hope has constricted human imagination."[87]

Among other shortcomings in its account of the nature of reality, the myth of progress cannot account for evil.[88] Hope, however, takes evil into account. The "fundamental structures of hope" are built upon belief in the goodness of creation, the nature of evil, and the plan of redemption.[89] Nowhere is evil more obvious than in suffering. The world of *The Road* is a world filled with suffering and the never-ending attempt to escape or minimize it—the very goal of the man and boy's journey. Placing human suffering in a new and startling context shocks us into recognition of truths we often work hard to avoid.

Yet the doctrine of progress in the modern age does not make room for suffering. Rather, the notion of progress suggests "that the great evils heretofore experienced in history are passing phenomena, not enduring characteristics of human existence."[90] The entire project of progress, as noble as it is untenable, is to eliminate suffering. *The Road* demonstrates the impossibility of such an idea. Yet, in so doing, it demonstrates the triumph of hope. Hope exists only where there are obstacles to achieving the good, and the good that one seeks in hope is arduous.

Flourishing is another way of talking about the modern notion of progress, which cannot accommodate the problem of evil. No world other than the postapocalyptic one can depict more dramatically the limits of insistence on human flourishing. "Flourishing is good," Taylor writes;

"nevertheless, seeking it is not the ultimate goal" for the believer.[91] *God* is the highest good for the Christian believer. Or goodness for another kind of believer.

The man in *The Road* is this other kind of believer. His reassurances to the boy that they will never become like the cannibals they must hide from shows the man's recognition of goodness and transcendence, even in such a horrific world, for he would rather they die (not flourish) than become that evil.

And if we accept the central metaphor of the story—carrying the fire—then we see that, after the man's death (but even before), the boy does carry it forward and, in so doing, extends in some way the man's natural life. The boy's sensitivity toward the transcendent is even stronger than the man's. It is the boy who, in his innocence, seeks to help others that the man, in his greater experience, rejects out of fear. It is the boy who, when they stumble upon a great store of food in a safe bunker underground, insists upon giving thanks—somehow, to someone—before they eat. Later, when they have reached their destination of the sea and they find a flare gun and the man explains its purpose to the boy—to show others where you are—the boy wonders if somebody "like God" might see it. "Yeah," his father answers. "Maybe somebody like that."[92]

Somebody like that does see the boy. After the father's death, a family who has been watching them comes to the boy's aid. They are a father, a mother, and two children. When the boy asks if they are "the good guys," they assure him they are. And they are. They take him in.

And sometimes the woman—the mother—talks to the boy about God.

"Ivan's Folly"

Chapter seven

Love

THE DEATH OF IVAN ILYCH

by Leo Tolstoy

And now these three remain: faith, hope and love.
But the greatest of these is love.

—1 Corinthians 13:13

In the film *Cast Away*, a FedEx engineer named Chuck Noland, played by Tom Hanks, survives a plane crash and washes up alone on an island. He manages to find sufficient means of survival. He also discovers in the plane's wreckage a volleyball. He marks it up to look like a face and names it Wilson. The closest thing Noland has to a companion, Wilson becomes a source of solace and comfort, a guard for his sanity, and even a well of strength, which helps him guard against giving up when being rescued seems impossible. The film powerfully shows how love and companionship—even if only in the form of a volleyball—are nearly as necessary to human survival as food, water, and shelter.

The Necessity of Friendship

Aristotle says friendship "is an absolute necessity in life." No one "would choose to live without friends, even if he had all the other goods" that life offers.[1] In *The Art of Loving*, psychologist Erich Fromm claims that the "deepest need of man" is "the need to overcome his separateness, to leave the prison of his aloneness."[2] This need is so strong, Fromm writes, that if it goes unmet, it will result in insanity. We need companionship—*love*—so badly that if we lack it, we will create the illusion of it, as Noland does with his volleyball named Wilson, just to survive.

Research backs this up. Various studies have shown how poorly children do in institutions where their physical requirements are met but their need for love is not. One study showed that children raised by their mothers in prison did better than children raised by highly trained professionals in a well-equipped institution.[3] Another study found that the lack of love can actually be fatal for children.[4] Harvard Medical School's famous Grant Study, which followed the lives of hundreds of men for seventy-five years, concluded that the most significant factor in life satisfaction is warm and loving relationships throughout one's life. The study's director summarized the findings this way: "Happiness is love. Full stop."[5]

It is love, as Dante famously says in the last line of *The Divine Comedy*, that "moves the sun and the other stars."[6] But we don't need ancient Greek philosophers or medieval Italian poets, or even modern-day sociologists (not to mention just about every pop song ever written), to tell us how necessary love is to human flourishing or our individual happiness; we just know. In *Faith, Hope, Love*, Josef Pieper puts it this way: "What matters to us, beyond mere existence, is the explicit confirmation: It is *good* that you exist; how wonderful that you are! In other words, what we need over and above sheer existence is: to be loved by another person."[7]

Too Many Loves

When it comes to love, we who communicate with the English language are at a great disadvantage. We have essentially one word to cover a wide variety of loves. We love our children; we love our dogs; we love mint-chip ice cream (at least, I do!); we love summer; and we love our spouses. All of these are, obviously, different kinds of loves. We have to rely on context in order to know that the word *love* when we talk about "making love" does not have the same meaning as when we say we "love" our grandmother. (Nor did it as far back as 1880, when Henry James used the phrase "making love" in *Portrait of a Lady*.)

Other languages have more words for love. The Indian language of Boro has a word for the kind of love that is temporal. Chinese has a word for the kind of love that is eternal. Danish has a word for the sense of falling in love. Hindi has a word for the realization of love that comes only from being separated. Portuguese has a word for the love felt for someone who was part of your past. Spanish has a word for the love of things, as opposed to people. And Greek has several words for the forms of love that define various human relationships.

It's more than simply a vocabulary problem, however. In each of these usages above, the context makes the meaning clear. However, when a single word bears the weight of so many different meanings, the distinctions between those meanings are inevitably blurred. When Wayne Pacelle, president and CEO of the Humane Society of the United States, met NFL player Michael Vick for the first time while Vick was imprisoned for convictions related to his dog-fighting operation (which involved horrific abuse of the animals, along with other crimes), Vick insisted to Pacelle that he "loves" dogs. As that conversation unfolded, it became clear that Vick, sadly, was confusing pride in possession with love.[8] He's not entirely to blame. The meaning of the word *love* has become so broad that the incoherent slogan "Love is love is love is love is love . . . ," proclaimed by the lead in a wildly successful Broadway show, has become the mantra of a generation.[9]

Both the Greek language and the Christian tradition offer a sharp contrast to this linguistic and moral fuzziness. The Greek of the New Testament uses a variety of words to refer to various kinds of love. In his book *The Four Loves,* C. S. Lewis famously explored four types of love, each associated with words from the Greek language: empathy (*storge*), friendship (*philia*), desire (*eros*), and godly love (*agape*), the highest form of love.

Godly love or *agape* is the kind of love meant in the First Epistle of John when it says that God is love (4:8). The King James Bible often translates *agape* as "charity" (e.g., 1 Cor. 13), which comes from a root word meaning "valued" or "dear." *Agape,* or charity, is the love that reflects the nature and character of God. It is sacrificial, self-giving, and righteous. Such love reflects the "triune God who is a communion of persons in self-giving love [who] created all things out of love. All persons are created to be in union with God in ultimate happiness."[10]

Happiness here, it's important to note, "is not some vague sense of goodwill," but is attained only "with a rich and complete understanding of what is truly good, in an ultimate sense."[11] This ultimate good is "union with God, which is true happiness."[12] Aquinas sums up the virtue of charity by calling it simply friendship with God,[13] and stating that the "perfection of the Christian life consists radically in charity."[14] Indeed, Paul says in 1 Corinthians 13:13, only faith, hope, and love (or charity) are everlasting—but "the greatest of these is love."

Charity perfects all the other virtues and contains all the virtues. The definition of charity given by Paul in 1 Corinthians 13 encompasses the virtues of patience, kindness, contentment, humility, temperance, justice, purity, honesty, wisdom, courage, faith, generosity, and perseverance. The definition reflects the very character of God.[15] The form of all the virtues is love. Charity "gives shape to (or trans-forms) acts of all the virtues by directing them toward the ultimate goal of union with God."[16] Only when we love as God loves can we heed the beautiful exhortation of Augustine: "Love, and do what you will: whether you hold your peace, through love hold your peace; whether you cry out, through love cry out; whether you correct, through love correct; whether you spare, through love do you spare: let the root of love be within, of this root can nothing spring but what is good."[17]

Charity perfects all the other virtues and contains all the virtues.

Agape: Supernatural Love

Clearly, not all that we call "love" is this kind of love, charity. Charity is "loving God first, and all else in God."[18] Charity, therefore, has its source in God. Such love is not natural to human beings but is supernatural.[19] It is a gift from God. Having the capability of this kind of love is part of what it means to be made in God's image.

Yet being capable of this love does not necessarily translate into possessing it. In fact, two of the profoundest miracles in my life consisted of God granting me supernatural love for two people for whom I could not muster love from my own strength despite my great effort to do so. Both were fellow Christians with whom I worked closely. Both were people whose personalities simply rubbed against mine. I willed myself to love them in my own strength, but I could not. Finally, I asked God to give me a supernatural love for both of these people. It did not happen overnight. I did not feel it taking place. But in both cases, after a few months passed, I suddenly realized that my attitude and feelings toward these people had gradually but completely transformed. I loved them. And in loving them, I came to see them completely differently. Nothing about them had changed. Everything in me had utterly changed. This was supernatural love. It reflects what Lewis writes in *Mere Christianity*: "He will give us feelings of love if he pleases. We cannot create them for ourselves."[20]

The Vice of Cupidity

This supernatural, theological love is a powerful theme in Leo Tolstoy's short novel *The Death of Ivan Ilych*. In the story, charity sharply contrasts with the empty, self-centered lives that populate the story. Ivan's life in particular is characterized not by the virtue of charity but by another kind of love: the vice of cupidity.

Most of us connect the word *cupidity* with its source, Cupid, the god of desire and erotic love in classical mythology. We associate Cupid with romance and Valentine's Day, but this sort of desire is not all that cupidity entails. Within ancient Christian tradition, cupidity was associated with lust and ambition, the counterpart of the virtue of charity or godly love. Augustine explains that love is the "impulse" to "enjoy God on his own account and one's neighbor on account of God." In contrast, cupidity (or lust) is "the impulse of one's mind to enjoy oneself and one's neighbor and any corporeal thing not on account of God."[21] While charity is desire that moves us toward God, cupidity is desire that moves us away from God. Thus, while there are many kinds of loves that are proper and many things that are proper to love, to love well requires the proper ordering of these loves, Augustine says.

> The person who lives a just and holy life is one who is a sound judge of these things. He is also a person who has ordered his love so that he does not love what it is wrong to love, or fail to love what should be loved, or love too much what should be loved less (or love too little what should be loved more), or love two things equally if one of them should be loved either less or more than the other, or love things either more or less if they should be loved equally.[22]

There is no tyranny like the tyranny of a desire that draws us away from God.

Ivan Ilych has spent his life in pursuit of such desires. In his youth "he succumbed to sensuality, to vanity" and "liberalism." He was a sycophant, "by nature attracted to people of high station as a fly is drawn to the light, assimilating their ways and views of life and establishing friendly relations with them."[23] He ordered his life around a received vision of how a successful life should go: "easily, pleasantly, and decorously."[24] His life was most markedly characterized, in fact, by decorum, a standard that, by definition, is based on surface appearances determined by ever-changing and fickle taste and manners.

Ivan's ontological orientation toward decorum is conveyed materially in his obsession with decor. As his successes in career and income increase, so too do his concerns over the appearance of his home (which is ironic, given the lack of familial love within the home). Even while at work, Ivan finds himself, despite liking his job and being successful at it, contemplating his furniture, curtains, and cornices. And it is while *decorating* that Ivan Ilych suffers his literal (and metaphorical) fall. Hanging drapery in his newest home, the grandest one yet, he slips and falls, bruising his side. The injury turns out to be fatal.

Ironically, tragically, Ivan's obsessive decorum is not even close to the accomplishment he fancies it to be: "In reality it was just what is usually seen in the houses of people of moderate means who want to appear rich, and therefore succeed only in resembling others like themselves: there are damasks, dark wood, plants, rugs, and dull and polished bronzes—all the things people of a certain class have in order to resemble other people of that class. His house was so like the others that it would never have been noticed, but to him it all seemed to be quite exceptional."[25] As the most famous line from the novel says, "Ivan Ilych's life had been most simple and most ordinary and therefore, most terrible."[26] There is perhaps no more apt object of pity than he who thinks himself exceptional but turns out to be merely ordinary. The tragedy, of course, is not in failing to be exceptional but in the greater loss of rejecting the glories of everyday gifts.

One of these great gifts that Ivan rejects is friendship. The love between friends is called *philia* in Greek (from which we get the word *filial*). This kind of love refers to the mutual affection, respect, and interconnectedness that "seeks the well-being of humanity"[27] that marks deep friendship. Many think that we in modern Western culture have lost much of the richness of this kind of brotherly love or deep friendship, particularly in the church, where both opposite and same-sex friendships are surrounded by anxiety because of our culture's tendency to equate nearly all forms of love with sex. Lewis mourns this loss. Because friendship is not necessary to human existence in the way that food and sex are, Lewis says, it should be valued all the more in being "freely chosen."[28]

Ivan Ilych clearly does not have this kind of love. The story begins with the announcement of his death at age forty-five. The opening focuses primarily on the responses of Ivan's colleagues and acquaintances to his premature death. These people cannot properly be called friends, and it quickly becomes clear that throughout his life Ivan utterly lacked the experience of the love of true friendship. It is a most unsettling start, striking an opening note of coldness that permeates nearly the entire story, beginning with that of those left to remember Ivan. Where we expect to find sadness and grief, we find selfishness and greed. Where we hope to witness love and loss, we witness callousness and complacency. Of all those ruminating on the death of Ivan, we read, "Each one thought or felt, 'Well, he's dead but I'm alive!'"[29]

Those closest to Ivan, whom the story refers to as "his so-called friends" and who are hardly close at all, are bothered more by the inconvenient obligations of paying condolences and attending the funeral than by Ivan's death. They find solace for their inconvenience in the fact that his death will open up a position that may allow some of them to advance in their careers.

A Life without Love

The reader naturally feels pity for Ivan to have been surrounded by such people. But as the story goes on, we learn that Ivan structured his life in such a way as to keep people at a distance both at work and at home. At work he "would maintain the semblance of friendly human relations." But "as soon as the official relations ended, so did everything else." He prided himself on his "capacity to separate his real life from the official side of affairs and not mix the two," managing these distinct relations "easily, pleasantly, correctly, and even artistically."[30] He maintained this distance even with those in his social circle, which consisted not of real friends but merely of "acquaintances among the best people and . . . people of importance." As for the rest, the "shabby friends and relations," Ivan, his wife, and their eldest daughter "were entirely agreed, and tacitly and unanimously kept at arm's length," shaking them off until "only the best people remained."[31] The startlingly cold reception of the news of Ivan's death turns out to be the fruit of what Ivan's life has sown.

Sadly, this same lovelessness also characterizes Ivan's marriage. The Greek term for the kind of love at the center of a romantic or sexual relationship is *eros*, from which we get the English word *erotic*. In Greek, the word refers to deep desire and is usually associated with sexual love. But Plato discusses *eros* more broadly to refer to the kind of intense desire that draws us out of ourselves toward the transcendent. For Plato such transcendence referred to the Ideal. But for Christians this transcendent desire—whether rooted in sexual desire for another person or in the longing caused by an object of beauty or visions of the good life cast by literature, film, or even advertising—points to God as the source of all beauty and goodness. Ivan seems to lack this kind of deep desire for something beyond and outside of himself, whether for another person or for God.

Ivan seems never to have experienced erotic desire. He had dalliances in his youth, we learn, but as with all his accomplishments, the proverbial sowing of Ivan's wild oats was rather like the fulfillment of some proper duty more than arising from some deep, if illicit, desire: "all done with clean hands, in clean linen, with French phrases, and above all among people of the best society and consequently with the approval of people of rank."[32] Even Ivan's marriage to Praskovya Fedorovna stems from duty rather than desire. After achieving professional success, Ivan attracts her at the local dances. At first Ivan doesn't even intend to marry, but when Fedorovna falls in love with him he says to himself, "Really, why shouldn't I marry?" After all, it is a match that offers Ivan "personal satisfaction" and meets the approval of "the most highly placed of his associates." "So," rather anti-climactically, "Ivan Ilych got married."[33]

The start of marriage for Ivan is "very pleasant." He enjoys the "conjugal caresses, the new furniture, new crockery, and new linen." But this pleasantness ends with the most natural of events: his wife becomes pregnant. And "from the first months of his wife's pregnancy, something new, unpleasant, depressing, and unseemly, and from which there was no way of escape, unexpectedly showed itself."[34] Ivan cares nothing about the birth and subsequent care of mother and child and withdraws from his family with the exception of "rare periods of amorousness which still came to them at times but did not last long."[35] Such moments are "islets at which they anchored for a while and then again set out upon that ocean of veiled hostility which showed itself in their aloofness from one another." Eventually, Ivan seeks from his wife and family only "those conveniences—dinner at home, housewife, and bed—which it could give him, and above all that propriety of external forms required by public opinion."[36]

Ivan's life lacks the love of both friendship and erotic desire. And when his children come along, we see he lacks even the love of family members for one another, which the Greek language calls *storge*.

Three of the children Ivan's wife bears die, and they are barely mentioned. Three children live. Eventually, when Ivan lies dying in his room, his eldest daughter is annoyed that his condition interrupts her evening plans. "Is it our fault?" she asks her mother. "It's as if we were to blame! I am sorry for papa, but why should we be tortured?"[37] Ivan's wife has a similar attitude. When Ivan falls ill and his sufferings increase unbearably, his wife thinks only of how miserable he has made her life: "She began to feel sorry for herself, and the more she pitied herself the more she hated her husband. She began to wish he would die; yet she did not want him to die because then his salary would cease. And this irritated her against him still more."[38] When Ivan tries to tell her the most recent doctor's report, she listens only until their daughter comes in, dressed to go out, and they depart, leaving Ivan alone. "Those about him did not understand or would not understand it," Ivan realizes, three months into his sickness. "His wife, his daughter, his son, his acquaintances, the doctors, the servants, and above all he himself, were aware that the whole interest he had for other people was whether he would soon vacate his place, and at last release the living from the discomfort caused by his presence and be himself released from his sufferings."[39]

Their lack of love "tormented Ivan Ilych more than anything."[40] Worse than his tremendous physical pain is his realization that he must "live thus all alone on the brink of an abyss, with no one who understood or pitied him."[41] No one feels compassion for him.

The Difference between Empathy and Compassion

While not the same as love, compassion is connected to love. Moral philosopher Martha Nussbaum explains that compassion is more than empathy.[42] Empathy allows someone to imagine what the experience of the sufferer might be like, but compassion goes beyond empathy. Compassion characterized Jesus's earthly ministry, leading him time and time again to heal or help those suffering. To have compassion is, literally, to "suffer with" someone (*com* meaning "with" and *passion* meaning "suffer"). Compassion involves "a sense of mature judgment and an understanding of the relatedness of life" and "directs our attention to life and the suffering of others."[43] Psychologist Paul Bloom, author of *Against Empathy*, argues that compassion—love, concern, and motivation to help others in their suffering—is more helpful and healthy than empathy—the ability to feel another's pain.[44] Charity is the bridge between mere empathy and compassion. Charity "orders our lives and our loves toward God and, subsequently, the whole of creation"[45] and "always seeks the best for its beloved."[46]

Ivan's colleague Peter Ivanovich illustrates the difference between empathy and compassion. He initially feels some sorrow and a sense of horror at the thought of Ivan's suffering. But it soon is evident that Peter

Ivanovich's fear is really for himself: "'Three days of frightful suffering and the death! Why, that might suddenly, at any time, happen to me,' he thought, and for a moment felt terrified." He takes comfort "that this had happened to Ivan Ilych and not to him, and that it should not and could not happen to him."[47] Peter Ivanovich feels enough empathy to imagine Ivan's suffering and to fear it for himself. He does not feel the compassion that would have led him to suffer with Ivan on Ivan's behalf.

Love Grounded in Reality

But even Ivan himself is guilty of denial of his own mortality. He knows "in the depth of his heart" the truth that he is dying, but his mind cannot accept it. He recalls a lesson from his youth: "The syllogism he had learnt from Kiesewetter's Logic: 'Caius is a man, men are mortal, therefore Caius is mortal,' had always seemed to him correct as applied to Caius, but certainly not as applied to himself. That Caius—man in the abstract—was mortal, was perfectly correct, but he was not Caius, not an abstract man, but a creature quite, quite separate from all others." Facing the reality of his life and his death requires Ivan to see himself not in the abstract but in the particular:

> He had been little Vanya, with a mamma and a papa, with Mitya and Volodya, with the toys, a coachman and a nurse, afterwards with Katenka and with all the joys, griefs, and delights of childhood, boyhood, and youth. What did Caius know of the smell of that striped leather ball Vanya had been so fond of? Had Caius kissed his mother's hand like that, and did the silk of her dress rustle so for Caius? Had he rioted like that at school when the pastry was bad? Had Caius been in love like that? Could Caius preside at a session as he did? "Caius really was mortal, and it was right for him to die; but for me, little Vanya, Ivan Ilych, with all my thoughts and emotions, it's altogether a different matter. It cannot be that I ought to die. That would be too terrible."[48]

Ivan's physical condition, caused by his literal fall, is emblematic of his spiritual condition, one we all share in being mortal. Charity—

godly love—cannot be separated from truth. Not just lofty transcendent truths, but the truth about the here and now and all the reality it entails—including our mortality. Truth is true and love is loving only in application.

But Ivan is not the only one having difficulty facing the truth. The people around him are in denial too, and this only makes his sickness even harder to bear: "What tormented Ivan Ilych most was the deception, the lie, which for some reason they all accepted, that he was not dying but was simply ill. . . . This deception tortured him—their not wishing to admit what they all knew and what he knew, but wanting to lie to him concerning his terrible condition, and wishing and forcing him to participate in that lie."[49] To love something for its own sake requires being truthful about what it is. Shakespeare expresses this poignantly in Sonnet 73. Addressed to the lover who sees the beloved's life nearing death, the poem closes with these two lines: "This thou perceivest, which makes thy love more strong, / To love that well which thou must leave ere long."[50] Augustine points to the necessity of truth to love when he says, "What is not loved for its own sake is not loved at all."[51] To face a beloved's weaknesses, including his mortality, is necessary to loving that person well by giving what is truly needed. Ivan wants—and needs—compassion (which is often, as here, translated as *pity*): "Apart from this lying, or because of it, what most tormented Ivan Ilych was that no one pitied him as he wished to be pitied. At certain moments after prolonged suffering he wished most of all (though he would have been ashamed to confess it) for someone to pity him as a sick child is pitied. He longed to be petted and comforted. . . . This falsity around him and within him did more than anything else to poison his last days." He yearns to shout at them, "Stop lying! You know and

Charity—godly love—cannot be separated from truth. Not just lofty transcendent truths, but the truth about the here and now and all the reality it entails—including our mortality. Truth is true and love is loving only in application.

I know that I am dying. Then at least stop lying about it!" But he lacks the will to do so. And so those around him reduce his dying to a mere "unpleasant" and "indecorous incident."[52]

Ironically, this state of affairs is the result of "that very decorum which he had served all his life long" in his self-deception. But finally, after one of many doctor's visits, as he tries to decipher the doctor's inscrutable medical jargon, Ivan is finally willing to face the most important questions honestly: "Is my condition bad? Is it very bad? Or is there as yet nothing much wrong?"[53]

To love something for its own sake requires being truthful about what it is.

The answer, yet unknown to him, is that his condition, both physical and spiritual, is very bad. The cavalier philosophy of the Latin *carpe diem*—eat, drink, and be merry, for tomorrow you die—is only half true. Tomorrow you die: so how you live today may determine who tends to your most basic needs in your dying days. And for Ivan, this turns out to be not his wife or his child or a friend, but the family's servant, Gerasim.

Servant Love

Gerasim is mentioned briefly in the opening chapter, but his real introduction occurs in the most humiliating circumstance for Ivan: "For his excretions also special arrangements had to be made, and this was a torment to him every time—a torment from the uncleanliness, the unseemliness, and the smell, and from knowing that another person had to take part in it."[54] Yet, the next line says, "through his most unpleasant matter, Ivan Ilych obtained comfort." Ivan speaks apologetically to Gerasim:

> "That must be very unpleasant for you. You must forgive me. I am helpless."
>
> "Oh, why, sir," and Gerasim's eyes beamed and he showed his glistening white teeth, "what's a little trouble? It's a case of illness with you, sir."
>
> And his deft strong hands did their accustomed task, and he went out of the room stepping lightly. Five minutes later he as lightly returned.[55]

In the midst of the most universal, most humbling, most unpleasant, and most human situation, Ivan finds the charity that has been absent most of his life. Only Gerasim faces the truth about Ivan's condition. Thus he is the only one capable of offering charity—love that seeks the good of the other in the knowledge that what is good is also true. Consequently, Ivan feels "at ease only with him." Gerasim tells Ivan the truth about us all, truth that others in the story shield themselves from: "We shall all of us die, so why should I grudge a little trouble?" Gerasim does not "think his work burdensome, because he was doing it for a dying man and hoped someone would do the same for him when his time came."[56] Gerasim understands that charity "is love received and given."[57] Gerasim's is a love that "rejoices with the truth" (1 Cor. 13:6).

> *Only in truth does charity shine forth,* only in truth can charity be authentically lived. Truth is the light that gives meaning and value to charity. That light is both the light of reason and the light of faith, through which the intellect attains to the natural and supernatural truth of charity: it grasps its meaning as gift, acceptance, and communion. Without truth, charity degenerates into sentimentality. Love becomes an empty shell, to be filled in an arbitrary way. In a culture without truth, this is the fatal risk facing love. It falls prey to contingent subjective emotions and opinions, the word "love" is abused and distorted, to the point where it comes to mean the opposite.[58]

This is what Flannery O'Connor means by her startling claim, "In the absence of faith, we govern by tenderness. . . . When tenderness is detached from the source of tenderness, its logical outcome is terror." Such tenderness, O'Connor says, "leads to the gas chamber."[59] When love is unmoored from unchanging truth, it becomes mere sentiment or tenderness. Sentiment and tenderness are opposed to suffering and can do anything to avoid pain. And the only end to earthly pain is death. Tenderness prefers death over suffering. Charity chooses to "suffer with," the literal meaning of *compassion*. Gerasim has true compassion for Ivan, a love rooted in acknowledgment of the truth of Ivan's condition.

As the weeks and months pass, one symptom leads to another, the doctors are unable to arrive at a diagnosis, and pain takes over. In the face of his family's indifference, Ivan begins to feel hatred toward them. His physical pain increases, as too his spiritual and emotional anguish that nothing he has achieved in his life means anything. He comes to see the deceptiveness of his whole life that has kept love from his life: "'This is wrong, it is not as it should be. All you have lived for and still live for is falsehood and deception, hiding life and death from you.' And as soon as he admitted that thought, his hatred and his agonizing physical suffering again sprang up, and with that suffering a consciousness of the unavoidable, approaching end."[60]

As his death draws near, Ivan's torments increase. Opium helps some of the physical suffering, but there seems to be no relief from his spiritual anguish. One night he cries out in anger to the God he had ignored his whole life:

> "Why hast Thou done all this? Why hast Thou brought me here? Why, why dost Thou torment me so terribly?" . . . And in imagination he began to recall the best moments of his pleasant life. But strange to say none of those best moments of his pleasant life now seemed at all what they had then seemed. . . . "It is as if I had been going downhill while I imagined I was going up. And that is really what it was. I was going up in public opinion, but to the same extent life was ebbing away from me. And now it is all done and there is only death."[61]

As his condition worsens, he discovers, rather accidentally, that his pain is alleviated when Gerasim holds up his legs. One night, gazing into Gerasim's face, Ivan Ilych suddenly wonders, "What if my whole life has been wrong?"[62] In facing this question, his mental sufferings became even worse than his physical pain.

> For the last three days of his life, Ivan screams.
>
> In the midst of this, two hours before his death, he finally asks himself, "But what is the right thing?" And upon asking this question, . . . he felt

that someone was kissing his hand. He opened his eyes, looked at his son, and felt sorry for him. His wife came up to him and he glanced at her. She was gazing at him open-mouthed, with undried tears on her nose and cheek and a despairing look on her face. He felt sorry for her too. . . .

And suddenly it grew clear to him that what had been oppressing him and would not leave him was all dropping away at once from two sides, from ten sides, and from all sides. He was sorry for them, he must act so as not to hurt them: release them and free himself from these sufferings. "How good and how simple!" he thought. "And the pain?" he asked himself. "What has become of it? Where are you, pain?" He turned his attention to it. "Yes, here it is. Well, what of it? Let the pain be." "And death . . . where is it?" He sought his former accustomed fear of death and did not find it. "Where is it? What death?" There was no fear because there was no death. In place of death there was light. "So that's what it is!" he suddenly exclaimed aloud. "What joy!"

To him all this happened in a single instant, and the meaning of that instant did not change. For those present his agony continued for another two hours. Something rattled in his throat, his emaciated body twitched, then the gasping and rattle became less and less frequent. "It is finished!" said someone near him.

He heard these words and repeated them in his soul. "Death is finished," he said to himself. "It is no more!" He drew in a breath, stopped in the midst of a sigh, stretched out, and died.[63]

These are the last words of the story. In death, Ivan Ilych finds a true vision for the good life. Indeed, he finds life itself. "We know that we have passed from death to life, because we love each other" (1 John 3:14).

In his sermon "On Love," John Wesley makes two important claims about love. First, Wesley says, "Without love nothing can so profit us as to make our lives happy." He explains further: "By happiness I mean, not a slight, trifling pleasure, that perhaps begins and ends in the same hour; but such a state of well-being as contents the soul, and gives it a steady, lasting satisfaction." Surely, by the end of his life, Ivan has learned this truth. Without love, Wesley says, "nothing can make death comfortable."[64]

It so happens that my most recent rereading of *The Death of Ivan Ilych* took place amid intimations of mortality in my own life. I think I am like most of us in wanting to shield myself from the intimate, uncomfortable, messy processes that mark the ending stages of life. We live in a culture that keeps death, dying, and aging as far from most of us for as long as possible. Geography often separates us from the aging of our elders, and medical science from our own aging.

I have been given the gift, however, of having my aging parents brought back into close proximity, and with their proximity has come the bodily, physical presence of the sights, sounds, scents, and servitude of illness and aging. And so it happened that the day before I bore helpless witness, quite recently, to my father's groanings in a hospital bed, I had only just reread the pages of Ivan Ilych's final fear- and scream-filled days.

Reading them prepared me for something I didn't know I needed to be prepared for. Facing something terrible, I could behold something less terrible, something good even, because I knew from reading *The Death of Ivan Ilych* that it is a terrible but wonderful thing that binds all of humanity together: the bearing of one another's burdens.

My father is now well. But one day, he—like all of us here—won't be. Death will come. And when he does, he will not be a stranger. Death is the shadow that has trailed us all our days, and comes 'round to meet us at the front door. No lock can keep him out forever.

How we die will depend on how we live and how we love, as *The Death of Ivan Ilych* helps us see. Its vision of charity—love given and received—is the image of the servant who, by tending the feet of others, bears their suffering.

Part Three

The Heavenly Virtues

"Dancing with Mattie"

Chapter Eight

Chastity

ETHAN FROME

by Edith Wharton

You have heard that it was said, "You shall not commit adultery." But I tell you that anyone who looks at a woman lustfully has already committed adultery with her in his heart.

—Matthew 5:27–28

I vividly remember the first time I heard the word *chastity*.

I was about ten years old. Arriving home after school one day, I walked into the living room where the television was tuned in to an afternoon talk show. That day's guest was Cher, a singer who made up one half of the popular seventies folk duo Sonny and Cher. She and the show's host were discussing the couple's young daughter, whose name was Chastity. I'd never heard that name or word before, but it didn't strike me as odd—not, that is, until the host asked Cher, with a sly voice, "Have you explained to your daughter what her name means?" Cher laughed, and I realized that the adults seemed to be sharing some kind of a naughty joke. As soon as I had a chance, I looked up *chastity* in the dictionary and still didn't get the joke. But I felt sorry for the little girl whose name the adults treated like something dirty.

"The Most Unpopular of the Christian Virtues"

Chastity, C. S. Lewis quipped, is "the most unpopular of the Christian virtues."[1] Augustine's view of chastity was a bit more favorable—but not favorable enough for him to wish it upon himself. "Oh Lord," he prayed, as the Lord was drawing Augustine to himself, "Give me chastity and continence, but not yet."[2]

Of all the virtues, chastity is one of the most misunderstood. It tends to be idealized—both negatively and positively, either abhorred or idolized. The high esteem in which chastity was held in ancient pagan and Christian cultures, for example, evolved into reverence for perpetual virginity, epitomized by Mary, whose virginity was imitated by those in the church taking vows of celibacy. Such idealization for chastity would not last, however. Percy Bysshe Shelley, the atheistic Romantic poet, gave chastity a backhanded compliment in book 9 of his poem *Queen Mab*, an epic-length poem setting forth Shelley's revolutionary philosophy.

Calling chastity "dull and selfish," the poem goes on to describe it dismissively as that "virtue of the cheaply virtuous / Who pride themselves in senselessness and frost."[3] In his novel *Eyeless in Gaza,* Aldous Huxley refers to chastity as "the most unnatural of all the sexual perversions."[4]

Sex is, of course, quite natural, as is sexual desire. Human vitality is characterized by our natural desires for self-preservation, reproduction, pleasure, and community. Just as individuals need food to live, the human race depends on human vitality, or the creational impulse, in order to continue. Sexual desire is good because it is part of how God designed human beings. God made the continuation of the human race dependent on communion with and desire for one another.

Of all the virtues, chastity is one of the most misunderstood. It tends to be idealized—both negatively and positively, either abhorred or idolized.

Temperance disciplines all the human appetites. As a kind of temperance, chastity tempers in particular the part of human vitality related to our desire to reproduce and to experience companionship. Temperance moderates according to the dictates of reason, which is why Augustine calls chastity, or purity, "a virtue of the mind,"[5] locating it in desire rather than action.[6] Like temperance, chastity demands more than mere suppression or denial for healthy discipline. Chastity is the proper ordering of one good thing (sexual desire) within a hierarchy of other good things.

However, even within the church, the importance of chastity is more often assumed than understood. Chastity is not the same as virginity or celibacy. Within Christianity, it is something both married and single people are called to. The person who is raped is not guilty of being unchaste. On the other hand, the consumer of pornography is. Chastity, most simply, is fidelity.

Chastity is the proper ordering of one good thing (sexual desire) within a hierarchy of other good things.

But beyond a proper definition of this virtue, the greater question is, Why does chastity even matter?

This question has gone so unexamined in the contemporary church that some years ago, Lauren Winner, a thoughtful adult convert to Christianity, had to research and write her own book in order to answer this question. *Real Sex: The Naked Truth about Chastity* is an insightful exploration of how chastity isn't just a negation: it's a positive good.

Chastity is a positive discipline that involves the whole person and affects the whole person. As one philosopher explains, chastity "is a quality of one's character, evident in all areas of life." It is a discipline oriented toward "becoming a person with an outlook that allows one to selflessly appreciate good and attractive things—most especially bodies and the pleasures they afford—by keeping those goods ordered to the good of the whole person and his or her vocation to love."[7] If sex "is about persons being bodies together,"[8] then chastity is about the right bodies being together at the right time. Chastity, then, is "not the mere absence of sex but an active conforming of one's body to the arc of the gospel."[9] Properly understood, chastity is not withholding but giving. As G. K. Chesterton enthuses, "Chastity does not mean abstention from sexual wrong; it means something flaming, like Joan of Arc."[10]

Properly understood, chastity is not withholding but giving.

Fidelity to another person, particularly in marriage, is more than physical. Sexual unfaithfulness wreaks certain pain and irreparable damage to a relationship. Yet so too does emotional infidelity, as *Ethan Frome* powerfully shows. This novel tells the story of disordered desires that are allowed to grow in their distortion until a marriage and three lives are ruined—even without the ultimate act of sexual betrayal taking place.

The Unchastity of Ethan Frome

Ethan Frome is set near the turn of the twentieth century. We first encounter Ethan through the eyes of the narrator, a visitor to the town who slowly discovers the events of years ago that have formed Ethan as we find him in the present day. The frame narrative is similar to that used in *The Great Gatsby*. The narrator, who visits the town on business, meets Ethan Frome when Ethan is an old and broken man. Even then, Ethan is "the most striking figure" in rural Starkfield, Massachusetts. At age fifty-two, "stiffened and grizzled,"[11] he looks much older, and is "but the ruin of a man."[12] The narrator learns that an accident years ago (the "smash-up") caused the atrophy of Ethan's right side and the jeering red scar on his forehead. Beyond these disfigurements, Ethan's face bears a "pained look," one that "neither poverty nor physical suffering could have put" there.[13] Clearly, Ethan's suffering is rooted less in the state of his circumstances than in the state of his soul. From the beginning, we see that his physical and spiritual condition contrasts sharply with the vitality of healthy human desire.

Undisciplined sexual desire is lust. Living in a modern culture in which sexual lust is so rampant and its destructiveness so woven into the social fabric, we see this vice a bit differently than earlier Christians did. The desert fathers understood lust more broadly as any excessive desire, not only wanton sexual desire. They viewed lust as "a sin of weakness, not a sin of malice."[14] This is why in *The Divine Comedy* Dante places those guilty of the sin of lust in the second circle, which is the first circle within hell (limbo being the first circle), reflecting the medieval church's view that lust is the least deadly of the deadly sins. The punishment for lust is, correspondingly, the lightest within hell: the souls damned for their lust spend eternity bandied about by strong gusts of wind, never able to rest, a fitting symbol of the sin of giving in to their carnal desires.

Ethan Frome's lust embodies each of the kinds of lust the Bible warns against: "the lust of the flesh, the lust of the eyes, and the pride of life" (1 John 2:16). David L. Allen explains that the Greek term for *lust* that is used in this passage carries the sense of being "hot after something," and it denotes things sought apart from God. "Lust of the flesh" refers to the worldly desires of our corrupted human nature as opposed to the will of God. The phrase "describes what it means to live life dominated by the senses" and neglectful of spiritual things. "Lust of the eyes" refers to desires for the things we can see—whether material possessions, beautiful persons, or successful status—again, pursued apart from God's will. It describes the condition of being consumed by outward appearances. Finally, "the pride of life," Allen explains, "describes the arrogant spirit of self-sufficiency."[15]

In sum, lust of the flesh centers on temptations that originate within the body, with our inner appetites (sexual or otherwise), and lust of the eyes on temptations originating externally, with things we perceive and then desire to possess. The pride of life combines the two, appealing to the internal desire to be like God and seeking fulfillment of this through external shows of power. Each of these lusts is at work in Ethan. His story depicts how chastity involves the whole person and, within the context of a marriage, every aspect of the marriage: physical, emotional, and spiritual.

Chastity involves the whole person and, within the context of a marriage, every aspect of the marriage: physical, emotional, and spiritual.

As a young man, Ethan's formal schooling was cut short by his father's death, followed by his mother's illness and eventual death. Ethan bears out the truth of Alexander Pope's famous line in *An Essay on Man* that "a little learning's a dangerous thing," for his short time at school only "fed his fancy and made him aware of huge cloudy meanings behind the daily face of things."[16] His schooling was just enough to raise his expectations, only to see them go unfulfilled, breeding in him frustration, resentment, and a sense of being ill-suited to those around him. His mind was all dressed up but given no place to go.

Ethan returned home to care for his mother. His cousin Zenobia (Zeena) Pierce (as with Pierce, whose piercing personality turns Ethan cold, the names in this book often resonate with meaningful associations) came to assist in nursing Ethan's mother, and for a time, Ethan's oppression lifted. Zeena brought understanding, order, and laughter into Ethan's life. They married.

But his happiness quickly vanished. Like Ethan's mother, Zeena "too fell silent."[17] Within a year, Zeena became sick with hypochondria. Their union grew as cold as the snow that blankets the cold New England town for much of the year.

Then Mattie Silver arrived.

A poor relation of Zeena's, Mattie is introduced to the reader through Ethan's perspective years before the narrative begins as he waits for her outside the church where she is attending a dance. He watches her through the window, a flimsy barrier against the lust of his eyes. He searches the crowd inside "for a glimpse of the dark head under the cherry-colored scarf" and is jealous at spotting Mattie dancing a reel with a handsome, lively partner. The scene is rich with the sensory detail Ethan's eyes take in as he seeks, is tempted, and finally consumed by his carnal desires: "As she passed down the line, her light figure swinging from hand to hand in circles of increasing swiftness, the scarf flew off her head and stood out behind her shoulders, and Frome, at each turn, caught sight of her laughing panting lips, the cloud of dark hair about her forehead, and the dark eyes which seemed the only fixed points in a maze of flying lines."[18]

At first, Ethan's desire is not solely, or even primarily, sexual. It is, rather, materialistic, possessive, and covetous: the lust of the eyes. What Ethan wants at this point is less Mattie herself than for him to be in the scene he now observes as an outsider looking in: "The dancers were going faster and faster, and the musicians, to keep up with them, belabored their instruments like jockeys lashing their mounts on the home-stretch; yet it seemed to the young man at the window that the reel would never end. Now and then he turned his eyes from the girl's face to that of her partner, which, in the exhilaration of the dance, had taken on a look of almost impudent ownership."[19]

The envy Ethan feels of Mattie's dance partner—a suitable match for Mattie—fuels his illicit desire for her. When the dance ends, Mattie has to choose whether to accompany her dance partner or Ethan home; she chooses Ethan. This walk is like countless others they've taken, filled with sensory experiences that knit together their emotions, exquisite sensations: ". . . the cold red of sunset behind winter hills, the flight of cloud-flocks over slopes of golden stubble, or the intensely blue shadows of hemlocks on sunlit snow. When she said to him once: 'It looks just as if it was painted!' it seemed to Ethan that the art of definition could go no farther, and that words had at last been found to utter his secret soul."[20] When they arrive home from the dance, Ethan feels through "his tingling veins" that just "one sensation throbbed: the warmth of Mattie's shoulder against his."[21]

Lust of the eyes—desire for things external to oneself, prompted by any of the sense organs—is connected to lust of the flesh—desire rooted in needs from deep within. Ethan's sexual desire for Mattie is connected to deeper desires for the intimacy of friendship and companionship, which he lacks, even with his wife. Ethan is "more sensitive than the people about him." He feels isolated and lonely, not knowing "whether any one else in the world felt as he did." With Mattie he feels he has found someone who shares in his appreciation for beauty and wonder, and he relishes the opportunity to gaze at the stars with her or stand "entranced before a ledge of granite thrusting up through the fern."[22] Mattie's attentiveness to Ethan and her admiration for him also feed his malnourished ego.

The novel paints a sympathetic picture of Ethan. He is a sensitive man whose desires, although not rightly ordered, are good: he values companionship, nature, knowledge, and beauty. He has been self-sacrificing in his care for his parents and acted honorably by marrying Zeena after she came to help. In his desires for beauty, friendship, affirmation, and respect, Ethan is like all of us. His situation is hard. He is a man born into hard conditions, with untapped potential, exposed to just enough of life beyond the narrow constraints of the life he inherited so as to dream, only to see those dreams frustrated. Even so, he epitomizes the definition of "lust of the flesh," desire rooted in one's fallen human nature, in inner needs he seeks to fulfill apart from the will of God.[23]

Ethan's lust of the flesh arises from seeing in others qualities he lacks and, in seeing this lack, desires. He is naturally awkward and is intensely aware of this. He admires "recklessness and gaiety in others" and feels pleasure from the sociability that does not come easily to him. The contrast "between his outer situation and his inner needs," the narrator observes, is "poignant."[24] But Mattie's arrival brought "a bit of hopeful young life" that was "like the lighting of a fire on a cold hearth."[25]

The Wife of His Youth

It is, ironically, at Zeena's request that Ethan accompanies Mattie to and from social events in town on her occasional nights off. The practice becomes a ritual that brings him increasing anticipation and delight, and the "fact that he had no right to show his feelings" only heightens his pleasure more.[26] By the time Ethan and Mattie face an unexpected opportunity to be alone for an extended time, their desires have been whetted, and temptation proves to be more than they are willing to resist.

In contrast to Ethan, Zeena is painted most unsympathetically, rousing our compassion for Ethan's situation all the more. Zeena is full of complaints, which she delivers in a "flat whine." She is rigid in both body and personality. She has false teeth and lashless eyelids. During one dinner she tells repugnant stories of the "intestinal disturbances among her friends and relatives."[27] Ethan and Zeena are two people who seem to bring out the worst in each other. Sadly, we all know couples like this. He feels he must "wear out all his years at the side of a bitter querulous woman," and she becomes "a hundred times bitterer and more discontented than when he had married her."[28]

It's important, however, to note that early in their relationship, Ethan and Zeena experienced laughter and hope. The illnesses that began to plague Zeena a year after their marriage changed that. But the dynamics of a relationship are determined by two people, not one. The rudder that turns the ship of a relationship in the way that will either bring it safely home or send it straight into the deathly glacier need not be large to direct it one way or the other. As Mattie says to Ethan just before the two of them later sail down the snow bank to their tragedy, "It takes two to coax it round the corner."[29]

The marital relationship is singular in the way each partner shapes and forms the other. The good habits practiced by one partner contribute to the positive formation of the other. The same is true of bad habits. This mutuality doubles the effects of one person's habits, whether positively or negatively. Thus, to reject the partner you once chose, as Ethan does, is, in a way, a kind of rejection of oneself. This is the idea expressed in Ephesians 5 when it says that "husbands ought to love their wives as their own bodies. He who loves his wife loves himself. After all, no one ever hated their own body, but they feed and care for their body" (vv. 28–29). Caring for one's spouse as one would care for oneself makes it possible to fulfill the purpose of marriage, described earlier in this same chapter of Ephesians, which is to love your wife "just as Christ loved the church and gave himself up for her to make her holy, cleansing her by the washing with water through the word, and to present her to himself as a radiant church, without stain or wrinkle or any other blemish, but holy and blameless" (vv. 26–27).

While Zeena bears responsibility for the habits that have made her difficult to love, Ethan too has contributed to her character formation. If a husband's care for his wife helps in her sanctification, then the reverse is true, as well. The mutuality that is part of every relationship is magnified in the marital relationship, in which two bodies become one flesh. Marriage to Ethan has made Zeena worse, not better. Whatever else might have been the cause for this, Ethan surely has a part. His response to the problem is to pursue lust.

The mutuality that is part of every relationship is magnified in the marital relationship, in which two bodies become one flesh.

Ethan's lack of chastity begins with giving Mattie time and attention that he should not give: "At first she was so awkward that he could not help laughing at her; but she laughed with him and that made them better friends. He did his best to supplement her unskilled efforts, getting up earlier than usual to light the kitchen fire, carrying in the wood overnight, and neglecting the mill for the farm that he might help her about the house during the day."[30] Early on, he develops habits of attentiveness toward her that he did not for his wife. This internal orientation is manifested outwardly by as small—and as significant—a habit as beginning after Mattie's arrival to shave every day. He makes a garden for her. He imagines what a good wife she might become to someone someday. Eventually, he cannot imagine her being that for anyone other than him. These efforts of fondness toward Mattie shift his orientation away from Zeena. It's the age-old story, the paradox of the extramarital affair, confirmed by research: had the time, attention, and emotion spent on the affair been invested in the marriage instead, the affair might never have occurred.[31] Zeena is not blind to these attentions. Once, after Ethan cleaned the kitchen floor in one of many efforts to cover for Mattie's inadequate work, Zeena "surprised him at the churn and had turned away silently, with one of her queer looks."[32]

Primed by the shorter moments he and Mattie share together, when Zeena announces unexpectedly that she will be gone for an entire day to see a new doctor out of town, Ethan envisions what extended time alone with Mattie might be like. He imagines their evening meal unhindered by Zeena's presence. The connection between the appetite for food and the appetite for sex is one that the desert fathers recognized.[33] The romantic meal Ethan and Mattie share proves to be both the height and the pit of their illicit love, a reminder that "sin entered the world through the bodily act of eating."[34]

Their evening together is as idyllic as Ethan hopes it will be. Even their mutual shyness enhances its honeymoon quality. Ethan attributes his feelings of awkwardness not to his wrongdoing but to his natural reserve. Yet his sexual lust is outweighed by his lust of the flesh: that little voice inside him that tells him he is inferior and must, therefore, prove himself to himself.

The evening is marred by just one small incident. In preparing the dinner table, Mattie uses Zeena's special pickle dish kept on the top shelf of the china closet. Zeena's cat—who has been a lingering reminder of her owner throughout the evening—knocks it over, breaking the dish into pieces. The broken dish not only precipitates the tragic outcome of the plot but is laden with symbolism. It is red, the color of the scarf Mattie wore in her hair at the dance, and the color of blood and harlotry. It was a wedding gift to the Fromes, one so special to Zeena that she never used it (suggestive of another kind of marital "disuse" that characterizes their marriage). The smashing of the dish is a stark symbol of Ethan's breaking of his marriage vows and foreshadows the greater "smash-up" to come, one that will forever change and define the relationship of these three people.

The fantasy ends when Zeena returns. And with a new medical diagnosis, she has the perfect excuse to put Mattie out in order to make room in the house for a more helpful boarder. "I never bargained to take her for life!" Zeena tells Ethan when he protests.[35] This is, of course, exactly what Ethan pledged in his marriage vows to Zeena—to take her for life. He is the one violating a vow, not Zeena.

Ethan is a man lacking even a healthy sense of control over his life. Yet he overlooks the very thing he can exert control over: his treatment of Zeena. Failing that, his sense of his lack of control over his life spirals out in the ensuing hours to its crisis point.

He and Mattie rashly determine to exert ultimate control over their lives by sledding down a hill and into a great tree at the bottom, thus ending their lives. Their decision is the inevitable culmination of unchastity: the pride of life that is the "arrogant spirit of self-sufficiency." But even this is out of their control, and it all goes wrong. Ethan and Mattie are left alive but gravely and permanently injured. Their foolish, romantic vision of dying together gloriously is met by harsh reality.

It could have turned out so much differently if Ethan had loved—purely, faithfully, and chastely—both his wife and Mattie. Although easy to miss amid all the misery portrayed, small details in the story suggest that Ethan and Zeena's marriage might have been brighter.

Ethan had married Zeena, seven years his elder, out of a sense of obligation, and she recognized this. A bad beginning worsened over time: "Perhaps it was the inevitable effect of life on the farm, or perhaps, as she sometimes said, it was because Ethan 'never listened.' The charge was not wholly unfounded. When she spoke it was only to complain, and to complain of things not in his power to remedy; and to check a tendency to impatient retort he had first formed the habit of not answering her, and finally of thinking of other things while she talked."[36]

The night of his dinner with Mattie, after Zeena returns from the new doctor and shares the dismal diagnosis with Ethan, he experiences a rare moment of compassion for her. He notices, looking at her, she "looked so hard and lonely, sitting there in the darkness with such thoughts."[37] Not long afterward he tells her, regretfully but defensively, "You're a poor man's wife, Zeena; but I'll do the best I can for you."[38] Yet this is a lie. He is not, and has not been, doing the best for her.

But what if he had?

Oh, their marriage would not have been perfect. It likely would always have been hard. Neither a good marriage nor a bad marriage is, in most cases, owing to just one thing, but to an accumulation of things that reach a tipping point that tilts toward better or worse. But at some point in the modern age, people were led to think that while some things might be hard and so must be worked at—things like work, school, raising children, maintaining health, even life itself—a marriage that is hard must be quit.

What a sharp contrast is painted by the biblical vision of marriage, rooted in love that is patient, kind, protective, and selfless. Recognizing the natural temptation to let time take its toll, Proverbs 5:18 exhorts a man to "rejoice in the wife of [his] youth." No exemptions are given for a wife who is sick, cranky, petulant, or needy. In fact, in Malachi 2:14, unfaithfulness to the wife of one's youth is one reason given for the Lord's rejection of the sacrifice offered to him. Whatever it was that was good enough in a woman to make a man want her in youth, these verses seem to imply, ought to be good enough in old age.

The virtue of chastity is both a recognition of this relational reality and a safeguard. Ethan and Mattie never have sex with one another. But they do not practice true chastity. Chastity is less about control of oneself than about love of the other. Ethan's love, both for his wife and for Mattie, falls short. If he had loved and not merely lusted for Mattie, and if he had sought for her good, he would have wanted what was good and right for her—the chance for a lawful husband, not an illicit lover. This understanding is reflected in the words of Pope John Paul II: "Only the chaste man and the chaste woman are capable of true love."[39] Zeena too, it might be argued, in the treatment of her husband has not been chaste because, in its broadest sense, *chaste* means "morally pure."[40] Love seeks the good of the other. Lust does not.

I have a single friend who, years ago, became infatuated with a male coworker who was in a difficult marriage. The two had a natural rapport and shared commitment to their work, which was meaningful to both of them. Because they were both committed Christians, the prospect of an affair seemed, ultimately, unlikely to my friend, but for a time she struggled. She was sure the attraction she felt was mutual. Many Christian leaders and authorities advise believers to run from such situations (even shunning opposite-sex friendships altogether to avoid them), and my friend seriously considered giving up a job she loved in order to flee temptation. But, as she worked through her feelings of desire, she came to realize that she did, in fact, love this man. She loved him as a Christian brother and wanted the best for him. She loved him enough to vow that no matter how strong her feelings grew, she would not harm her brother by entangling him in sin. And she didn't. By the time her coworker moved away for another job, her lust for him had subsided. But her pure love remained.

Chastity is less about control of oneself than about love of the other.

It's a common observation that over time married people begin to look like one another. One theory for this phenomenon is that shared emotions produce similar facial patterns that become etched into both faces over the years, making them resemble each other more.[41] *Ethan Frome* offers an ironic twist on this truth. The injuries Mattie receives in the smash-up render her forever dependent on the woman she and Ethan betrayed. At the story's end, she has grown so similar to Zeena in appearance and demeanor that when the narrator enters the Frome house for the first time many years later, he is uncertain at first which one is Ethan's wife and which his near mistress. Slowly, it becomes clear that the more crippled, complaining one is Mattie, who is now under Zeena's care. Ethan now lives not with one whiny, querulous woman but with two.

The description of the last scene that takes place in the Frome house—in the kitchen—is filled with things that are rough, soiled, and broken. Echoing Zeena's words earlier in the novel, Ethan tells a visitor, apologetically, "My, it's cold here! The fire must be 'most out."[42] Coldness permeates the Fromes' marriage, kitchen, house, town, and community. The place is as wrong for them as they are for one another.

Chastity and Community

Just as marriage takes place before and is upheld within community, so too does chastity, whether that of a married person or a single one. Thus the novel's setting is a significant element of the story.

Ethan and Zeena's alienation from one another is rooted in the alienation that characterizes life in Starkfield (another of the novel's resonant names). Starkfield is a cold place, both geographically and emotionally. Its citizens uphold the real-life stereotype of New Englanders: rigidly stoic, intensely private, and exceedingly independent. (I hail from New England. I know my people well.) Besides the chill of winter and snow, Starkfield is characterized by silence. The silence freezes Ethan's spirit even more than does the weather or his wife, who goes silent on Ethan after they marry. When they first married, Ethan fancied that having Zeena as his wife would help him find his place in the world, but it didn't. She, on the other hand, was disappointed in life on an isolated farm.[43] In marriage, they find themselves alone together.

Just as marriage takes place before and is upheld within community, so too does chastity, whether that of a married person or a single one.

While chastity is formed in and sustained in community, lust "thrives in privacy and alienation, and lustful people often feel alone."[44] Alienation is the opposite sense of knowing another and being known. Frederick Buechner explains that "the hunger to know someone sexually is the hunger to know and be known by that person humanly."[45] Lust derives from a feeling of lack, and nothing feels more lacking than a sense of isolation. It is probably not coincidental that the technology that makes pornography omnipresent is the very technology that is isolating human beings from one another more and more and generating greater loneliness.[46] Ethan's lusts are rooted in his loneliness.

Marriage forms a little society. And the health of that little society depends to some degree on the health of the larger surrounding society.

Tellingly, the closest he comes to changing course and remaining chaste occurs because of a rare moment of compassion from a neighbor when Ethan makes a desperate appeal to her. "It was a long time since any one had spoken to him as kindly. . . . Most people were either indifferent to his troubles, or disposed to think it natural that a young fellow of his age should have carried without repining the burden of three crippled lives. But Mrs. Hale had said, 'You've had an awful mean time, Ethan Frome,' and he felt less alone with his misery." This unexpected, uncommon kindness deters Ethan from his plan to request a loan under false pretenses. For the moment, Ethan sees his situation clearly and chooses to accept it rather than do wrong: "With the sudden perception of the point to which his madness had carried him, the madness fell and he saw his life before him as it was. He was a poor man, the husband of a sickly woman, whom his desertion would leave alone and destitute; and even if he had had the heart to desert her he could have done so only by deceiving two kindly people who had pitied him."[47] If Ethan had kept this resolve, he might have found his way to some fulfillment. But this rare experience of community is not enough.

Lauren Winner explains, "The community is not so much cop as it is storyteller, telling and retelling the foundational stories that make sense of the community's norms."[48] Marriage is not only about mutual companionship and romantic love, but it is the institution "out of which cultures and societies are formed."[49] Marriage "is about children, and household economy, and stability. And marriage is also about God."[50] Marriage forms a little society. And the health of that little society depends to some degree on the health of the larger surrounding society.

Unlike abstention, an act of an individual, chastity is a form of community, and chastity depends on community. We can't always choose where we place our roots, but when we can, it's important to choose well. The ancient monastics took their vows of chastity within a community. Whether or not we realize it, we do as well.

"Diligent Christian"

CHAPTER NINE

Diligence

PILGRIM'S PROGRESS

by John Bunyan

And we desire that every one of you do shew the same diligence to the full assurance of hope unto the end: That ye be not slothful, but followers of them who through faith and patience inherit the promises.

—Hebrews 6:11–12 (KJV)

After a frustrating rehearsal one day, violinist Mischa Elman and his wife were leaving Carnegie Hall by the backstage entrance when they were approached by two tourists looking for the hall's entrance. Seeing Elman's violin case, they asked, "How do you get to Carnegie Hall?" Without looking up, Elman replied, "Practice."[1] Other versions of this story (there are many) ramp up the punch line to "Practice, practice, practice!"

Whether this urban legend is true or not, it conveys the powerful truth that most accomplishments in life require the tedium of time and effort. This is true of expertise in one's craft, proficiency in a new language, and the depth of a good friendship, as it is for most other things. The secret ingredient to most success is diligence.

The word *diligence* comes from a Latin word that once meant "to single out, value highly, esteem, prize, love." From this meaning, diligence later came to mean "attentiveness" or "carefulness." This evolution in meaning is logical since one usually renders care and attention to things one values and esteems. From this intermediate meaning, it is a short skip to our current sense of diligence as "steady, persistent effort."[2]

The Most Boring Virtue

Diligence is the most humble, perhaps even the most boring, of virtues. Diligence is so humdrum that it doesn't get nearly as much attention in moral philosophy as the other virtues. Some of its near cousins, such as perseverance and constancy, get more coverage, but neither of these mean quite the same thing. On the other hand, the Bible mentions diligence a considerable number of times (particularly in the King James translation). And as with all the virtues, diligence is not virtuous unless it is put toward a virtuous end. Persistence in planning a robbery or harassing strangers on the internet isn't a virtue any more than loyalty is virtuous when it's given to a mobster or a Klansman.

Diligence must also, like other virtues, represent a mean between an extreme of excess and an extreme of deficiency. It's easy to see how insufficient diligence is a vice, but an excess of effort is also a vice. Such excess could take various forms. One form might be the workaholic. Working too hard at one good thing (e.g., a job) while neglecting other important things (e.g., family) is a vice. Perfectionism is another example of caring to a detrimental degree. Another form of excessive effort might manifest as obsessive-compulsive disorder. Too much care and attention given to social media notifications might be another example of excessive care and attention that constitutes a vice. (Guilty!)

In the Bible, diligence is often presented in contrast to its opposite, sloth. For example, Proverbs 12:24 says, "The hand of the diligent shall bear rule: but the slothful shall be under tribute" (KJV). Sloth has received considerable examination by moral philosophers, so to understand the virtue of diligence, it's helpful to examine its opposing vice of deficiency.

Sloth is commonly thought of as laziness, but it's much more than that. (We saw in chapter 6 that sloth opposes magnanimity, for example.) Sloth involves not only a lack of effort but also a lack of care. In fact, the Greek word for sloth, *acedia*, literally means "without care" or "careless." It's similar to a word we use more commonly today, *apathy*. One of the seven deadly sins, sloth was nicknamed by the early monks as the "noonday devil," after that sense of dullness or languor that commonly sets in at midday. (College professors find this languor most prevalent in their classes right after lunch.)

> Sloth involves not only a lack of effort but also a lack of care.

Just as the original meaning of *diligent* connoted desire, the slothful person is, in contrast, without appetite or desire. Such a condition clearly goes against both our design and the one who designed us. Aquinas considered sloth to be "an oppressive sorrow," which "so weighs upon man's mind, that he wants to do nothing." Sloth refers not only to "a certain weariness of work" but also to "a sluggishness of the mind which neglects to begin good." This is why Aquinas defined sloth as "sorrow for spiritual good."[3] It is a mortal sin in "robbing us of our appetite for God, our zest for God, our interest and enjoyment in God. Sloth stops us from seeking God, and that means we do not find him."[4] Paradoxically, then, the busiest people can be the most slothful. Frenetic activity can be what most effectively keeps us from what we are supposed to be doing, particularly seeking God and his righteousness. Being busy is easier than being good. This is why sloth's being "a sin of omission, not commission," by one way of thinking, "makes it deadlier."[5]

It's a tough thing to balance, giving just the right amount of care and attention to a task, not more or less than is warranted, not only in terms of the task itself but more so in how that task fits into the larger picture of one's life. A diligent approach to reading means one thing for the seminary student, another for the man with heavy work responsibilities and five children at home. For the former, diligence in reading might mean reading two books a week; for the latter, a few pages a night. Likewise, diligence in a sport looks very different on the part of a professional player than it does for a young child. Such differences point out the strength of virtue ethics over rules or outcome-based approaches. Human excellence varies from person to person, whereas rules do not.

Although applied to a goal, diligence itself isn't measured by outcome. I've often told my students that effort is like a muscle. Sometimes I ask my personal trainer about how far to bend or turn in a new exercise. When she answers, "Until it hurts," I have to chuckle because it all hurts at first! As a beginner, I found it harder to leg press 70 pounds than a more fit person would find pressing 150 pounds. The student not accustomed to studying at all will feel that cramming for thirty minutes before an exam is a lot of effort. The one who studies two hours every day for a class will in contrast not even notice an extra sixty minutes to refresh before the same exam. Diligence is subjective in this way. The relative luxury of twenty-first-century American life compared to most of human history has made us soft.

Diligence is probably both the hardest and the easiest virtue to cultivate. It's easy in the sense that it's inherently simple: whatever it is you are doing, keep at it with care and attention, and then keep at it some more. Care can be faked when necessary (one can answer the phone all day with a cheerful voice even if one doesn't really feel cheerful), but the attention part can be so hard. So many things vie for our attention, many of them good and important things, like work and family and friends and fine films and good books—but of course, many of them are unimportant and negligible things, like social media and games and gossip, and the list goes on. Nevertheless, diligence consists of taking one step at a time toward the goal, not getting distracted, and not giving up. No wonder diligence is mentioned so much in the Bible.

Diligence and the Christian Life

Fittingly, diligence is the virtue at the core of one of Christianity's greatest classics, the most popular story ever published, in fact: *Pilgrim's Progress.*

For three centuries, this allegory by John Bunyan has been almost as familiar as the great stories of the Bible. Christian, encumbered by the burden of sin on his back, heeding the words of Evangelist, flees his unbelieving wife and family in the City of Destruction to journey to the Celestial City. Along the way, he must resist the temptations of mockers, pass through the narrow Wicket Gate, and overcome many obstacles by exercising the muscle of his faith before finally arriving at the city gates.

After the Bible, *Pilgrim's Progress* is the most read book in English. Since its first publication in 1678, it has never gone out of print. (Bunyan published a second part of the story in 1684, which narrates the pilgrimage of the family Christian left behind on his journey in the first part, but the second part was never as successful or as beloved as the first.) Countless variations of the original—children's versions, abridged editions, annotated editions, and modernized English versions—are still being published today. Most of us know the story in one form or another (although, sadly, many who own watered-down versions are not even aware of the theological and artistic superiority of the original).

Not only is *Pilgrim's Progress* the allegory of every Christian's life, but it also reflects Bunyan's own life—so well, in fact, that it is almost impossible to separate the story itself from the story of its author. Born in 1628, Bunyan served the parliamentary army during the English Civil War, which pitted the Puritans against the Royalists. By 1655, he had undergone a genuine conversion to Christianity and was preaching to dissenting Puritan congregations—so called because they relied on the pure Word of God and believed the established Church of England needed further purification from the influence of the Roman Catholic Church, from which it had broken under King Henry VIII in 1534. In 1649, the Puritans gained power when Oliver Cromwell's army tried, convicted, and executed King Charles. However, when the eleven-year interregnum ended in 1660 with the restoration of the monarchy, religious tolerance of dissenters ended. The Act of Uniformity, which required both Anglican ordination and use of the *Book of Common Prayer* to lead worship, made Bunyan's preaching illegal. Rather than ceasing, Bunyan surrendered to arrest and ended up experiencing one of the longest jail terms ever served by a dissenter in England.[6] In jail, he was able to keep a copy of the Bible and Foxe's *Book of Martyrs*. There he wrote his famous spiritual autobiography, *Grace Abounding to the Chief of Sinners*, and began the work that would become *Pilgrim's Progress*. In 1672, by decree of King Charles II, Bunyan was freed along with thousands of other imprisoned nonconformists. Bunyan's life attests to his belief that diligence is necessary to a virtuous life but is insufficient apart from the work of Christ. This is also the message of *Pilgrim's Progress*.

Few stories in literature demonstrate in the protagonist the kind of diligence demanded by Christian. This emphasis on diligence is directly connected to the Calvinist theology of Bunyan's Puritan faith. One essential tenet of that belief is known as perseverance of the saints. It expresses the idea that those whom God calls to salvation cannot lose their salvation but will persevere until the end and display the fruits of their salvation. The word *persevere* is no accidental term, of course. Traditional Christianity (unlike some modern iterations) emphasizes the fact that salvation does not promise ease and comfort but is more likely, as church history shows (particularly that period of history surrounding Bunyan's lifetime), to bring suffering and trial. The virtue of diligence is necessary, therefore, to persevere. If perseverance is successfully staying afloat in the water, diligence is the treading feet that make floating possible. Perseverance is the what; diligence is the how.

The aspect of diligence as, like all virtues, a mean between two extremes is reinforced by various pairings within *Pilgrim's Progress,* representative of extremes one must be diligent to navigate between. Colorful yet insightful dyads such as Obstinate and Pliable, Formalist and Hypocrisy, and Pope and Pagan offer the reader sets of vices between which the mean Christian virtue is found.

Perseverance is the what; diligence is the how.

Diligence through Trials and Tribulations

Many of Christian's trials and tribulations are drawn directly from biblical language (such as the perilous journey through the Valley of the Shadow of Death), but many are created out of Bunyan's imagination. It is this extraordinary combination of biblical foundation and soaring imagination (along with its solid theology) that gained the work the longevity and fame it deserves. Over and over, Christian faces obstacles in his journey that would make turning back seem to be the most reasonable course. Yet, through diligence, Christian perseveres through trials that symbolize both outer obstacles and internal temptations.

One of these outer temptations is Vanity Fair. This term, original to Bunyan, captures perfectly what the place represents both literally and symbolically: a carnival of human flesh and wickedness (*carnival,* of course, comes from the word *carnal*). Vanity Fair has become so ingrained in our cultural imagination that it became the title of a novel by William Makepeace Thackeray in the nineteenth century and of a glossy, high-end American magazine in the twentieth century. Bunyan's version is much more terrifying: Christian's traveling companion Faithful is martyred there, and Christian barely escapes.

Other external pressures to give up come in the form of people Christian encounters along his way who would lead him astray, such as Mr. Worldly Wiseman, Ignorance, and Talkative. Some actively attempt to dissuade Christian from his journey, while others merely distract him.

But the character who symbolizes every Christian's battle—sin itself—provides one of Bunyan's most acclaimed depictions.

The warrior Apollyon—a fierce creature, a hybrid being with the wings of a dragon, the feet of a bear, the scales of a fish, and the mouth of a lion—confronts Christian and claims that he is lord over Christian. Apollyon attempts at first to dissuade Christian from "persisting in his way," as Bunyan's gloss on the text says.[7] Failing this, Apollyon then employs darts and a sword against Christian. Christian resists all of these attacks, not through any particular feats of wit or strength, but rather through sheer diligence.

However, an even greater obstacle than the outer, physical obstacle Apollyon presents is an internal one. Apollyon taunts Christian for his imperfect service and devotion to Christ (an imperfection all Christians bear). The place of this conflict Bunyan aptly names the Valley of Humiliation, for Christian is truly humiliated here for his failures to his Lord. Yet because Christian's earlier diligence has made him spiritually stronger, he is able to endure these accusations and respond with the truth: "All this is true, and much more which thou hast left out; but the Prince whom I serve and honor is merciful, and ready to forgive."[8]

This scene is one of the most praised in the book, deservedly so because of Bunyan's vivid characterization of the villain and skillful use of allegorical language. C. S. Lewis finds in it the "supreme example" of Bunyan's incarnational approach to allegory, capturing profound spiritual truths in the language of common, everyday experience. When Christian explains to Apollyon why he has chosen to serve another master rather than him, he says that Apollyon's wages are "such as a man could not live on." Here, of course, as Lewis points out, Bunyan simply alters slightly the text found in Romans 6:23, which states that the wages of sin is death.[9] Bunyan's allegorical language is like poetry in casting the familiar in a new light, bringing spiritual truth down to earthly level, not simply to leave it there but to lift the reader toward the spiritual truth.

Christian has to work hard but also carefully, the essence of diligence. Even the smallest error can and does have disastrous effects. Traveling with Hopeful to the Celestial City after surviving Vanity Fair and countless other trials, Christian suggests they veer off the narrow path and walk through a meadow that appears to offer an easier way. This turns out to be a grave error. The meadow belongs to a giant named Despair who captures the pair and throws them into the dungeon of Doubting Castle. There, subjected to merciless beatings and deprivation, Christian comes the closest to giving up than he comes during his entire journey. The giant's wife, Diffidence (an archaic term that in Bunyan's day meant "lack of faith"), tells her husband to persuade Christian and Hopeful to kill themselves, which he tries to do. In the clutches of despair and doubt, Pilgrim is sorely tempted to take the giant Despair's advice, but Hopeful persuades him not to give up. Then, in my favorite moment in the story, after a time of prayer Christian suddenly realizes that all along he has had a key called Promise in his pocket and uses it to quickly free them from Doubting Castle.

Human Diligence and God's Grace in Partnership

I am thankful never to have experienced the kind of despair that would tempt me to take my life, but the scene rings true for me in other ways. It captures perfectly the mysterious relationship between diligence, despair, prayer, and divine intervention at just the moment when we not only need it but are actually ready for it.

The virtue of diligence has been fairly easy for me to cultivate in my life for a couple of reasons. First, I was born to parents who instilled the practice in me through both their words and their example. Second, I am blessed in lacking any natural talents that would allow me to excel at anything without painstaking effort and practice. Everything good in my life that I have accomplished, I've done only through prolonged diligence. Writing books, especially, takes me to the limits of my diligence. My ideas don't pour out like champagne from a bottle that bursts open with a pop. For me, writing is more like chipping away at stone, hour after hour, day after day, month after month, whittling away until the shape of a thought begins to emerge, then whittling away some more. In this and all other endeavors (even the study of literature, my livelihood), I have cultivated the virtue of diligence throughout my life through sheer necessity.

There's something about those promises offered to us in the Bible. They are always there, but until life prepares us to receive them, they are just like the key Christian had in his pocket all along but didn't remember until he was ready to use it. Diligence and providence are like human will and God's sovereignty, two sides of the coin that is the mystery of God's created order.

Diligence and Allegory

The diligence modeled by *Pilgrim's Progress* is its own sort of two-sided coin. Diligence is advanced not only in the content of the story but in its form as well. The reader must practice diligence in order to gain the greatest grasp of the work's meaning.

Pilgrim's Progress is one of the most exemplary allegories ever written. In simple terms, an allegory is a story that is symbolic. Allegory doesn't just *contain* symbols, as many literary works do, but it is *wholly* symbolic. Allegory works on two levels, the literal and the symbolic. On the surface, *Pilgrim's Progress* is the story of Christian's journey from one city to a better city. The people he meets along the way function just as characters in any story do. But as an allegory, all of these characters and events have symbolic meaning, and it is, of course, the symbolic level—in this case, the Christian doctrine—that carries the real meaning of the work.

Bunyan chose the form of allegory, in part, due to Puritan objections to fiction as mere lies. Because allegory does not make up a fictional story but uses symbols that correspond directly with truth, allegory (before the existence of our modern literary categories) was not considered fiction in the way that we think of fiction today. Even so, Bunyan felt the need to justify his work through a defense of his method in a poem that serves as the story's preface.

Allegory can be deceptively simple, and *Pilgrim's Progress* is as straightforward as allegory can be. Christian is a Christian. Mr. Worldly Wise is a person who relies on worldly rather than godly wisdom. Hopeful and Faithful are characters who symbolize exactly those things. Mr. Talkative is, well, talkative. And so on. This easy correspondence can be challenging to modern readers because it seems so simple. But closer analysis reveals that diligence is required of the reader in order to see the deeper truths revealed by the allegorical mode.

One way to consider the richness of allegory is to compare it to a nonsymbolic exposition of the same truths contained in the symbol. Bunyan might have written a treatise simply stating his doctrinal view that a Christian must set his sights on eternity rather than this world, must not listen to worldly wisdom nor stray from the narrow way, and so forth. But an allegory, like all stories, shows rather than tells. In adding the layers of significance and meaning inherent in all symbols and, in fact, in language itself, allegory makes more explicit the way that all language functions. Language is indirect or mediated in a way that images and pictures are not. All language is, in a certain sense, metaphorical, and allegory simply amplifies this aspect of language. The dependence of allegory on the resonances of language to convey its layers of meaning helps to explain the difficulty of a good film adaptation of allegory. Replacing metaphorical language with literal depictions erases most of the significance of allegory, the content of which resides in the form. The same is true of all literary works, which use language as an artistic medium, not merely a form of communication.

From Plato's *Allegory of the Cave* in the classical era to Bunyan's *Pilgrim's Progress* in the seventeenth century, and a wide array of allegorical works throughout the medieval age in between, we see a worldview in which such layers of meaning, not only in literature but in the world itself, were both assumed and understood. As C. S. Lewis explains in *The Discarded Image*, this allegorical way of thinking was based on a notion of truth that transcended the modern categories of history and fiction.[10] Like the parables told by Christ, allegorical stories didn't have to be true; they pointed to truth just as Christian's companion Hopeful points the wavering pilgrim to the truths of Scripture as they both cross the River of Death before finally entering the Celestial City.

For the Puritans, literary critic J. Paul Hunter explains, the world constituted a "book of nature" filled with emblems pointing to spiritual truth. This truth might be discovered through interpretation, based on the logic that underlies an understanding of how similitudes (such as symbols and analogies) work. Despite being iconoclasts who eschewed graven images, the Puritans inherited from the medieval worldview "mental habits of conceiving abstractions pictorially." Interpretations arising from observations of the book of nature were seen not as creating fictions but rather as simply uncovering meanings already inhering in the world by God's design. Such a "metaphorical mode of thinking" was prone to producing and appreciating allegory.[11] Allegory depends on a thick understanding of the physical world and the language that bridges that world with the spiritual one. Whereas the modern fiction writer creates out of her imagination, the premodern allegorist translated from the book of nature.

Modern ways of thinking cultivate a flatter approach to language and stories—as well as to the world and truth—than the ancients had. This modern preference for the literal over the symbolic, metaphorical, and poetic lends itself to a fundamentalism that the Puritans would never have recognized. For the Puritans, the world, even language itself, was charged with meaning both originating in and pointing toward God. For example, it is impossible to understand the meaning of marriage apart from an understanding of how marriage is an emblem for the relationship of Christ and the church. To separate the poetic nature of marriage (as allegorical and anagogical) is to change its meaning altogether. When the ties between layers of meaning inherent in language are broken, then our own ability to know and grow in truth is hindered. Allegory employs double-minded language that requires more shrewdness in the reader (and the writer) than the literal-minded like to admit.

Even the word *progress* in the title *Pilgrim's Progress* is suggestive of how allegory functions. Allegory operates on a built-in expectation that readers will "progress" from the literal, material level of the story to the symbolic, spiritual truth beyond. It has an explicit assumption of interpretation that is implicit in all literary writing, indeed in all writing and all use of language. In other words, allegory requires and assumes the exercise of diligence by readers.

Another sense of progress is connected to the proverbial "Puritan work ethic." Although diligence has been considered a virtue since ancient times, it has a particular connection to the period that birthed *Pilgrim's Progress* and this emphasis on the importance of work. As a result of the Enlightenment and the advances of scientific inquiry that accompanied it, the notion of progress became one of the defining concepts of the age, as seen in chapter 6 on hope. However, progress did not refer exclusively to scientific and technological advancements; it was about human progress as well. The doctrines of the Protestant Reformation—and later, Puritanism—contributed significantly to the idea that individuals can progress beyond their given condition, whether that condition is spiritual, social, or economic. The Puritan (or Protestant) work ethic is the indirect offspring of a doctrinal emphasis on the role of the individual in his or her own salvation, sanctification, and Scripture reading. The work ethic both depends on and cultivates the careful attentiveness and desire at the heart of diligence. Of course, as we saw in chapter 6 while considering the virtue of hope, even progress—and the work that achieves it—has its limits.

Allegory requires and assumes the exercise of diligence by readers.

The most significant sense of progress in *Pilgrim's Progress* is its overarching theological theme: sanctification. While there are various debates about the exact point in the story at which Christian is saved, this question misses the larger concern of the story. Bunyan wasn't writing in a time in which the evidence of salvation was in the documentation of the exact day and hour at which one "receives Jesus in one's heart." Bunyan's Calvinist belief emphasized not the moment of salvation but the work of ongoing sanctification that is evidence of salvation. Anyone can raise a hand, repeat a prayer, and go forward to the altar, but only a truly regenerated heart will bear the fruit of sanctification and persevere until the end. This is the real progress that *Pilgrim's Progress* is about. Christian's diligence in the faith is a picture of the admonition to believers in Philippians 2:12 to work out our faith in fear and trembling.

Such diligence requires care and attention, which, in turn, depend on the cultivation of godly desire. *Pilgrim's Progress* is an invitation to the reader to practice diligence in both the reading and the application.

"Longsuffering Anne"

Chapter ten

Patience

PERSUASION

by Jane Austen

The end of a matter is better than its beginning,
and patience is better than pride.

—Ecclesiastes 7:8

Whenever I'm asked to give advice about life to young people, I give the same answer: be patient.

What I mainly mean when I say this is: Slow down. Don't be in a hurry. Life is long. Work hard, and the rewards will come. The dreams you have—some of them—will come true; those that don't will be replaced by others, maybe even better ones.

In the context of everyday life, we think of patience in more mundane terms. Being patient is what we aim for (or fail at) when sitting in traffic, standing in line, or waiting for a table. But the virtue of patience entails much more than merely waiting. The essence of patience is the willingness to endure suffering.

Patience as Suffering

That "suffering" is the meaning of the root word for *patience*[1] is made clear by the fact that we also use the word *patient* to refer to someone under medical care. The patient is someone "suffering" from an ailment—not merely waiting. *Patient* shares the same root as the word *passion,* which also means "suffering." Someone who has a passion—a passion for music, a passion for soccer, a passion for a person—suffers on behalf of that love. When we speak in the church about "the passion of Christ," it literally refers to the suffering of Christ on the cross on our behalf. The overlap between the words *suffering* and *patience* can be seen in another meaning of both words: "permit." When Jesus said, "Suffer little children . . . to come unto me" (as Matthew 19:14 is rendered in the King James), he meant "permit" them to come. And when we speak of women's suffrage, we refer to women

The virtue of patience entails much more than merely waiting. The essence of patience is the willingness to endure suffering.

being permitted to vote. The word *permit* in these contexts suggests willingness; the willingness to endure suffering is the meaning of the word *patient*. The expression "the patience of Job," describing the great test of faith Job underwent in the Bible, refers to Job's suffering, not merely his endurance. As connected as patience is to suffering, it is no wonder that, as theologian N. T. Wright points out, we "applaud patience but prefer it to be a virtue that others possess."[2]

Suffering is not something we do well in the modern age. It's certainly not something I do well. This is why patience is, as they say, a virtue. Since suffering is inevitable in this world, it might seem silly to consider the willingness to endure it as a virtue. But while suffering is inevitable, we can choose how we bear it. Patient character has everything to do with our will, as opposed to our circumstances.

Like all virtues, patience is the mean between an excess and a deficiency. The excessive vice related to suffering is wrath. Evil and suffering should result in a righteous anger. To fulfill the admonition of Paul to "be angry and do not sin" (Eph. 4:26 ESV) requires patience that is the fruit of the Spirit. Patience is a virtue, not in overlooking wrong, but in refusing to do wrong in overcoming wrong. But untempered by patience, such an impulse becomes wrath. On the deficient side of the scale is a lack of spirit or carelessness or sloth. If in the face of evil or suffering one simply does not care, no patience is required. But such lack of care is, like wrath, a vice. Patience is not inaction. As the Bible says in James 5:11, patience is not passivity but perseverance. When faced with suffering or wrong, the virtuous person responds neither with wrath nor with stoicism but with patience. A person who has true patience is "angrily virtuous,"[3] whether that means giving time for the emotional heat to subside before acting or simply waiting for the slow wheels of justice to turn.

Patience is not inaction.

The character most famous in literature for patience is the legendary Griselda of ancient folklore. Her story is best known in the telling found in Boccaccio's *Decameron*, but it is retold with more Christian overtones by the clerk in Chaucer's *Canterbury Tales*, and other variations appear throughout world literature. In this story, a nobleman who spends all his time hunting and hawking resentfully gives in to his subjects' desires for him to marry by choosing as his wife the daughter of a poor cottager. Her beauty, graciousness, and exemplary character only draw her husband's ire, and he subjects her to the cruelest tests of constancy: he orders their first and then their second child to be put to death; he tells her he has gained papal permission to divorce her and remarry; he brings home a young woman he introduces as his new bride. Through all of this, Griselda responds graciously and submissively. At this point, her husband reveals all has been but a test. The girl is their daughter. He reunites Griselda with their children and takes her back as his faithful and beloved wife. Her character is known as the Patient Griselda. Griselda may represent some male fantasies of a patient wife, but her patience is not the virtuous kind.

A Virtuously Patient Character

In contrast to Griselda, Anne Elliot of Jane Austen's novel *Persuasion* may be one of the most virtuously patient heroines in literature. She is exemplary of the virtue of patience that comports with both the classical and the biblical understanding of that quality.

Patience isn't the most obvious theme in *Persuasion*. Just as *Pride and Prejudice* is about pride and prejudice, and just as *Sense and Sensibility* is about sense and sensibility, so too the central theme of Austen's last novel, published posthumously in 1817, is captured straightforwardly by the title (which was chosen by her brother after her death). Most of the characters in the novel can be evaluated in terms of how easily and by whom they are persuaded,[4] beginning with Anne's father, a baronet who must be persuaded to reduce his expenses in light of his dwindling fortune. Anne, we soon learn, was persuaded several years before the story's beginning to make a decision that dramatically altered the course of her life, a decision she has come to regret.

When she was nineteen, Anne fell in love with and quickly became engaged to Frederick Wentworth. While Wentworth was honorable and hardworking and fully returned Anne's affection, he was also a naval officer—not a member of the aristocracy. A trusted and beloved family friend, Lady Russell (who is "able to persuade a person to anything!"[5]), convinced Anne that her engagement to Captain Wentworth was ill-suited and that she could make a better match. Young and trusting, Anne followed this advice. When the novel opens eight years afterward, Anne is twenty-seven, still unmarried (a spinster by the standards of the day), and possesses a face and figure from which the bloom of youth has slipped away. Anne is painfully conscious of all of these facts, yet she is forbearing of her lot.

Then Captain Wentworth reenters the scene. He too has remained single. But unlike Anne, time has improved his station and allure, and he is ready to seek love again.

The social circle at the center of the story includes, along with Wentworth, a number of eligible women and men, each bent on settling down with a marriage partner from among many possibilities and rivals in love. It's not difficult to imagine the acts of persuasion that ensue with such a cast of characters. When one of the would-be lovers, an impatient Louisa Musgrove, failing to be persuaded not to do so, jumps off a step—expecting to be caught by Captain Wentworth, who is a beat too late—she is knocked unconscious as her head hits the stone surface. This fall precipitates a series of consequences that shifts the dynamics of the budding romances, each one involving persuasions of various levels and types.

However, underneath this surface-level theme of persuasion runs an even more interesting theme. Anne's virtuous patience is what makes her such an intriguing character and what makes *Persuasion*, I think, the most artful of Austen's novels.

Anne is unlike most of Austen's heroines and heroes because, as C. S. Lewis points out in an essay on Austen, she does not undergo illumination or enlightenment; but, in contrast to these other characters, she has no need to. Anne, as Lewis says, "commits no errors."[6] Too-perfect characters are rarely, if ever, interesting. But Anne's passion, insight, maturity, and fortitude make her a winsome character despite her lack of a great flaw,[7] a characteristic modern readers expect. An additional feature that makes

Anne—and the novel—most interesting is her patience. She is called to practice patience because she suffers.

It is, as the narrator explains early in the story, Anne's "usual fate" to have "something very opposite from her inclination fixed on."[8] In everything from her father's financial irresponsibility to her family's resulting removal from the country home she loved to the city of Bath that she detested, from one sister's insufferable hypochondria and the other sister's egocentric snobbery to being left alone as caregiver for her sick nephew, from serving as sounding board for family members' complaints about one another to having lost the chance to marry the one man she loved, Anne suffers. And she suffers alone. C. S. Lewis calls Anne a "solitary" heroine, one who suffers in solitude.[9] But she suffers virtuously. Anne is not the doormat Griselda who passively accepts the wickedest of wrongs. Nor does Anne succumb to the vice of wrath in spite of recognizing the suffering she and others around her experience as the direct consequence of evil or foolish decisions.

Because Anne suffers virtuously, she doesn't let her pain cause her to turn inward upon herself. Rather, her patient bearing of suffering allows her to recognize the suffering of others. When the recently widowed Captain Benwick joins their party, Anne's patience draws him out as others have been unable to do. Following a conversation with the bereft widower, Anne is persuaded she has "given him at least an evening's indulgence in the discussion of subjects which his usual companions had probably no concern in" as well as guidance about "the duty and benefit of struggling against affliction."[10] Captain Benwick gratefully accepts Anne's recommendations of reading to help him better bear his pain—a list that includes the "best moralists" as well as letters and memoirs by "the strongest examples of moral and religious endurances." When the evening ends, Anne is "amused at the idea of her coming to Lyme to preach patience and resignation to a young man whom she had never seen before." She thinks, "like many other great moralists and preachers, she had been eloquent on a point in which her own conduct would bear ill examination."[11] She suffers, yet does not recognize the virtuous way in which she bears it.

When Louisa Musgrove, who has lately received the attentions of Anne's former suitor Captain Wentworth, falls and knocks herself unconscious, of all the company in attendance it is Anne whose patience brings order to everyone else's panic and confusion. Time and time again, when others are rude or catty or neglectful or demanding, Anne's patience is shown in graciousness that is gracious because it is not blind.

Anne's greatest patience, however, is in bearing over the years her regret at breaking off her engagement to Wentworth. It would be easy for her to be bitter—bitter at her fate, at herself, or at Lady Russell for being the one to advise the break. But again, Anne exhibits true patience precisely because she is not blind. Her patience prevents her from hurriedly accepting a subsequent offer of marriage and from too hastily accepting the courtship of a new suitor, who, as it turns out, has ill motives. As a result, Anne is still free, and readier, all these years later, when her beloved Wentworth returns, better situated now than before and even more convinced of his love and desire for Anne. In the years that have passed, Anne, "forced into prudence in her youth, . . . learned romance as she grew older: the natural sequence of an unnatural beginning."[12] She has come to recognize that time is required "to be wise and reasonable"[13] and is wise enough to recognize when she is not.

No Regrets

When she and Wentworth finally overcome the many obstacles to reuniting after all these years and are on their way to their reasonably-happy-ever-after, Anne explains to Wentworth how unavoidable her past decision was:

> I have been thinking over the past, and trying impartially to judge of the right and wrong, I mean with regard to myself; and I must believe that I was right, much as I suffered from it, that I was perfectly right in being guided by the friend whom you will love better than you do now. To me, she was in place of a parent. Do not mistake me, however. I am not saying that she did not err in her advice. It was, perhaps, one of those cases in

> which advice is good or bad only as the event decides; and for myself, I certainly never should, in any circumstance of tolerable similarity, give such advice. But I mean that I was right in submitting to her, and that if I had done otherwise, I should have suffered more in continuing the engagement than I did even in giving it up, because I should have suffered in my conscience. I have now, as far as such a sentiment is allowable in human nature, nothing to reproach myself with; and, if I mistake not, a strong sense of duty is no bad part of a woman's portion.[14]

Anne is confident that she made the right decision in being guided by Lady Russell, a good and rightful (if not infallible) authority in her life. "If I was wrong in yielding to persuasion once," she tells Wentworth, "remember that it was to persuasion exerted on the side of safety, not of risk. When I yielded, I thought it was to duty."[15]

Patience is a virtue only if the *cause* for which that person suffers is good.

Anne's reasoning reflects a quality of patience insisted on by Augustine in order for patience to be considered virtuous. "When therefore you shall see any man suffer anything patiently, do not straightway praise it as patience; for this is only shown by the cause of suffering. When it is a good cause, then is it true patience."[16] Patience is a virtue only if the *cause* for which that person suffers is good. Yet the *source* of suffering might not always be good. We cannot—in the name of patience—ask someone to endure abuse, since the cause of such suffering is evil, not noble. Anne suffers because she made a right decision to take the reasonable and well-intentioned advice of the mother figure in her life. The advice proves to have been wrong, but Anne's patient bearing of the consequences of her decision to follow the advice is virtuous.

Patience and Future Pleasures

While others in the novel are eager to locate the cause of their suffering, and therefore to assign blame, Anne is more concerned with what future pleasures might possibly arise from difficulty. When Captain Wentworth marvels at Anne's desire to visit Lyme again, on account of it being the location where Louisa took her terrible fall, Anne explains,

> "The last few hours were certainly very painful," replied Anne; "but when pain is over, the remembrance of it often becomes a pleasure. One does not love a place the less for having suffered in it, unless it has been all suffering, nothing but suffering, which was by no means the case at Lyme. We were only in anxiety and distress during the last two hours, and previously there had been a great deal of enjoyment. So much novelty and beauty! I have travelled so little, that every fresh place would be interesting to me; but there is real beauty at Lyme; and in short," with a faint blush at some recollections, "altogether my impressions of the place are very agreeable."[17]

Anne's perspective of suffering, in the words of Augustine, sees beyond what is "temporal and brief,"[18] seeking instead what is greater and more lasting. I had a similar perspective, even as a child. Because I read so much and loved stories from an early age, when I encountered some sort of difficulty—teasing or getting in trouble for wrongdoing or disappointment in a friend or crush—I always had a sense that there was a story in the making. Although I didn't find whatever unpleasantness I was in any happier because of it, simply wondering how the story would resolve gave me patience to bear it a little better. This seems to be Anne's tack too.

I always had a sense that there was a story in the making. Simply wondering how the story would resolve gave me patience to bear it a little better.

A subtle contrast can be seen in the book between Anne's posture, which transcends merely temporal concerns, and that of her father, Mr. Elliot, who makes constant observations about the effects of both time and suffering on people's faces, complexions, and lives (particularly those of a lower class). Numerous connections are made throughout the novel between time and patience (or lack thereof). "How quick come the reasons for approving what we like!" the narrator observes concerning Lady Russell's eagerness to leave the Elliot's country estate and remain in Bath.[19]

Persuadability, too, is connected to time. While Anne's rival Louisa Musgrove brags that she is not easily persuaded, Anne questions whether firmness of character is always ideal, arguing that "a persuadable temper might sometimes be as much in favour of happiness as a very resolute one."[20] Here we see a hint of the connection between persuasion and patience—both rooted in time, easily subject to it but also able to transcend it. As Anne remarks hopefully about the mourning of the widowed Captain Benwick, "We know what time does in every case of affliction."[21] When she realizes the corrupt character of her relation, the younger Mr. Elliot, she is patient in allowing his character to reveal itself rather than forcing the matter herself. She realizes, too, the effect of time on "pain, once severe, but now softened."[22]

Anne's transcendent view of persuasion and patience owes to what Alasdair MacIntyre says in *After Virtue* is her "teleological perspective,"[23] a perspective that keeps ultimate purpose and end in mind. As we have seen, *After Virtue* explores what it means to live in a modern world that no longer believes in the essential part of virtue in human flourishing. MacIntyre points to Austen as one of the last modern writers whose worldview remains shaped by virtue ethics. Such principles are, MacIntyre says, "essential to Jane Austen's art" and form a "grammar of conduct"[24] within the world of her novels, a world newly characterized by social mobility, ideological flux, and increasing skepticism toward authority. In contrast to the modernity overtaking the world she lived in, Austen was Aristotelian in her view of happiness, drawing together in her novels Aristotelian and Christian themes[25] that unite in an emphasis on "cheerful moderation."[26] Her novels demonstrate that the "virtues and the harms and evils which the virtues alone will overcome provide the structure both of a life in which the *telos* can be achieved and of a narrative in which the story of such a life can be unfolded."[27]

MacIntyre attributes to Austen one virtue particular to her world, one not emphasized in most catalogs of classical virtues: constancy. Constancy is an important virtue in the world of Austen's characters, according to MacIntyre, because of the emphasis their world places on two other qualities found liberally throughout Austen's novels: amiability and agreeableness. Agreeableness is an impression one makes by conforming to expected manners (which, notably, was reflected in Austen's original title for *Pride and Prejudice*: *First Impressions*). Amiability, however, is deeper and more genuine than mere agreeableness. Amiability "requires a genuine loving regard for other people as such, and not only the impression of such a regard embodied in manners."[28] A world of many rules and expectations lends itself to outward conformity that makes an impression—an impression that need not be in agreement with internal nature. The more appearances matter, the more counterfeits abound.

As a writer of comedies of manners, Austen is concerned with what MacIntyre calls counterfeit virtues. As with all counterfeits, those who are most often taken in by them are those in possession of them. Austen's novels show that the antidote to counterfeit virtue is self-knowledge. Constancy depends on self-knowledge, "a recognition of a particular kind of threat to the integrity of the personality in the peculiarly modern world." Constancy is what holds all other virtues together. Constancy is "reinforced by and reinforces" patience, which "involves a recognition of the character of the world."[29] This is exactly the patience—and constancy—Anne Elliot displays.

The nature of the world is that it is fallen—but will be created anew. Because it is fallen, the world is filled with people who are fallen—but who have the possibility of redemption. Nevertheless, pain, suffering, wrongdoing, and injustice are, because of this fallenness, inevitable. Failure to recognize either the current condition of the world or the promise of its future will lead to either of the vices that patience moderates: wrath owing to an unwillingness to accept this reality of the world or dispiritedness that is a form of withdrawal from this reality. Anne Elliot may be a character who doesn't change over the course of the book, but she is interesting because she embodies in her patience this tension.

Recognizing the true character of the world requires recognition of the God who made it and his character. The most perfect patience grows out of not only teleology but eschatology too. "The end of a matter is better than its beginning, and patience is better than pride. Do not be quickly provoked in your spirit, for anger resides in the lap of fools" (Eccles. 7:8–9). N. T. Wright says about the virtue of patience: "Those who believe in God and the creator and in the eventual triumph of his good purposes for the world will not be in a hurry to grasp at quick-fix solutions in their own life or in their vocation and mission—though they will not be slow to take God-given opportunities when those arise."[30] Because God is sovereign over all, even over natural phenomena, James Spiegel explains, "all patience or impatience is ultimately patience or impatience with someone." This fact helps to explain how impatience is ultimately rooted in egocentrism. Patience is difficult because it "concerns what philosophers call the 'egocentric predicament,' which is the natural human condition of being immediately aware only of one's own thoughts and feelings." He further explains: "I know, however, only my own thoughts and am intimately aware of only my own needs, which naturally incline me to put myself first. The result is frustration that I'm not first, and this strongly tempts me to be impatient." Patience "is not a fundamental virtue so much as a complex of other virtues," particularly generosity, self-control, and humility.[31] These are virtues necessary to take us out of our natural, human egocentrism.

Failure to recognize either the current condition of the world or the promise of its future will lead to either wrath or dispiritedness.

Even more than character and theme, the literary form of Austen's novels embodies the decentering of self that is necessary to achieving the habit of patience. The satirical mode Austen uses depends on the double perspective of irony. Irony occurs when the intended meaning is the opposite of the stated meaning. Understanding irony requires the reader to accommodate both levels of meaning, the stated and the intended meaning, thereby forcing the reader out of the single perspective that defines most of one's interior life. In this way, such a narrative form cultivates the virtue of patience.

Furthermore, for a Christian writer such as Austen, this technique has a specifically Christian purpose. As MacIntyre explains, "Jane Austen's moral point of view and the narrative form of her novels coincide. The form of her novels is that of ironic comedy. . . . She is a Christian and she sees the *telos* of human life implicit in its everyday form. Her irony resides in the way that she makes her characters and her readers see and say more and other than they intended to, so that they and we will correct ourselves."[32]

Patience and the Possession of One's Soul

N. T. Wright says that patience is required in order to attain the other virtues.[33] "Patience is one of the places where faith, hope, and love meet up," he writes.[34] Augustine describes patience as the virtue by which "we tolerate evil things with an even mind." The patient person, he continues, chooses to bear evil rather than to commit further evil in response to it. Patience keeps us from yielding to evils that are "temporal and brief" and from losing "those good things which are great and eternal."[35] Patience is a high virtue, that's certain. No wonder patience is traditionally understood to be a subvirtue of courage. Indeed, all the virtues, Aquinas says, "are directed to the good of the soul." He continues: "Now this seems to belong chiefly to patience; for it is written (Luke 21:19): 'In your patience you shall possess your souls.' Therefore patience is the greatest of the virtues."[36]

Of all Austen's characters, Anne Elliot is the one who is most lovable and most admirable. Elizabeth Bennet is lovable, but until she overcomes her pride, she is not entirely admirable. Fanny Price and Elinor Dashwood are perhaps Austen's two most admirable characters, but they are too passionless to be greatly lovable. Anne Elliot is both of these. She is so because she is self-possessed. In her patience, she possesses her soul.

"Kin"

Chapter Eleven

Kindness

"TENTH OF DECEMBER"

by George Saunders

Anyone who withholds kindness from a friend
forsakes the fear of the Almighty.

—Job 6:14

On Monday, June 19, 2017, a fifteen-year-old girl from rural Pennsylvania hung herself.

Her family made the unusual decision to include the cause of her death in the teen's obituary. Suicide is always surrounded by guilt, shame, and an extra burden of pain beyond what accompanies any other death. Thus it is seldom acknowledged in this sort of public way. But, the obituary explained, the family wanted to dispel rumors about the girl's death with facts. In addition to the cause of death, the obituary adds this background:

> If you take a minute and look at Sadie's family dynamics you will see that a large percent of the people in her life were not related to her by blood but she was sent to us by God who knew this child needed a family. Sadie had a tough life and until a recent incident at school she handled everything life served her. For a young lady so excited about going to the High School things sure went terribly wrong for her. For the bullies involved, please know you were effective in making her feel worthless.

The obituary ends with the family suggesting, in lieu of flowers, "that you be kind to one another."[1]

Kindness Isn't Natural or Nice

Kindness is unlike other virtues in that "we know exactly what it is, in most everyday situations; and yet our knowing what it is makes it easier to avoid."[2] We "are profoundly ambivalent about kindness" in that we "are never as kind as we want to be, but nothing outrages us more than people being unkind to us."[3]

Kindness isn't natural to most of us, which is why it is a virtue that needs to be taught and cultivated. When I was a child, my parents and a couple of my teachers "encouraged" (read: "pressured") me to give time and attention to the children in my class and neighborhood who were often overlooked or left out. I wasn't always happy then about being made to do this, but I am thankful now. Teaching me compassion and attentiveness toward others was one of the greatest gifts the adults in my life gave me as a child. The ones who give such kindness, particularly to "the least of these," will be even more blessed than the ones who receive it.

Kindness isn't sexy. It doesn't dazzle you with wit and charm and verve. We want to be with the kind, even if we don't want to be the kind. People envy the rich, the beautiful, the powerful, the courageous, and the wise. Do we ever envy the kind?

Kindness isn't natural to most of us, which is why it is a virtue that needs to be taught and cultivated.

Envy, in fact, is the vice that, in the classical tradition, opposes kindness. Perhaps this seems strange until we look at what kindness truly is.

Kindness isn't mere niceness. Although *kind* and *nice* are nearly synonymous now, the history of both words shows a once-sharp difference that is still helpful to consider today. *Nice* comes from a Latin word that means "unknowing" or "ignorant" and in Middle English came to mean "senseless" or "foolish."[4] The linguist Henry Watson Fowler opines, in his characteristically colorful way, that the current meaning of *nice* as similar to *kind* came about when *nice* became "too great a favourite with the ladies who have charmed out of it all its individuality and converted it into a mere diffuser of vague and mild agreeableness."[5]

In its etymology, *kind* means something radically different from mere agreeableness. Indeed, *kind*, rightly understood, can include all sorts of disagreeableness. *Kind* comes from the same root from which we get the word *kin*. To be kind, then, is to treat someone like they are family. To possess the virtue of kindness is to be in the habit of treating all people as if they were family.

Kindness is like love. The love we have for family members takes different forms. It is not all Christmas mornings and movie nights. But it is always seeking and celebrating the good of that person. The same is true of kindness. As Augustine says of the virtuous life in *City of God*, a life characterized by kindness "is social, and for its own sake values the good of friends as its own, just as it wishes for them, for their own sake, what it wishes for itself." Augustine then explains that by "friends" he means members of the family, household, community, and world—even the angels.[6] All are kin.

Envy: The Opposite of Kindness

The connection between kindness and kinship helps make sense of the reason for envy being the vice that opposes kindness. Aquinas calls envy "sorrow for another's good."[7] Unless the relationship is marred by some dysfunction, it is natural for us to celebrate a family member's happiness or success. When something good happens to someone in our family, it is like it has happened to us. We share in that good rather than envy it. To seek and celebrate the good for others is then to treat them as family in this way. This is what it means to be kind.

> To seek and celebrate the good for others is to treat them as family. This is what it means to be kind.

Jesus's parable of the good Samaritan in Luke 10 demonstrates kindness well. The question Jesus asks after telling the story of the beaten man who was helped—not by the religious leaders but by the Samaritan, who belonged to a class of people despised for not upholding the Jewish law—has to do with who acted as neighbor to the beaten man. Neighbor in this context is very similar to kin: the person near you, associated with you. The person who acted as kin—kindly—was, of course, the lowly Samaritan.

Another, more subtle observation about kindness can be made from the story of King Solomon's wise judgment in the dispute between two women, each claiming an infant as her own (1 Kings 3:16–28). One woman had accidentally smothered her child in the night and swapped her dead child for the other woman's living child. Unable to tell which woman was the true mother of the living child, Solomon stated he would settle the matter simply by dividing the child in two and giving one half to each. The woman who agreed to this horrific solution obviously was not the child's mother. She would prefer for the living child to be dead than for the other woman to have what she no longer had. Her response reveals both her envy and her lack of kinship to the child. The child's true mother reveals both her kinship and her kindness in desiring the good of the child, his very life, even if the other woman were to have him instead of her.

It's not a very nice story. But this story that illustrates kindness also illustrates how kindness is not always *nice*. If kindness means treating someone like family, then kindness must include all the varieties of ways that family members show love for one another through the entire range of circumstances, conditions, and situations they find themselves in. Sometimes loving a family member requires gentleness. Sometimes toughness. Often forbearance. Always honesty and truth.

Kindness must include all the varieties of ways that family members show love for one another through the entire range of circumstances, conditions, and situations they find themselves in.

This is another way being kind and being nice differ. Niceness has no inherent link to truth. Indeed, being connected etymologically to ignorance, niceness might have no connection to truth at all. Even the current sense of *nice*—agreeable or pleasant—can be at odds with the truth. The truth is often not pleasant or agreeable. A mere acquaintance might be nice enough to say that your new hairstyle is attractive even if it isn't, but a true friend—someone who is more like family—would be kind to point out that another style is more suited to you. The virtue of kindness simply cannot be separated from truth.

Kind to Be Cruel

Even "a harsh truth can be compassionate in the sense that it speeds us along from falseness to truth,"[8] explains George Saunders, one of today's most remarkable writers. Saunders is a satirist, treating vice and folly humorously for the purpose of correction, but his satire is not as straightforward as what we saw in Henry Fielding's *Tom Jones*. The classical satirist sits outside in judgment, much like the omniscient narrator of *Tom Jones*. But Saunders stoops down to get inside his characters, to inhabit them, and to correct the errors of both the character and the reader by modeling sincere loving-kindness rather than distant mockery.

In one interview, Saunders was asked about his statement that "satire is a way of saying, 'I love this culture.'" He explained: "It's hard to be sufficiently involved in satirizing something you don't like. That's just sneering. Satire is, I think, a sort of bait-and-switch. You decide to satirize something, so you gaze at it hard enough and long enough to be able to say something true and funny and maybe angry or critical—but you first had to gaze at it for a long time. I mean, gazing is a form of love, right?"[9]

Saunders relates that when he was growing up, telling funny stories about people was part of his family and social life, "ostensibly for laughs, or to mock somebody out." But behind these "odd little Zen parables," as he calls them, "were deeper questions looming—like who we are, and what the hell are we doing here, how should we love, what should we value, how are we to understand this veil [*sic*] of tears?"[10]

> Being kind is so much more than being sensible, reserved, or mild. It is so much more than being *nice*.

Saunders's fame exploded even beyond his impressive literary reputation (he has won many of the world's most prestigious literary awards) with his 2013 commencement speech at Syracuse University, which went viral. In the speech's most moving and memorable line, Saunders tells the graduates, "What I regret most in my life are *failures of kindness.*" Such failures include, Saunders goes on to explain, "those moments when another human being was there, in front of me, suffering, and I responded . . . sensibly. Reservedly. Mildly."[11]

Being kind—being like family—is so much more than being sensible, reserved, or mild. It is so much more than being *nice*.

Think about what family members do for and with one another: Family members share space and meals. They share bathrooms and bedrooms. They witness one another's bodily sounds and smells. They argue over who should get the last red velvet cupcake, who they should vote for to be president, and whose turn it is to clean up the dog's vomit on the living-room rug. Family members share funny and embarrassing stories about one another. They infuse one another's memories into one another, and their stories get passed down time and time again through the years until they aren't even sure who had the experience and who merely observed and retold it. Family members wipe the noses and change the diapers of younger (or much, much older) family members. They are there when other members are born, win success, find love, grow old, get sick, and when they die.

This is the sort of hard kindness that permeates Saunders's literary art. His stories are often bizarre, even surreal. They contain elements of the obscene and profane. Some might find it hard to look past these rough edges to see the kindness that is the central characteristic of Saunders's art. But kindness, in its inherent connection to truth, must be grounded in the *real.* And in a postvirtuous culture, the foil that offsets kindness will be very dark indeed. It takes little for a glimmer of kindness to burn bright in such an age. One psychoanalytic study of kindness suggests, "Perhaps it is one of the perils of secularization, that if we no longer believe in God—in a Being who is himself invulnerable and so is capable of protecting us—we cannot avoid confronting our own relative helplessness and need for each other."[12]

But kindness, in its inherent connection to truth, must be grounded in the *real*.

In Saunders' short story "Tenth of December," such kindness transforms not only the receivers of kindness but those who give it as well.

Into the Woods

"Tenth of December" begins with a young boy named Robin trekking into the woods on a cold December day, embarking on an imaginary adventure in which he plays the hero who will rescue a damsel in distress (played in his imagination by a lovely classmate who doesn't even know his name). As he moves along in his made-up adventure, Robin's thoughts reveal that he is teased at school but loved at home. Eventually, Robin finds some (real) tracks in the snow and, weaving their presence into his imaginary adventure, follows them until they take him to an abandoned, but still warm, winter coat. Robin is animated by his instinctive kindness. "Something is wrong here," Robin realizes. "A person needed a coat," he thinks. "Even if the person was a grown-up."[13] The coat belongs to Don Eber, a fifty-three-year-old terminally ill man who has come into the woods intending to end his life.

Using a remarkable combination of third-person and stream-of-consciousness narration, the story toggles back and forth between Robin's point of view and Don's point of view. Saunders's masterful skill in capturing the distinct voice of each character allows us to enter their interior world as they experience and process the events of the story. In this way, the reader directly experiences the inner story the character tells himself about what is happening as it is happening, a technique that re-creates the way we tell our own stories in our heads in our real lives.

Yet, at the same time, the reader knows more than the characters know. We are simultaneously inside a character's head and outside it. We can thus see three stories at once: Robin's, Don's, and the larger story of the world beyond their inner experience. While we participate in the stories Robin and Don imagine for themselves, empathizing and feeling kinship, we also see beyond the stories they imagine, recognizing the limits and distorted perceptions of their stories, the same kind of limits and distorted perceptions that are part of our own stories that we tell ourselves about our own lives.

As the narrative point of view shifts to that of Don, we learn that he loves his family and wishes to spare them from further pain in his suffering. This is what a loving husband and father does, he thinks: "eases the burdens of those he loves."[14] Like Robin, Don wants to be a hero too.

It's not just this, of course. Don is suffering, and his sufferings promise only to increase in coming days. Ending his life is a way for him to seize control and preempt "all future debasement."[15] Don reflects on his father's lack of kindness earlier in his life. Don's father and his father's friend had "switched spouses, abandoned the switched spouses, fled together to California." He fantasizes about forgiving them for leaving him and his mother in exchange for some "solid manly advice."[16] He also thinks about his stepfather, Allen, who was a good father to Don and a good husband to Don's mother. Until he got sick. The dementia that set in turned Allen into a near monster. It is this terror that Don wishes to avoid in taking his own life, before his sickness does the same to him—and to his family.

Everyday kindness can be the greatest sort of heroism.

He has seized this particular moment when his wife has left the house to get his medicine and he still (barely) has strength to drive the short distance and walk into the woods and do the deed. He wants to end it now. "Clean. Cleanly."[17] It is his "incredible opportunity to end things with dignity."[18]

Both Robin and Don imagine that their current courses of action are heroic. But what both they and the reader will see when the characters' paths converge is that everyday kindness can be the greatest sort of heroism. Kindness changes the stories we imagine for ourselves by letting in other people who will change the outcome of the story.

When Don spies the boy carrying his coat in search of him, even his weakened mind is troubled at the thought of a child stumbling across the scene of death he is about to create. He doesn't want to traumatize a child like this. After all, he has two kids of his own, grown now. He has thought to end his life so as to spare "the ones he loves from painful last images that might endure for a lifetime."[19] Yet here is this boy, not one of his loved ones, but a total stranger. If he kills himself here in the woods as planned, then he will be imposing on this stranger, a mere child who might stumble upon him, a painful image that would likely endure for a lifetime. "That could scar a kid," he thinks.[20] He remembers how when he was a kid he found a picture of his father naked with a woman who wasn't his mother and how this traumatized him.

As he contemplates this unexpected obstacle to his suicide plan, he suddenly sees that the boy has fallen through the ice on the pond in his attempt to find him and bring him his coat. As sick and feeble as he is in body, mind, and spirit, Don reacts:

> Suddenly he was not purely the dying guy who woke nights in the med-bed thinking, Make this not true make this not true, but again, partly, the guy who used to put bananas in the freezer, then crack them on the counter and pour chocolate over the broken chunks, the guy who'd once stood outside a classroom window in a rainstorm to see how Jodi was faring with that little red-headed s—— who wouldn't give her a chance at the book table, the guy who used to hand-paint bird feeders in college and sell them on weekends in Boulder, wearing a jester hat and doing a little juggling routine he'd—
>
> He started to fall again, caught himself, froze in a hunched-over position, hurtled forward, fell flat on his face, chucked his chin on a root.
>
> You had to laugh.
>
> You almost had to laugh.
>
> He got up. Got doggedly up.[21]

In giving up death in order to save the life of a stranger, Don recovers his true self, the one that includes his dying but doesn't forget his life, his living. His kindness to the boy reminds him of his kinship with his family, with whom he belongs both in life and in death.

> In giving up death in order to save the life of a stranger, Don recovers his true self.

When he finally reaches the pond, the boy has reached the shore on his own but is at risk of losing his life to hypothermia. Don takes the wet clothes off the boy (remembering, as he does so, undressing his own children for bed years ago), removes his own outer garments, puts them on the boy, and urges him toward home "in a grave fatherly way."[22]

Robin breaks from Don and runs across the field home, and doing so, he experiences an epiphany, an important turning point. Still in shock from his near drowning and near freezing, he cannot yet recollect or process his physical ordeal. But he suddenly, quietly realizes that his reason for entering the woods this day—to immerse himself in a fantasy game—has been mere foolishness. He sees how "stupid" it was, "talking in your head to some girl who in real life called you Roger."[23]

Robin's adolescent-sized epiphany points to the larger one in the story, the one in which all the meaning of the tale culminates. Robin's release of his romantic, illusory thinking parallels the epiphany Don has as a result of this day, this ordinary day, the tenth of December.

Out of the Woods

Just before Robin's mother finds him shivering in the cold, Don, having sacrificed his own warmth in order to cover Robin with his clothes, realizes how wrongheaded he'd been in thinking he would serve his family by ending his life. "You couldn't leave a couple of little kids behind,"[24] he realizes in horror. "What a cruel thing. Suddenly he saw clearly how cruel it was. And selfish. Oh God."[25] Robin's mother takes Don, this stranger who has saved her son's life, to her home. There Don begins to realize what he had done in choosing life, both his own and Robin's. He is filled with a renewed joy in life: "What a thing! To go from dying in your underwear in the snow to this! Warmth, colors, antlers on the walls, an old-time crank phone like you saw in silent movies. It was something. Every second was something. He hadn't died in his shorts by a pond in the snow. The kid wasn't dead. He'd killed no one. Ha! Somehow he'd got it all back. Everything was good now."[26]

Robin comes into the room, sheepish and still shivering. He takes Don's hand in his and apologizes for running from him in fear. Don responds, "You did amazing. You did perfect. I'm here. Who did that?"

Then he thinks to himself, "There. That was something you could do. The kid maybe felt better now? He'd given the kid that? That was a reason. To stay around. Wasn't it? Can't console anyone if not around? Can't do squat if gone?"[27]

Choosing life is also about receiving love.

This is merely the outer edge of Don's epiphany. As we move closer to the end of the narrative, we move to the heart of the story. Choosing life is about more than sticking around to give love to others, as priceless a part of life as this is. Choosing life is also about receiving love. When his wife arrives in search of her missing husband, she is weighted with all the emotions a human being might know:

> She came in flustered and apologetic, a touch of anger in her face. He'd embarrassed her. He saw that. He'd embarrassed her by doing something that showed she hadn't sufficiently noticed him needing her. She'd been too busy nursing him to notice how scared he was. She was angry at him for pulling this stunt and ashamed of herself for feeling angry at him in his hour of need, and was trying to put the shame and anger behind her now so she could do what might be needed.
>
> All of this was in her face. He knew her so well.
>
> Also concern.[28]

He knew her so well. "Kindness is a way of knowing people beyond our understanding of them."[29] It is "the ability to bear the vulnerability of others, and therefore oneself."[30] Such knowing and being known comes only in the tedium of day-to-day life together:

> When they were first married they used to fight. Say the most insane things. Afterward, sometimes there would be tears. Tears in bed? Somewhere. And then they would—Molly pressing her hot wet face against his hot wet face. They were sorry, they were saying with their bodies, they were accepting each other back, and that feeling, that feeling of being accepted back again and again, of someone's affection for you always expanding to

> encompass whatever new flawed thing had just manifested in you, that was the deepest, dearest thing he'd ever—
>
> Overriding everything else in that lovely face was concern.
>
> She came to him now, stumbling a bit on a swell in the floor of this stranger's house.[31]

The connection between the house of a stranger and the kinship of love is powerful and paradoxical. Kindness "opens us up to the world (and worlds) of other people in ways that we both long for and dread."[32] Kindness makes us vulnerable. It's an acknowledgment of our interdependence and therefore risky.[33] Yet the very thing "we have in common is our vulnerability."[34] Being kind brings other people into the stories that are in our heads. This can change their lives, and our own, in ways we can't predict.

"Kindness is a way of knowing people beyond our understanding of them."

Earlier, just before his reunion with his wife, Don pauses one more time to consider whether he really wants to continue living, knowing the days he has left are numbered and will be filled with great pain. "Oh, Lord," he thinks, "there was still all that to go through."

> Did he still want it? Did he still want to live?
>
> Yes, yes, oh, God, yes, please.
>
> Because, O.K., the thing was—he saw it now, was starting to see it—if some guy, at the end, fell apart, and said or did bad things, or had to be helped, helped to quite a considerable extent? So what? What of it? Why should he not do or say weird things or look strange or disgusting? Why should the s—— not run down his legs? Why should those he loved not lift and bend and feed and wipe him, when he would gladly do the same for them? He'd been afraid to be lessened by the lifting and bending and feeding and wiping, and was still afraid of that, and yet, at the same time, now saw that there could still be many—many drops

Being kind brings other people into the stories that are in our heads.

> of goodness, is how it came to him—many drops of happy—of good fellowship—ahead, and those drops of fellowship were not—had never been—his to [withhold].[35]

I've read this passage many times. It pierces me each time.

You see, I am so terribly, terribly afraid of dying. My own dying and other people's dying and animals' dying. I am afraid of the lifting and bending and feeding and wiping to come. I am afraid of the blood and the fluids and the suffering and the pain. I am afraid of being weak, sick, immobile, demented, blind, deaf—whatever of these might come to me and to those I love.

I know such fears are natural and normal. But I know, too, that these fears are amplified by the false values of a culture that idolizes youth, beauty, health, and—most of all—productivity. I was raised on the Protestant work ethic, and productivity is my love language. Such values get absorbed by our minds and are poured back out in the way we order our lives.

And the way we order our deaths.

Suicide has hit my family and me hard. The death of my father-in-law was eerily like the one that Don Eber planned for himself. Unlike Don, my father-in-law went through with his plans. Stoic and independent to a fault, my father-in-law thought the most rational thing he could do when he became terminally ill would be to treat himself like the animals he sometimes found in the traps placed in the woods where he often roamed: put them out of their misery.

Like Don, he waited until his wife went on a brief errand, leaving him alone in the home where he figured he was going to die anyway. Don Eber realized in time the sort of impact a scene of self-inflicted death has on those who come upon it. My father-in-law did not.

The physical aftermath he left for his grown children, including my husband, to tend to is, I suppose, the kind of thing soldiers go through, find impossible to talk about, and carry with them for the rest of their lives. His widow and children have had to bear feelings of guilt, wondering what they could have done that might have influenced my father-in-law not to make this choice. My husband has had to go without a father for nearly all of his adult life.

For those so sick or scared or depressed that they think their loved ones would be better off without them, I so wish for them to know what Don Eber came to know: caring for these bodies we inhabit for a while—whether that care is of our own or someone else's body—isn't a distraction from what life is all about. It is what life is all about.

In lieu of death, be kind to one another.

"Ruby before Swine"

Chapter twelve

Humility

"REVELATION" AND "EVERYTHING THAT RISES MUST CONVERGE"

by Flannery O'Connor

Humble yourselves therefore under the mighty hand of God, that he may exalt you in due time.

—1 Peter 5:6 (KJV)

"Mrs. Turpin always noticed people's feet."[1]

Like all good writers of fiction, Flannery O'Connor shows rather than tells. She is exquisitely good at it. This skill is what can make her stories so difficult to understand at first. O'Connor refuses to tell her readers very much. But like a photographer with a keen eye and a high-quality lens, she captures telling details about her characters, focusing our attention on the concrete shell around the inner nut of meaning, on the manners that reveal the mystery. Indeed, as O'Connor explains in *Mystery and Manners,* a collection of essays and lectures on the thinking and technique behind her craft, manners (the tangible, observable details) reveal the mystery (the essence, truth, and universals) of being. And those few simple words—"Mrs. Turpin always noticed people's feet"—capture the essential nature of the main character of O'Connor's "Revelation." They also capture her central problem: namely, in order to see someone's feet, you have to look down on them. Mrs. Turpin looks down on everyone.

We Are All Mrs. Turpin

As with many of O'Connor's characters, Ruby Turpin's prevailing sin is pride. In Ruby's case, this is a twofold irony: first, Mrs. Turpin thinks she is humble, but she is not; second, the qualities she judges others for are ones she shares. But this is the universal truth, the mystery that O'Connor reveals behind the particular example: none of us has reason to look down on anyone else. Yet we do. We are all Mrs. Turpin.

To be human is to struggle with pride. A few have too little of it; most, too much. There is a good sense of pride, of course, such as having pride in one's work or one's children. Aristotle means this sort of pride when he speaks of it as a virtue. In the Christian tradition, pride is understood as the excess of this good pride, what Aristotle terms *vanity*. Both the Aristotelian and the Christian tradition call for the proper proportion of esteem of oneself. Aquinas defines pride, simply, as "inordinate self-love." He explains that "every man's will should tend to that which is proportionate to him"; therefore, pride goes against right reason.[2]

Pride may be simple and it may be human, but it is a devastating vice. The root of pride, according to Aquinas, is lack of submission to God; pride, therefore, is "the beginning of all sin."[3] Pride is the sin attributed to the fall of Lucifer, who sought to ascend to the throne of God and be equal with the Most High (Isa. 14:12–15). Pride is the sin of Adam and Eve, who sought, in eating the forbidden fruit, to be like God (Gen. 3:5). The New Testament teaches that "God opposes the proud but shows favor to the humble" (1 Pet. 5:5; cf. Prov. 3:34). No wonder Pope Gregory I in the sixth century named pride the "root of vices," the deadliest of the deadly sins.[4] It has since then been recognized as such throughout church history.

To be human is to struggle with pride. A few have too little of it; most, too much.

Accordingly, moral philosophers have long considered the virtue that opposes pride—humility—to be the foundation of all other virtues.

John Chrysostom calls humility the "mother, and root, and nurse, and foundation, and bond of all good things: without this we are abominable, and execrable, and polluted."[5] Or as Peter Kreeft writes, "The greatest virtue keeps us from the greatest vice."[6]

Without humility, without an understanding of our proper place within the order of creation, we cannot cultivate the other virtues. We cannot even come to Christ, or to true knowledge, apart from humility. Augustine wrote in one of his letters that the way to truth begins and ends with humility:

> In that way the first part is humility; the second, humility; the third, humility: and this I would continue to repeat as often as you might ask direction, not that there are no other instructions which may be given, but because, unless humility precede, accompany, and follow every good action which we perform, being at once the object which we keep before our eyes, the support to which we cling, and the monitor by which we are

> restrained, pride wrests wholly from our hand any good work on which we are congratulating ourselves.[7]

But do we know what true humility is? "Nothing is more deceitful," says Fitzwilliam Darcy in *Pride and Prejudice*, "than the appearance of humility. It is often only carelessness of opinion, and sometimes an indirect boast."[8] False humility so abounds that we often distrust humility when we think we see it: The celebrity or athlete who gestures to heaven following a stellar performance. The humblebrag posted on social media ("I'm struggling so much more to learn Russian than I did learning French, Spanish, and Japanese!"). The public figure who accepts a greater honor with the obligatory announcement that it is "humbling" to do so. The church leader who "humbles" himself by making a dramatic public confession of some petty and popular sin that serves only to make him more endearing and relatable. None of these examples portray how truly, well, *humiliating*, real humility is.

Without humility, we cannot cultivate the other virtues.

Humility Is Being Grounded

It's helpful, as is often the case, to look at the etymology of the word. One thing I love about words is how their own stories can reveal so much about the history of ideas and worldviews, along with a deeper understanding of the concept. *Humility* is one such word. The ancient root from which we get the word, along with its sister *humble*, means "earth" or "ground." Eugene Peterson explains, "This is the Genesis origin of who we are: dust—dust that the Lord God used to make us a human being. If we cultivate a lively sense of our origin and nurture a sense of continuity with it, who knows, we may also acquire humility."[9] Implicit in the word *humility* is the acknowledgment that we "all come from dust, and to dust all return" (Eccles. 3:20). Like the earth itself, the humble person is lowly. The person of humility is—literally and figuratively—*grounded*.

Thus humility is the recognition that we are all *human*—another word that comes from the same root—and that none of us are God. Remembering our position as earthly creatures who are not gods is the essence of humility. The virtue of humility, most simply defined, is an accurate assessment of oneself. And, of course, it is impossible to assess oneself rightly apart from God.

While the definition of humility is simple, achieving this accurate assessment of oneself is not easy. In fact, in "Revelation," it comes only through an act of divine grace. Through Mary Grace, to be exact.

Like the earth itself, the humble person is lowly. Humility is the recognition that we are all *human*.

Mary Grace is the name of a young woman Ruby Turpin encounters in the doctor's waiting room where she sits with her husband, Claud, who is there to seek treatment. Mrs. Turpin's "little bright black eyes [take] in all the patients" in the crowded and dirty room. She passes the time by making haughty, scornful judgments on them. The irony is that Ruby Turpin is not a well-to-do, polished, genteel lady observing the hoi polloi from a lofty place of privilege. No. Mrs. Turpin and her husband are farmers—pig farmers, to be exact. But they have just enough more than some for Mrs. Turpin to feel justified in looking down upon the black people they hire as day laborers and the common folk she observes in the waiting room. She's so proud of herself and her station in life that she tells one of the women during a conversation in the waiting room, "Our hogs are not dirty and they don't stink."[10]

No pride could be more blinding than the kind that makes you think your pigs don't stink.

Pride has traditionally been associated with blindness, all the way back to Oedipus Rex, the famous hero of Sophocles's ancient Greek drama. Oedipus's tragic flaw of pride ultimately compels him to blind himself in an act of poetic justice for unknowingly killing his father and marrying his mother. His self-imposed physical blindness serves as both a reminder of the pride that kept him from an accurate assessment of himself (humility) and an emblem of the self-knowledge now in his possession, gained at great cost.

Pride is always a way of not seeing oneself properly, whereas humility is "self-knowledge perfected."[11] And if knowing oneself is not already difficult enough (indeed, even impossible given the deceitful nature of the human heart), true humility requires not only an understanding of oneself but also an understanding of objective reality outside of oneself. As Josef Pieper explains, "The ground of humility is man's estimation of himself according to the truth."[12]

Pride is always a way of not seeing oneself properly.

Mrs. Turpin isn't physically blinded in the story, as Oedipus is, but she comes close. Like Oedipus, her spiritual blindness is her downfall. She is blind both in her high estimation of herself and in the limitations of her knowledge of others. Her blindness leads to excessive pride. This pride is like a coin: one side is Mrs. Turpin's elevated view of herself; the other side is her low view of others.

> To help anybody out that needed it was her philosophy of life. She never spared herself when she found somebody in need, whether they were white or black, trash or decent. And of all she had to be thankful for, she was most thankful that this was so. If Jesus had said, "You can be high society and have all the money you want and be thin and svelte-like, but you can't be a good woman with it," she would have had to say, "Well don't make me that then. Make me a good woman and it don't matter what else, how fat or how ugly or how poor!" Her heart rose. He had not made her a n—— or white-trash or ugly! He had made her herself and given her a little of everything. Jesus, thank you! she said. Thank you thank you thank you![13]

Mrs. Turpin is, in a sense, merely an exaggerated version of Jane Austen's Elizabeth Bennet in *Pride and Prejudice*, who also places too much confidence in her own perceptiveness. The two characters and their stories are worlds apart, but they are similar in exposing the folly of pride. Whereas Elizabeth Bennet's pride is subtle and even appealing in its relatability, Mrs. Turpin's arrogance is shocking: "There was nothing you could tell her about people like them [white trash] that she didn't know already." Significantly, the story specifies in the next sentence that she "knew all this from her own experience."[14] Experience is, of course, a way of knowing that sharply contrasts with revelation, as the story makes clear by the end. Experience is rooted in the self and is thus a source of knowledge that is ripe for pride.

Soon Mrs. Turpin can't help but say out loud what she had just been thinking, and she tells the woman she's been chatting with in the waiting room, "When I think who all I could have been besides myself and what all I got, a little of everything, and a good disposition besides, I just feel like shouting, 'Thank you, Jesus, for making everything the way it is. . . . Oh thank you, Jesus, Jesus, thank you!'"[15]

Moment of Revelation

Mrs. Turpin gives thanks for her good standing in life. Then we read: "The book struck her directly over her left eye."[16]

This burst of unexpected violence is a signature move for O'Connor: sudden, inexplicable, and disorienting. But such violence in O'Connor is never gratuitous or unnecessary. No, with O'Connor it is always the most necessary violence of all, reflecting the violence of Christ's crucifixion, the means God uses to offer the grace that saves. O'Connor explains her use of violent and grotesque characters this way: "When you can assume that your audience holds the same beliefs you do, you can relax and use more normal means of talking to it; when you have to assume that it does not, then you have to make your vision apparent by shock—to the hard of hearing you shout, and for the almost-blind you draw large and startling figures."[17]

For O'Connor, both her audience and her subject matter reflect conditions characteristic of what she termed a "Christ-haunted" culture. There are various qualities of such a society, bereft of Christ, but one quality that stands out is pride. Not the most obvious kind of pride, perhaps, but the kind that is most difficult to detect and therefore to shake: that quiet and persistent pride of placing faith in oneself. We see this pride in many of the characters in O'Connor's stories: Hulga in "Good Country People," the grandmother in "A Good Man Is Hard to Find," Mrs. Cope in "A Circle in the Fire," and Ruby Turpin in "Revelation."

The book is hurled at Mrs. Turpin by Mary Grace, the daughter of the woman she was speaking to moments before. Mrs. Turpin had scorned her for her acned face and surly attitude, but the girl seems to have seen right through Mrs. Turpin, lobbing angry glances at her while looking up from reading her book until she finally throws it at her. The chaos that follows ends with Mary Grace restrained, medicated, and taken away as a lunatic and with Mrs. Turpin, injured and stunned, returning home in a daze.

Unable to shake the shock of the attack, Mrs. Turpin senses that God has given her a message in the horrible words Mary Grace hissed to her as she lay subdued on the floor, words she cannot get out of her mind: "Go back to hell where you came from, you old wart hog."[18] Restless, she finally goes to the pig parlor and begins to hose down the hogs. There she wrestles with God. "How am I a hog?" she demands of God. "If trash is what you wanted why didn't you make me trash?" she implores, her pride yet intact.[19]

But as she rages on at God, she gazes at the scene before her: her husband's truck on the highway, the pigs settled in the corner, the sun in the sky. Then a "visionary light settled in her eyes."[20] As is typical in O'Connor, first there is the storm of violence, then the light.

The vision Mrs. Turpin sees while standing there, hose in hand, baptizing the unclean pigs with water, is of a procession of people making their way into the Promised Land. The group is led by the very folks Mrs. Turpin had proudly disdained. "And bringing up the end of the procession was a tribe of people whom she recognized at once as those . . . like herself and Claud. . . . They were marching behind the others with great dignity, accountable as they had always been for good order and common sense and respectable behavior. They alone were on key. Yet she could see by their shocked and altered faces that even their virtues were being burned away."[21]

At last—by the violent means of grace—Mrs. Turpin understands that "the first shall be last." She and Claud may be last, but through the vision she at last understands that the order is of no importance at all. All that matters is that you come. And when you do, your virtues—those good deeds and good manners and good things in your possession—will count for nothing.

But until you have enough humility to accept that, you will never be able to come.

The story closes with Mrs. Turpin listening to "the voices of the souls climbing upward into the starry field and shouting hallelujah."[22]

But between the awakening violence and the redemptive vision is suffering. Suffering, as "a form of involuntary humility," is thereby "a form of divine grace."[23] The violent act of Mary Grace causes Mrs. Turpin to suffer. Her pain is not merely physical but mental and spiritual as well. In fact, her physical suffering is far less than the spiritual torment she experiences as she begs God to reveal the meaning of Mary Grace's cursing her to hell.

Humiliation and Affliction

In *Waiting for God,* Simone Weil draws a distinction between suffering and affliction. In Weil's terms, suffering involves physical pain, but affliction involves the anguish of the soul. Weil contrasts the deaths of the martyrs with the death of Christ to show the distinction between suffering and affliction: "Those who are persecuted for their faith and are aware of the fact are not afflicted, although they have to suffer. They only fall into a state of affliction if suffering or fear fills the soul to the point of making it forget the cause of the persecution. The martyrs who entered the arena, singing as they went to face the wild beasts, were not afflicted. Christ was afflicted."[24]

Mrs. Turpin experiences not only physical suffering but the greater anguish of affliction. She is wounded less in being struck by the book than by the conviction that God is chastening her through Mary Grace's horrible words. Mrs. Turpin, who looks down upon everyone she sees, struck (nearly) in the eye, now can see that her pride has been all for naught. This kind of true affliction, as Weil says, involves "social degradation or the fear of it in some form or another."[25] Mrs. Turpin's pride has depended on her view of herself in relation to others in her social world. Her redemption is in undergoing the humbling vision in which she has taken her proper place in heaven as last, not first.

Earlier in the waiting room, before being struck by Mary Grace's flying book, Mrs. Turpin was half listening to the piped-in music. "The gospel hymn playing was, 'When I looked up and He looked down,' and Mrs. Turpin, who knew it, supplied the last line mentally."[26] She knew the line. But until her moment of grace, she couldn't grasp its meaning. "Pride looks down, and no one can see God but by looking up."[27]

Humiliation is a form of affliction, not merely suffering. O'Connor's use of violence in her stories brings about the sort of affliction of the soul—the humiliation—that allows for repentance and redemption. Such humiliation, Weil says, is "a violent condition of the whole corporal being which longs to surge up under the outrage but is forced, by impotence or fear, to hold itself in check."[28] Consider the humiliation Christ endured through his suffering and affliction on the cross. Christ,

> being in very nature God,
> did not consider equality with God something to be used to
> his own advantage;
> rather, he made himself nothing
> by taking the very nature of a servant,
> being made in human likeness.
> And being found in appearance as a man,
> he humbled himself
> by becoming obedient to death—
> even death on a cross! (Phil. 2:5–8)

The rich layers of the word *humbled* in this passage reflect the depths of Christ's incarnation. On a literal level, the word denotes the fact that Christ became human (earthly). But it also suggests the meaning we associate with the word today: Christ degraded himself, stooped low, and gave up his rightful and lofty place in heaven in order to share our humanity with us. Both the literal and the accumulated meaning of *humiliation* capture Christ's action. Christ's own humiliation is the evidence moral philosophers give to explain why the virtue of humility is central to the good life.[29]

A Life of Humiliation

Flannery O'Connor knew humiliation well. Her very life was in many ways a humiliation. From a young age, she was unable to meet her mother's expectation for her to be a proper Southern belle. She described herself later as "a pidgeon-toed [*sic*], only-child with a receding chin and a you-leave-me-alone-or-I'll-bite-you complex."[30] As a girl, she had to wear corrective shoes and "had a distinctive kind of loping walk."[31] Later, her few, awkward attempts at romance were never fully requited. When she became ill with lupus, she had to give up the independent life she had carved out for herself as a writer in the Northeast, returning to her mother's home in Georgia until she died at age thirty-nine from the disease.

Of course, every humiliation of ours is but a pale shadow of Christ's humiliation. Comparing whatever we go through to what he did puts our afflictions in proper perspective. This is the beginning of humility. Humility is not, therefore, simply a low regard for oneself; rather, it is a proper view of oneself that is low in comparison to God and in recognition of our own fallenness.[32] "Humility is thinking less *about* yourself, not thinking less *of* yourself."[33]

The Beatitudes describe the characteristics of the humble: the poor in spirit, the meek, the mournful, the merciful, the pure in heart, the peacemakers, the ones who hunger and thirst for righteousness. But the Sermon on the Mount doesn't merely praise these qualities; it offers a paradoxical promise in which all of those who are last shall be first. (And the Mrs. Turpins of the world, as her revelation reveals, shall be last.) Christ's own humiliation is the most dramatic example of this. The passage from Philippians quoted above continues by describing Christ's reward for his sacrifice:

> Therefore God exalted him to the highest place
>   and gave him the name that is above every name,
> that at the name of Jesus every knee should bow,
>   in heaven and on earth and under the earth,
> and every tongue acknowledge that Jesus Christ is Lord,
>   to the glory of God the Father. (Phil. 2:9–11)

This is the "moral irony" of the virtue of humility: the "ironic biblical principle that humility ultimately results in exaltation."[34] The paradox of humility is that through it we are exalted (Matt. 23:12). And the paradox of pride is that through it we fall—a truth devastatingly portrayed in another of O'Connor's stories, "Everything That Rises Must Converge."

The Paradox of Pride

Julian Chestny is a recent college graduate who is living at home and selling typewriters until he can succeed as a writer. He and his mother live in a declining neighborhood in the newly integrated South. Julian's mother sacrificed a great deal for her son: her own "teeth had gone unfilled so that his could be straightened," and she "brought him up successfully and had sent him to college." But Julian is ungrateful to his mother. Because "gratitude recognizes and prizes the work that another does and who the other is,"[35] gratitude requires humility. Julian is not only ungrateful; he is proud. He thinks his failure to thrive professionally is because he is "too intelligent to be a success."[36] His pride and lack of gratitude contribute to the shame he feels about his mother. He is ashamed of her racism, her prejudice, her haughtiness, her backwardness, and her pride in their family's lofty past that means nothing now.

Julian's mother (she is always referred to this way in the story, not by her name) does possess these flaws. Her moral blindness and false pride are serious defects in character. They are also just plain annoying. "Your great-grandfather was a former governor of this state," she reminds Julian as they ride the bus one day to her weight-loss class at the Y. Julian must accompany her on the bus because, the story suggests, she won't ride alone now that the buses are integrated. "Your grandfather was a prosperous landowner. . . . Your great-grandfather had a plantation and two hundred slaves." When Julian reminds her of the dingy city where they now live and the fact that there are no more slaves, his mother responds, "They were better off when they were."[37] When she starts reminiscing fondly on the bus about her childhood nurse, "an old darky" named Caroline, and how she's "always had a great respect for my colored friends," Julian begs her to change the subject, aware of the hurt her words might cause if heard by fellow passengers. He is so pained by his mother's racism that whenever "he got on a bus by himself, he made it a point to sit down beside a Negro, in reparation as it were for his mother's sins."[38]

The reader can't help but be pained along with Julian as we witness such blind prejudice on the part of this woman who thinks herself so fine. We can't help but look down on her, which means, whether we realize it or not, thinking more highly of ourselves. And thus we have fallen into O'Connor's trap. For as Julian continues to think disdainfully about his mother, he elevates himself, just as the reader has herself, in his own mind, and to astonishing heights:

> The further irony of all this [he thinks] was that in spite of her, he had turned out so well. In spite of going to only a third-rate college, he had, on his own initiative, come out with a first-rate education; in spite of growing up dominated by a small mind, he had ended up with a large one; in spite of all her foolish views, he was free of prejudice and unafraid to face facts. Most miraculous of all, instead of being blinded by love for her as she was for him, he had cut himself emotionally free of her and could see her with complete objectivity. He was not dominated by his mother.[39]

As Julian continues to stew about his mother during their trip (belying his insistence that he is not dominated by her), something horrible about Julian slowly and steadily unfolds to the reader. He harbors a growing, sinister desire to "teach her a lesson." He imagines befriending and bringing home "some distinguished Negro professor or lawyer" just to make her blood pressure rise. He nurses fantasies that become shockingly violent.

> He imagined his mother lying desperately ill and his being able to secure only a Negro doctor for her. He toyed with that idea for a few minutes and then dropped it for a momentary vision of himself participating as a sympathizer in a sit-in demonstration. This was possible but he did not linger with it. Instead, he approached the ultimate horror. He brought home a beautiful suspiciously Negroid woman. Prepare yourself, he said. There is nothing you can do about it. This is the woman I've chosen. She's intelligent, dignified, even good, and she's suffered and she hasn't thought it fun. Now persecute us, go ahead and persecute us. Drive her out of here, but remember, you're driving me too. His eyes were narrowed and through the indignation he had generated, he saw his mother across the aisle, purple-faced, shrunken to the dwarf-like proportions of her moral nature.[40]

Julian characterizes his mother's morals as small and narrow, yet he does not recognize his own immorality in his treatment of her. He goes so far as to imagine slapping her, as he would a child. And when the bus ride is over, Julian's wishes will be tragically fulfilled.

After disembarking from the bus, his mother tries to give a penny to a small black child who had been sitting next to her. Shockingly, the child's mother, offended at Julian's mother's condescending posture, punches Julian's mother in the face. Yet even more shocking is Julian's response to this violence against his mother.

As she lies collapsed on the sidewalk, he responds by hissing at her, "I told you not to do that." Slathered in his own self-righteousness, he continues, "You got exactly what you deserved. Now get up." The vengeful fantasy he was nursing minutes before has come true: "I hope this teaches you a lesson," he admonishes her. His mother's response is heartrending: "She leaned forward and her eyes raked his face. She seemed trying to determine his identity. Then, as if she found nothing familiar about him, she started off with a headlong movement in the wrong direction."[41]

In the last few minutes of the narrative, Julian's mother's mind slips from reality into the past where she, tragically, has stored so much of her treasure. She calls out first for her father, then for the black nurse of her youth—the people who, unlike Julian, returned her love. Because he lacks humility, Julian lacks love. "True love presupposes humility; without humility, the self comes to occupy all the available space and sees the other person as an object . . . or as an enemy."[42] Indeed, while love is the "finest fruit of virtue," humility is its root.[43]

Julian's mother's delirium spirals until her body gives way and her very life slips from her, there on the pavement with Julian helplessly calling out. But it is too late. She gets, as Julian said earlier, "exactly what [she] deserved"—as we all do apart from the grace that comes only with humility. The story closes with Julian enveloped by swirling darkness that seems "to sweep him back to her, postponing from moment to moment his entry into the world of guilt and sorrow."[44]

A Proper Valuing of Oneself

The subtle hope of this last line can be seen in the pattern of O'Connor's works taken as a whole. Their collective vision shows that before there can be salvation, there must be recognition of guilt as well as sorrow for that guilt, which leads to humility or the "proper valuing of oneself in light of the real relationships one encounters."[45] Significantly, Julian defines himself in light of relationships he imagines having, rather than real ones. Earlier in the story we learn that he tries to befriend black people but only ones he imagines to be what they are not. They don't pass the prejudicial tests Julian doesn't see that he has. Ironically, his rejection of his mother because of her immoral racism is his immorality. He rejects the one real person most significant in his life, all because he lacks humility. To live "humbly before God means suffering and submitting to other sinful human beings,"[46] but Julian refuses this, imprisoning himself in his own pride. For, Hannah Anderson notes insightfully in *Humble Roots,* "As much as humility frees us from condemning ourselves, it also frees us from condemning others."[47] The story ends with a hint that Julian, forced to see what he wished for come to fruition, will achieve recognition of who he truly is and, therefore, redemptive grace.

Seeing who we really are—which requires seeing ourselves in relationship to God—is true humility. In *Mystery and Manners,* O'Connor says, "To know oneself is, above all, to know what one lacks. It is to measure oneself against Truth, and not the other way around. The first product of self-knowledge is humility."[48] But gaining humility—knowing who we are—isn't only about degradation and lack. It is about the exaltation offered in the freedom of knowing who we are and who we were created to be.

The awkward, pigeon-toed, sickly O'Connor beautifully demonstrated the exaltation of humility in her own life and work. Once, when asked by a student at a lecture, "Miss O'Connor, why do you write?" she answered, "Because I'm good at it."[49] At first glance, this reply might seem conceited or proud. But the truth is that knowing what we are good at and what we are not, doing what we are supposed to do and not what we aren't, being what we are supposed to be and not what we aren't, is the essence of true humility.

Before O'Connor knew for certain who she was and what she was good at, when she was struggling to learn this along with the craft of writing, she kept a prayer journal at school. In it, she wrote this prayer: "But dear God please give me some place, no matter how small, but let me know it and keep it. If I am the one to wash the second step everyday, let me know it and let me wash it and let my heart overflow with love washing it."[50] Humility is taking our place, no matter how small (or big), and fulfilling that place with a heart overflowing with love.

The good life begins and ends with humility.

Acknowledgments

I am grateful to the entire Brazos team—they were professional, personal, knowledgeable, warm, and encouraging. This project was a long time in the making—and writing. Without Bob Hosack's interest and support from the beginning, and his seasoned guidance throughout, this would have been an entirely different (and inferior) book. Eric Salo's investment of time and skill from start to finish was invaluable, as were his careful eye and attuned ear. Jeremy Wells is the pin holding all the parts together, and I'm very thankful for his enthusiasm and expertise.

Rebecca Konyndyk DeYoung—who, unlike me, is an expert and scholar in philosophy—was generous and gracious in directing me at the start of my research (and throughout) to the best contemporary sources in the field of virtue ethics.

Several graduate and undergraduate students assisted me with research and clerical tasks, allowing me to do much more than I could have accomplished without them. I'm grateful to Bailey Jarnagin, Emily Meadows, Rebecca Olsen, Emily Thompson, and Hannah Underhill—as well as to Liberty University for providing me with the support of these student workers and graduate research assistants (and the time to write).

Some of this book was drawn heavily from material I teach. Some of it came from research in areas new to me. Combining these threads in ways both accurate and (hopefully) compelling was a challenge, and I'm grateful for the many former students, colleagues, and friends who offered to read drafts of chapters and give me feedback. Thank you to Marybeth Baggett, Christy Chichester, Gina Dalfonzo, Paul Faust, Kathryn Harmon, Emily Beth Hill, Ginger Horton, Teri Hyrkas, Robert Joustra, Pam Keating, Lauren Lund, Dustin Messer, Adam Myers, Nick Olson, Leo Percer, Kelly Sauskojus, Kayla Snow, and Janna Campbell Wiersma. (And my sincere apologies go to anyone whose name I inadvertently omitted.) I must make particular mention of Jennifer Bolan Ulrich, who read several chapters and provided helpful feedback time and time again. So much of writing is a solitary act. But it is rooted in and offers fruit in community. I'm thankful to be surrounded by a rich and deep community of fellow readers and writers who make my work what it is and make me who I am.

To have my words adorned by the lush, bold prints of the talented Ned Bustard is a blessing and honor that only the Lord could have orchestrated. I'm thankful to share these pages with such a visionary artist.

Finally, I'm thankful to my family, who is so supportive of me, for giving me the time and space required to read and write, read and revise, and read and write some more—and for making sure I take time to do other things too, because moderation is a virtue after all.

Discussion Questions

Introduction: Read Well, Live Well

1. Why should we read "promiscuously"? Are there important reasons for Christians especially to do so?
2. In what ways is reading an activity that in itself cultivates virtue?
3. What are the obstacles to reading and to reading well? How can these obstacles be overcome?
4. How does literary language differ from everyday language? How can skill in literary language help us better use and appreciate everyday language?
5. What does it mean to consider the form of a literary work as opposed to its content? What is the difference between the aesthetic and the utilitarian value of a literary work?

Chapter 1: Prudence: *The History of Tom Jones, A Foundling* by Henry Fielding

1. What is the relationship between prudence and morality? Between prudence and immorality?

2. How does the virtue of prudence combat the obstacle that perfectionism presents to the good?
3. What is the excess of prudence? What is its deficit? What do these vices look like in real life? What does prudence look like in real life?
4. How does the form of *The History of Tom Jones, A Foundling* support the content of the story?
5. What are the strengths and weaknesses of satire?

Chapter 2: Temperance: *The Great Gatsby* by F. Scott Fitzgerald

1. How is temperance different from the other virtues?
2. Aristotle viewed temperance as related to the appetites humans share in common with animals. What are more expansive applications of temperance?
3. How is temperance related to the Christian life?
4. What role does temperance have in Jay Gatsby's life?
5. How does our nation's life and culture reflect temperance or its lack?

Chapter 3: Justice: *A Tale of Two Cities by Charles Dickens*

1. In what ways does justice depend on both communities and individuals? How does this make the virtue of justice different from the other virtues?
2. It is said that "the wheels of justice turn slowly." Why, if they turn too slowly, is justice ultimately thwarted?
3. Do the coincidences, romanticism, and Gothicism of *A Tale of Two Cities* advance or detract from the theme of justice? How so?

4. Was Sydney Carton's decision to take Charles Darnay's place at the guillotine justice or something else?
5. What is the relationship between justice and beauty?

Chapter 4: Courage: *The Adventures of Huckleberry Finn* by Mark Twain

1. What are the elements necessary for a risk taken to constitute the virtue of courage?
2. What real-life examples of courage have you seen?
3. What is it about a mob that makes its participants lack the qualities necessary for true courage?
4. How do Huck Finn, Tom Sawyer, and Jim show the virtue of courage (or not)?
5. What role does courage have in assisting other virtues?

Chapter 5: Faith: *Silence* by Shusaku Endo

1. In what way is faith as a theological virtue different from the classical virtues Aristotle wrote about?
2. What makes faith so difficult to measure and be certain of?
3. What various examples of faith are seen in the description of the story of *Silence*?
4. Is denouncing a symbol of one's faith the same as denouncing one's faith? Why or why not?
5. What does it mean to live with a "hidden faith"? Is such a thing possible? Does it make a difference if one is living where Christians are persecuted? Why or why not?

Chapter 6: Hope: *The Road* by Cormac McCarthy

1. What can a postapocalyptic world reveal about our own world and the human condition?
2. What is the difference between the natural passion of hope, shared by both humans and animals, and theological hope, which is unique to humans?
3. How can natural hope prepare a person to receive theological hope from God? How can the existence of natural hope in the world help us better understand supernatural hope?
4. Describe the relationship between the man and the boy. How does the man's hope help them to survive?
5. What role does ordinary, mundane goodness have in cultivating hope?

Chapter 7: Love: *The Death of Ivan Ilych* by Leo Tolstoy

1. What are various meanings of the word *love*? What do they have in common? How are they different?
2. How are friendship and companionship important to human flourishing?
3. Why does materialism so often replace love of people?
4. How are compassion and empathy different? How is charity or *agape* different from these?
5. Discuss Ivan Ilych's death and the role that both suffering and love played in it.

Chapter 8: Chastity: *Ethan Frome* by Edith Wharton

1. What are the positive and negative understandings of chastity?
2. Why is chastity so misunderstood?

3. How do the various kinds of lusts work against chastity, both in *Ethan Frome* and in real life?
4. What are the various ways Ethan was unchaste? How might he have changed the outcome of the story?
5. What role does the community have in cultivating chastity in its members? How can communities do a better job at this?

Chapter 9: Diligence: *Pilgrim's Progress* by John Bunyan

1. Why is diligence one of the least examined virtues?
2. What are examples of accomplishments in life that rely mainly on diligence?
3. How is diligence shown in *Pilgrim's Progress*?
4. Discuss the way allegorical language depends on and cultivates diligence.
5. What is the relationship between language, the physical world, and the spiritual world? How does allegory help demonstrate this?

Chapter 10: Patience: *Persuasion* by Jane Austen

1. How does the history of the word *patience* and its various applications help us better understand it as a virtue?
2. What, beyond waiting, are the necessary components of the virtue of patience?
3. How are situations from the mundane to the excruciating similar in requiring patience? How are they different?
4. In what ways does Anne Elliot's behavior exhibit the virtue of patience?
5. How does the form of *Persuasion* help the reader to practice patience?

Chapter 11: Kindness: "Tenth of December" by George Saunders

1. If kindness is so easy and simple, why is it so lacking around us?
2. How is *nice* different from *kind*?
3. How do the characters in "Tenth of December" show the virtue of kindness?
4. How does the way the story is narrated help the reader to practice kindness?
5. Where in the real world do you see the virtue of kindness needed or already at work?

Chapter 12: Humility: "Revelation" and "Everything That Rises Must Converge" by Flannery O'Connor

1. How does the etymology of *humility* illuminate what it means to be humble?
2. What is false humility? Why is it sometimes confused with true humility?
3. How does Christ's humiliation on the cross help us understand the virtue of humility?
4. How are suffering and affliction different?
5. How do you see O'Connor's Christian faith at work in these stories?

Notes

Foreword

1. Aristotle, *Poetics* 13.

2. Philip Sidney, *A Defense of Poetry*, in *English Essays from Sir Philip Sidney to Macaulay* (New York: Collier, 1910), 26, 32.

3. Ernest Hemingway, *Death in the Afternoon* (New York: Scribner, 1932), 4.

4. Oscar Wilde, preface to *Picture of Dorian Gray* (New York: Dover, 1993), vii.

5. C. S. Lewis, *English Literature in the Sixteenth Century: Excluding Drama* (Oxford: Oxford University Press, 1973), 346.

Introduction: Read Well, Live Well

1. John Milton, *Areopagitica: A Speech of John Milton*, 1644, The John Milton Reading Room, accessed November 1, 2017, https://www.dartmouth.edu/~milton/reading_room/areopagitica/text.html. I have modernized the spelling in the quoted passage.

2. Nicholas Carr, *The Shallows: What the Internet Is Doing to Our Brains* (New York: Norton, 2011), 10.

3. Paul Lewis, "Our Minds Can Be Hijacked: The Tech Insiders Who Fear a Smartphone Dystopia," *The Guardian*, October 6, 2017, https://www.theguardian.com/technology/2017/oct/05/smartphone-addiction-silicon-valley-dystopia.

4. For more on reading for enjoyment, see Alan Jacobs, *The Pleasures of Reading in an Age of Distraction* (Oxford: Oxford University Press, 2011).

5. Shane Parrish, "If You Want to Get Smarter, Speed-Reading Is Worse Than Not Reading at All," Quartz, January 23, 2017, https://qz.com/892276/speed-reading-wont-make-you-smarter-but-reading-for-deep-understanding-will.

6. Take encouragement in slow reading from the renowned scholar David Mikics in his Harvard-published book, *Slow Reading in a Hurried Age* (Cambridge, MA: Belknap, 2013).

7. Baxter, *Christian Directory*, part 3, "Christian Ecclesiastics," in *The Practical Works of the Rev. Richard Baxter* (London: James Duncan, 1830) 5:584, available at https://play.google.com/books/reader?id=MKcOAAAAQAAJ.

8. For a thorough treatment of marking up a book, see the classic, *How to Read a Book* by Mortimer J. Adler and Charles Van Doren (New York: Touchstone, 1972).

9. Tony Reinke, Facebook discussion, March 10, 2018.

10. Billy Collins, "Marginalia," available at https://www.poetryfoundation.org/poetrymagazine/browse?contentId=39493.

11. C. S. Lewis, *An Experiment in Criticism* (Cambridge: Cambridge University Press, 2000), 9.

12. Lewis, *An Experiment in Criticism*, 88.

13. Thomas Jefferson, "To Robert Skip with a List of Books," August 3, 1771, Yale Law School: Avalon Project, The Letters of Thomas Jefferson, accessed December 1, 2017, http://avalon.law.yale.edu/18th_century/let4.asp.

14. Paul A. Taylor, "Sympathy and Insight in Aristotle's *Poetics*," *The Journal of Aesthetics and Art Criticism* 66, no. 3 (Summer 2008): 268.

15. Taylor, "Sympathy and Insight in Aristotle's *Poetics*," 265–80.

16. George Saunders, lecture, Festival of Faith and Writing, Calvin College, Grand Rapids, April 15, 2016.

17. Taylor, "Sympathy and Insight in Aristotle's *Poetics*," 265.

18. Taylor, "Sympathy and Insight in Aristotle's *Poetics*," 266.

19. Taylor, "Sympathy and Insight in Aristotle's *Poetics*," 276.

20. For a more extensive discussion on formation versus mere information, see James K. A. Smith, *Desiring the Kingdom* (Grand Rapids: Baker Academic, 2009), beginning on page 18 and throughout.

21. Sir Philip Sidney, *A Defence of Poetry* (Oxford: Oxford University Press, 2006), 31–32.

22. Sidney, *Defence of Poetry*, 29.

23. Will Durant, *The Story of Philosophy* (New York: Simon & Schuster, 1926), 87.

24. Alasdair MacIntyre, *After Virtue: A Study in Moral Theory*, 3rd ed. (Notre Dame, IN: University of Notre Dame Press, 2007), 11–12.

25. MacIntyre, *After Virtue*, 5.

26. MacIntyre, *After Virtue*, 2.

27. Keith Oatley, *Such Stuff as Dreams: The Psychology of Fiction* (Sussex: Wiley-Blackwell, 2011), 28, 29, 30.

28. I am indebted to Jason Alvis for this phrase used about this verse, a point he makes in a different context in "How to Write a Christian Sentence: Some Reflections on Scholarship," *Faith and the Academy* 2, no. 2 (Spring 2018): 38–41.

29. Graham Ward, "How Literature Resists Secularity," *Literature and Theology* 24, no. 1 (March 2010): 82.

30. Ward, "How Literature Resists Secularity," 85.

31. Emily Dickinson, "I dwell in Possibility—," in *The Norton Anthology of Women's Literature*, 3rd ed., ed. Sandra M. Gilbert and Susan Gubar (New York: Norton, 2007), 1:1053.

32. Sidney, *Defence of Poetry*, 54.

33. Smith, *Imagining the Kingdom*, 133, 137.

34. Jacques Ellul, *The Humiliation of the Word*, trans. Joyce Main Hanks (Grand Rapids: Eerdmans, 1985), 53.

35. Marcel Proust, *Days of Reading* (London: Penguin, 2008), 70.

36. See my chapter on Madame Bovary in *Booked: Literature in the Soul of Me* (Ossining, NY: TS Poetry Press, 2012).

37. Mark Edmundson, *Why Read?* (New York: Bloomsbury, 2004), 112.

38. Edmundson, *Why Read?*, 73.

39. Marshall Gregory, *Shaped by Stories: The Ethical Power of Narrative* (Notre Dame, IN: Notre Dame Press, 2009), 20.

40. Smith, *Imagining the Kingdom*, 108.

41. Smith, *Imagining the Kingdom*, 116, 36.

42. Keith Oatley, *Such Stuff as Dreams: The Psychology of Fiction* (Sussex: Wiley-Blackwell, 2011), 112, 221.

43. Smith, *Imagining the Kingdom*, 108.

44. Martha Nussbaum, *Love's Knowledge: Essays on Philosophy and Literature* (Oxford: Oxford University Press, 1990), 3–4.

45. Nussbaum, *Love's Knowledge*, 5.

46. Nussbaum, *Love's Knowledge*, 47.

47. Joseph Epstein, *A Literary Education and Other Essays* (Edinburg, VA: Axios, 2014), 16.

48. Nussbaum, *Love's Knowledge*, 44.

49. Aristotle, *Nicomachean Ethics*, ed. Roger Crisp, rev. ed. (Cambridge: Cambridge University Press, 2014), 27.

50. Aristotle, *Nicomachean Ethics*, 29–31.

51. Baxter, *Christian Directory*, part 1, "Christian Ethics," in *The Practical Works of the Rev. Richard Baxter* (London: James Duncan, 1830) 2:151, available at https://play.google.com/books/reader?id=7XcAAAAAMAAJ.

Chapter 1: Prudence: *The History of Tom Jones, a Foundling* by Henry Fielding

1. *Catechism of the Catholic Church*, para. 1806, accessed October 17, 2017, http://www.vatican.va/archive/ccc_css/archive/catechism/p3s1c1a7.htm.

2. André Comte-Sponville, *A Small Treatise on the Great Virtues: The Uses of Philosophy in Everyday Life* (New York: Picador, 2002), 37.

3. W. Jay Wood, "Prudence," in *Virtues and Their Vices*, ed. Kevin Timpe and Craig A. Boyd (Oxford: Oxford University Press, 2014), 38.

4. Cicero, *The Cyclopaedia of Practical Quotations, English and Latin* (Funk and Wagnalls, 1889), 557.

5. Josef Pieper, *The Four Cardinal Virtues* (Notre Dame, IN: University of Notre Dame Press, 1966), 3.

6. Wood, “Prudence,” 37.

7. Pieper, *Four Cardinal Virtues*, 7.

8. Pieper, *Four Cardinal Virtues*, 4.

9. *Catechism of the Catholic Church*, para. 1806.

10. Alasdair MacIntyre, *After Virtue: A Study in Moral Theory*, 3rd ed. (Notre Dame, IN: University of Notre Dame Press, 2007), 39.

11. MacIntyre, *After Virtue*, 39.

12. It should be noted, however, that Fielding’s theological framework, latitudinarianism, itself reflected more modern than traditional impulses.

13. MacIntyre, *After Virtue*, 11–12.

14. Christian Smith, *Soul Searching: The Religious and Spiritual Lives of Emerging Adults* (Oxford: Oxford University Press, 2009).

15. Henry Fielding, *The History of Tom Jones, A Foundling* (Middletown, CT: Wesleyan University Press, 1975), 7. Use of capital letters has been modernized in quotations from the text.

16. Martin Battestin, introduction to *The History of Tom Jones, A Foundling*, by Henry Fielding (Middletown, CT: Wesleyan University Press, 1975), xxv.

17. “Prudence,” *Online Etymology Dictionary*, accessed January 15, 2018, https://www.etymonline.com/word/prudence.

18. Cicero, cited in Comte-Sponville, *Small Treatise on the Great Virtues*, 34.

19. Battestin, introduction to *History of Tom Jones*, xxv.

20. Pieper, *Four Cardinal Virtues*, 11.

21. MacIntyre, *After Virtue*, 70–74.

22. Comte-Sponville, *Small Treatise on the Great Virtues*, 37.

23. Fielding, *History of Tom Jones*, 8.

24. Fielding, *History of Tom Jones*, 316.

25. Pieper, *Four Cardinal Virtues*, 19; Wood, “Prudence,” 47.

26. “Prudence,” *Merriam-Webster Dictionary*, accessed October 17, 2017, http://www.merriam-webster.com/dictionary/prudence.

27. Fielding, *History of Tom Jones*, 165.

28. Pieper, *Four Cardinal Virtues*, 22.

29. Pieper, *Four Cardinal Virtues*, 21.

30. Wood, “Prudence,” 38.

31. Pieper, *Four Cardinal Virtues*, 37.

32. Augustine, cited in Comte-Sponville, *Small Treatise on the Great Virtues*, 295n19.

33. Augustine, *On Christian Teaching*, ed. R. P. H. Green (Oxford: Oxford World’s Classics, 1999), 21.

34. Fielding, *History of Tom Jones*, 960.

35. Fielding, *History of Tom Jones*, 165.

36. Pieper, *Four Cardinal Virtues*, 31.

37. Thomas Aquinas, *Summa Theologiae* II-II, Q. 47, Art. 1, in *Summa Theologiae of St. Thomas Aquinas*, 2nd and rev. ed., 1920, literally translated by Fathers of the English Dominican Province. Available online at http://www.newadvent.org/summa.

38. Stanley Hauerwas and Charles Pinches, *Christians among the Virtues: Theological Conversations with Ancient and Modern Ethics* (Notre Dame, IN: University of Notre Dame Press, 1997), 102.

39. Hauerwas and Pinches, *Christians among the Virtues*, 101–2.

40. Pieper, *Four Cardinal Virtues*, 20.

41. Pieper, *Four Cardinal Virtues*, 22.

42. Wood, "Prudence," 49.

43. Wood, "Prudence," 49.

44. Fielding, *History of Tom Jones*, 768.

45. Pieper, *Four Cardinal Virtues*, 20.

46. Fielding, *History of Tom Jones*, 141.

47. Pieper, *Four Cardinal Virtues*, 21.

48. Wood, "Prudence," 44–45.

49. MacIntyre, *After Virtue*, 53–54.

50. Fielding, *History of Tom Jones*, 960.

51. Fielding, *History of Tom Jones*, 981.

52. Wood, "Prudence," 38.

Chapter 2: Temperance: *The Great Gatsby* by F. Scott Fitzgerald

1. André Comte-Sponville, *A Small Treatise on the Great Virtues: The Uses of Philosophy in Everyday Life* (New York: Picador, 2002), 42.

2. William C. Mattison III, *Introducing Moral Theology: True Happiness and the Virtues* (Grand Rapids: Brazos, 2008), 76.

3. Mattison, *Introducing Moral Theology*, 76.

4. Aristotle, *Nicomachean Ethics*, ed. Roger Crisp, rev. ed. (Cambridge: Cambridge University Press, 2014), 54.

5. Aristotle, *Nicomachean Ethics*, 54–57.

6. *Catechism of the Catholic Church*, para. 1809, accessed October 17, 2017, http://www.vatican.va/archive/ccc_css/archive/catechism/p3s1c1a7.htm.

7. Thomas Aquinas, *Summa Theologiae* I-II, Q. 3, Art. 1, in *Summa Theologiae of St. Thomas Aquinas*, 2nd and rev. ed., 1920, literally translated by Fathers of the English Dominican Province. Available online at http://www.newadvent.org/summa.

8. Robert C. Roberts, "Temperance," in *Virtues and Their Vices*, ed. Kevin Timpe and Craig A. Boyd (Oxford: Oxford University Press, 2014), 99.

9. Comte-Sponville, *Small Treatise on the Great Virtues*, 39.

10. Postmodern philosophers such as Jean Baudrillard theorize that the real, including sex, will be supplanted by the hyper-real or technological stimulation and

simulation of the real. Indeed, recent declines in teen sexual activity and pregnancy may owe in part to the replacement of embodied relationships with technologically mediated ones.

11. *Prohibition,* directed by Ken Burns and Lynn Novick, aired 2011, on PBS, http://www.pbs.org/kenburns/prohibition.

12. Frank A. Salamone, "Prohibition," in S. Bronner, ed., *Encyclopedia of American Studies* (Baltimore: Johns Hopkins University Press, 2016), http://eas-ref.press.jhu.edu/view?aid=614; Robin A. LaVellee and Hsiao-ye Yi, "Surveillance Report #104: Apparent Per Capita Alcohol Consumption: National, State, and Regional Trends, 1977–2014," National Institute on Alcohol Abuse and Alcoholism, March 2016, https://pubs.niaaa.nih.gov/publications/surveillance104/CONS14.pdf.

13. F. Scott Fitzgerald, *The Great Gatsby* (New York: Scribner, 1992), 105.

14. Fitzgerald, *Great Gatsby,* 104–5.

15. Fitzgerald, *Great Gatsby,* 77.

16. Fitzgerald, *Great Gatsby,* 155.

17. Fitzgerald, *Great Gatsby,* 117.

18. William R. Leach, *Land of Desire: Merchants, Power, and the Rise of a New American Culture* (New York: Vintage, 1994), 7.

19. Fitzgerald, *Great Gatsby,* 83.

20. Fitzgerald, *Great Gatsby,* 96.

21. Fitzgerald, *Great Gatsby,* 42–43.

22. Leach, *Land of Desire,* xiii.

23. Leach, *Land of Desire,* 3.

24. Leach, *Land of Desire,* xiv.

25. Beth Teitell, "Today's Families Are Prisoners of Their Own Clutter," *Boston Globe,* July 9, 2012, https://www.bostonglobe.com/lifestyle/2012/07/09/new-study-says-american-families-are-overwhelmed-clutter-rarely-eat-together-and-are-generally-stressed-out-about-all/G4VdOwzXNinxkMhKA1YtyO/story.html.

26. Glenn Tinder, *The Fabric of Hope* (Atlanta: Scholars Press, 1999), 17.

27. Josef Pieper, *The Four Cardinal Virtues* (Notre Dame, IN: University of Notre Dame Press, 1966), 148.

28. Fitzgerald, *Great Gatsby,* 85.

29. Fitzgerald, *Great Gatsby,* 33.

30. "Temper," *Oxford Dictionary,* accessed January 15, 2018, https://en.oxforddictionaries.com/definition/temper.

31. "Temper," *Online Etymology Dictionary,* accessed October 17, 2017, http://www.etymonline.com/word/temper.

32. "Temper," *Online Etymology Dictionary.*

33. Fitzgerald, *Great Gatsby,* 116.

34. Fitzgerald, *Great Gatsby,* 117.

35. Fitzgerald, *Great Gatsby,* 68.

36. Fitzgerald, *Great Gatsby,* 130.

37. Fitzgerald, *Great Gatsby,* 189.

38. Fitzgerald, *Great Gatsby*, 181–82.

39. Benjamin Franklin, *The Autobiography of Benjamin Franklin* (New York: Houghton Mifflin, 1888), 101.

40. Franklin, *Autobiography*, 102.

41. Fitzgerald, *Great Gatsby*, 104.

42. Fitzgerald, *Great Gatsby*, 101.

43. Fitzgerald, *Great Gatsby*, 98.

44. Comte-Sponville, *Small Treatise on the Great Virtues*, 40.

45. Fitzgerald, *Great Gatsby*, 12.

46. Fitzgerald, *Great Gatsby*, 97–98.

47. Fitzgerald, *Great Gatsby*, 98.

48. Guy Debord, *Society of the Spectacle* (Detroit: Black and Red, 1983), thesis 17.

49. Debord, *Society of the Spectacle*, thesis 67.

50. Leach, *Land of Desire*, 42.

51. Fitzgerald, *Great Gatsby*, 167.

52. Fitzgerald, *Great Gatsby*, 5.

53. Fitzgerald, *Great Gatsby*, 188.

Chapter 3: Justice: *A Tale of Two Cities* by Charles Dickens

1. William Faulkner, *Requiem for a Nun* (New York: Vintage, 2011), 73.

2. Aristotle, *Nicomachean Ethics*, ed. Roger Crisp, rev. ed. (Cambridge: Cambridge University Press, 2014), 80.

3. Plato, *The Republic*, trans. Allan Bloom, 2nd ed. (New York: Basic Books, 1991), 124.

4. Michael Novak and Paul Adams, *Social Justice Isn't What You Think It Is* (New York: Encounter Books, 2015), 19.

5. Aristotle, *Nicomachean Ethics*, 79.

6. Gerard Manley Hopkins, *Hopkins: Poems and Prose* (New York: Knopf, 1995), 18.

7. Elaine Scarry, *On Beauty and Being Just* (Princeton, NJ: Princeton University Press, 1999), 93.

8. André Comte-Sponville, *A Small Treatise on the Great Virtues: The Uses of Philosophy in Everyday Life* (New York: Picador, 2002), 61.

9. Josef Pieper, *The Four Cardinal Virtues* (Notre Dame, IN: University of Notre Dame Press, 1966), 61–62.

10. Aristotle, *Nicomachean Ethics*, 81.

11. Pieper, *Four Cardinal Virtues*, 65.

12. Charles Dickens, *A Tale of Two Cities* (New York: Bantam Classic, 1989), 1.

13. Stephen Koch, afterword to *Tale of Two Cities*, 358.

14. Dickens, *Tale of Two Cities*, 53–54.

15. Dickens, *Tale of Two Cities*, 47.

16. Dickens, *Tale of Two Cities*, 2–3.

17. Dickens, *Tale of Two Cities*, 47.

18. Dickens, *Tale of Two Cities*, 53.

19. Aristotle, *Nicomachean Ethics*, 80.

20. Augustine, *On the Free Choice of the Will, On Grace and Free Choice, and Other Writings*, ed. and trans. Peter King (Cambridge: Cambridge University Press, 2010), 10.

21. Martin Luther King Jr., "Letter from a Birmingham Jail," April 16, 1963, accessed October 28, 2017, https://www.africa.upenn.edu/Articles_Gen/Letter_Birmingham.html.

22. Dickens, *Tale of Two Cities*, 53–54.

23. Dickens, *Tale of Two Cities*, 2.

24. Dickens, *Tale of Two Cities*, 95.

25. Dickens, *Tale of Two Cities*, 107.

26. Dickens, *Tale of Two Cities*, 102.

27. Dickens, *Tale of Two Cities*, 102.

28. Dickens, *Tale of Two Cities*, 143.

29. Dickens, *Tale of Two Cities*, 206.

30. Dickens, *Tale of Two Cities*, 206–7.

31. Dickens, *Tale of Two Cities*, 208.

32. Dickens, *Tale of Two Cities*, 252.

33. Dickens, *Tale of Two Cities*, 251.

34. Dickens, *Tale of Two Cities*, 294–95.

35. King, "Letter from a Birmingham Jail."

36. Similarly, in our own time, capital punishment in America has steadily narrowed in use and diminished in acceptability: over the years, public executions and executions of minors and the mentally challenged have been rejected, for example, with some states abolishing the death penalty altogether. See Shane Claiborne, *Executing Grace: How the Death Penalty Killed Jesus and Why It's Killing Us* (San Francisco: HarperOne, 2016), 156.

37. Dickens, *Tale of Two Cities*, 347.

38. Dickens, *Tale of Two Cities*, 344–45.

39. Dickens, *Tale of Two Cities*, 346.

40. Dickens, *Tale of Two Cities*, 71.

41. Dickens, *Tale of Two Cities*, 192–93.

42. Dickens, *Tale of Two Cities*, 193.

43. Comte-Sponville, *Small Treatise on the Great Virtues*, 83.

44. David Schmidtz and John Thrasher, "The Virtues of Justice," in *Virtues and Their Vices*, ed. Kevin Timpe and Craig A. Boyd (Oxford: Oxford University Press, 2014), 68.

45. Schmidtz and Thrasher, "Virtues of Justice," 67.

46. Koch, afterword to *Tale of Two Cities*, 364.

47. Dickens, *Tale of Two Cities*, 138.

48. Plato, *The Republic*, 118–19.

49. Dickens, *Tale of Two Cities*, 80.
50. Dickens, *Tale of Two Cities*, 191.
51. Dickens, *Tale of Two Cities*, 76.
52. Scarry, *On Beauty and Being Just*, 91.
53. Scarry, *On Beauty and Being Just*, 42.
54. Scarry, *On Beauty and Being Just*, 81.
55. Dickens, *Tale of Two Cities*, 351.
56. Dickens, *Tale of Two Cities*, 351–52.

Chapter 4: Courage: *The Adventures of Huckleberry Finn* by Mark Twain

1. "Brave," *Online Etymology Dictionary*, accessed October 17, 2017, http://www.etymonline.com/index.php?term=brave.
2. "Alex Skarlatos Says Gut Instinct, Military Training Helped Subdue Gunman in France Train Attack," *Oregon Live*, August 23, 2015, http://www.oregonlive.com/today/index.ssf/2015/08/alex_skarlatos_says_gut_instin.html.
3. William C. Mattison III, *Introducing Moral Theology: True Happiness and the Virtues* (Grand Rapids: Brazos, 2008), 180.
4. Mark Twain, *The Adventures of Huckleberry Finn* (New York: Penguin, 2003), 9.
5. Twain, *Adventures of Huckleberry Finn*, 19.
6. Of course, in the neoclassical eighteenth century when America was founded, happiness was understood in the Aristotelian sense, as inextricably connected to virtue. Now, as we saw in chapter 2, the American Dream has seen the happiness attainable only through virtue replaced with a happiness attainable through materialism.
7. Twain, *Adventures of Huckleberry Finn*, 48.
8. Twain, *Adventures of Huckleberry Finn*, 19.
9. Twain, *Adventures of Huckleberry Finn*, 158–59.
10. "We fear all evils, such as disgrace, poverty, disease, friendlessness, death, but not all of them seem to be the concern of the courageous person. For some things, like disgrace, it is right and noble to fear, and shameful not to fear: the person who fears this is good and properly disposed to feel shame, and the one who does not is shameless." Aristotle, *Nicomachean Ethics*, ed. Roger Crisp, rev. ed. (Cambridge: Cambridge University Press, 2014), 48.
11. Josef Pieper, *The Four Cardinal Virtues* (Notre Dame, IN: University of Notre Dame Press, 1966), 122.
12. Aristotle, *Nicomachean Ethics*, 49.
13. Ambrose, "On the Duties of the Clergy" 1.35, in *A Select Library of Nicene and Post-Nicene Fathers of the Christian Church*, 2nd series, ed. Philip Schaff and Henry Wace, 14 vols. (repr., Peabody, MA: Hendrickson, 1994), 10:30.
14. Daniel McInerny, "Fortitude and the Conflict of Frameworks," in *Virtues and Their Vices*, ed. Kevin Timpe and Craig A. Boyd (Oxford: Oxford University Press, 2014), 85.

15. As William Bennett reminds us in his chapter on courage in *The Book of Virtues* (New York: Simon & Schuster, 1993), 441.

16. Aristotle, *Nicomachean Ethics*, 49.

17. Pieper, *Four Cardinal Virtues*, 117.

18. Twain, *Adventures of Huckleberry Finn*, 247.

19. Twain, *Adventures of Huckleberry Finn*, 252.

20. McInerny, "Fortitude and the Conflict of Frameworks," 84.

21. Pieper, *Four Cardinal Virtues*, 123.

22. Pieper, *Four Cardinal Virtues*, 120.

23. Pieper, *Four Cardinal Virtues*, 124.

24. Pieper, *Four Cardinal Virtues*, 128.

25. Thomas Aquinas, *Summa Theologiae* I, Q. 79, Art. 13, in *Summa Theologiae of St. Thomas Aquinas*, 2nd and rev. ed., 1920, literally translated by Fathers of the English Dominican Province. Available online at http://www.newadvent.org/summa.

26. Henry Fielding, *The History of Tom Jones, A Foundling* (Middletown, CT: Wesleyan University Press, 1975), 171n.

27. Mattison, *Introducing Moral Theology*, 107.

28. Mattison, *Introducing Moral Theology*, 108.

29. Twain, *Adventures of Huckleberry Finn*, 240.

30. Twain, *Adventures of Huckleberry Finn*, 247–48.

31. Twain, *Adventures of Huckleberry Finn*, 167.

32. Twain, *Adventures of Huckleberry Finn*, 101.

33. Mattison, *Introducing Moral Theology*, 108–9.

34. Mattison, *Introducing Moral Theology*, 110.

35. Twain, *Adventures of Huckleberry Finn*, 103–4.

36. Twain, *Adventures of Huckleberry Finn*, 227.

37. Twain, *Adventures of Huckleberry Finn*, 228.

38. Pieper, *Four Cardinal Virtues*, 126.

39. Dietrich Bonhoeffer, *Ethics*, trans. Neville Horton Smith (New York: Simon & Schuster, 1995), 244.

40. McInerny, "Fortitude and the Conflict of Frameworks," 87.

41. Azar Nafisi, *The Republic of Imagination: America in Three Books* (New York: Viking, 2014), 142.

Chapter 5: Faith: *Silence* by Shusaku Endo

1. "What Is the Nature of True Saving Faith?," Grace to You, accessed October 12, 2017, https://www.gty.org/library/questions/QA164/what-is-the-nature-of-true-saving-faith.

2. Josef Pieper, *Faith, Hope, Love* (San Francisco: Ignatius, 2012), 99–100.

3. Pieper, *Faith, Hope, Love*, 33.

4. Thomas Aquinas, *Summa Theologiae* I-II, Q. 62, Art. 1, in *Summa Theologiae of St. Thomas Aquinas*, 2nd and rev. ed., 1920, literally translated by Fathers of

the English Dominican Province. Available online at http://www.newadvent.org/summa.

5. Karl Clifton-Soderstrom, *The Cardinal and the Deadly: Reimagining the Seven Virtues and Seven Vices* (Eugene, OR: Cascade, 2015), 42.

6. Clifton-Soderstrom, *The Cardinal and the Deadly*, 35.

7. "Faith Defined," Ligonier Ministries, accessed October 14, 2017, http://www.ligonier.org/learn/devotionals/faith-defined.

8. Chad Thornhill, personal correspondence, January 28, 2017.

9. Makoto Fujimura, *Silence and Beauty: Hidden Faith Born of Suffering* (Downers Grove, IL: InterVarsity, 2016), 85.

10. Philip Zaleski, "Book Awards: HarperCollins 100 Best Spiritual Books of the Century," LibraryThing, November 1999, https://www.librarything.com/bookaward/HarperCollins+100+Best+Spiritual+Books+of+the+Century.

11. Shusaku Endo, *Silence*, trans. William Johnston (New York: Picador, 2016), 38.

12. Endo, *Silence*, 56.

13. Endo, *Silence*, 182.

14. Endo, *Silence*, 183.

15. Endo, *Silence*, 183.

16. Endo, *Silence*, 183.

17. Endo, *Silence*, 204.

18. Shusaku Endo, *Journeying Together: Conversation between Shusaku Endo and Yasumata Sato* (Tokyo: Kodansha Bungei, 1991), 25, translated by and quoted in Fujimura, *Silence and Beauty*, 40.

19. Endo, *Silence*, 203.

20. Endo, *Silence*, 203–4.

21. James Martin, SJ, "Fr. James Martin Answers 5 Common Questions about 'Silence,'" *America: The Jesuit Review*, January 18, 2017, https://www.americamagazine.org/arts-culture/2017/01/18/fr-james-martin-answers-5-common-questions-about-silence.

22. Peter Epps, "Interpret Carefully: Balancing Caution and Hope in Responding to Shusaku Endo's Novel *Silence*," *Christ and Pop Culture*, January 20, 2017, https://christandpopculture.com/interpret-carefully-balancing-caution-hope-responding-shusaku-endos-novel-silence.

23. William Johnston, translator's preface to *Silence* by Shusaku Endo (New York: Picador, 2016), xix.

24. Fujimura, *Silence and Beauty*, 47–50.

25. Fujimura, *Silence and Beauty*, 48–49.

26. Fujimura, *Silence and Beauty*, 50.

27. Fujimura, *Silence and Beauty*, 41.

28. Shusaku Endo, *The Voice of Silence* (Tokyo: President Company, 1992), 86, quoted in Fujimura, *Silence and Beauty*, 80.

29. Fujimura, *Silence and Beauty*, 41.

30. Mark Jenkins, "Scorsese's 'Silence': A Clash of Cultures—and Creeds—in 16th Century Japan," NPR, December 23, 2016, http://www.npr.org/2016/12/23/506341698/scorseses-silence-a-clash-of-cultures-and-creeds-in-16th-century-japan.

31. Patricia Snow, "Empathy Is Not Charity," *First Things*, October 2017, https://www.firstthings.com/article/2017/10/empathy-is-not-charity.

32. "Oedipus: The Message in the Myth," OpenLearn, December 6, 2007, http://www.open.edu/openlearn/history-the-arts/history/classical-studies/oedipus-the-message-the-myth.

33. Joseph Schwartz, "Chesterton on the Idea of Christian Tragedy," *Renascence: Essays on Values in Literature* 53, no. 3 (2001): 227.

34. "The Real Life of 'Silence's' Characters," News and Events, Society of Saint Pius X (website), May 2, 2017, http://sspx.org/en/news-events/news/real-life-silences-character.

35. Snow, "Empathy Is Not Charity."

36. Sigmund Freud, *The Basic Writings of Sigmund Freud*, trans. A. A. Brill (New York: Random House, 1938), 307.

37. Aristotle, *Poetics* 14, par. 15.

38. Schwartz, "Chesterton on the Idea of Christian Tragedy," 227.

39. Fujimura, *Silence and Beauty*, 80.

40. Fujimura, *Silence and Beauty*, 81.

41. Fujimura, *Silence and Beauty*, 49.

42. Martin Luther, "Babylonian Captivity," quoted in Clifton-Soderstrom, *The Cardinal and the Deadly*, 41.

43. Todd E. Outcalt, *Seven Deadly Virtues* (Downers Grove, IL: IVP Books, 2017), 35.

44. R. Scott Clark, "Is Faith a Virtue?," *The Heidelblog*, June 28, 2014, https://heidelblog.net/2014/06/is-faith-a-virtue-2.

45. Clifton-Soderstrom, *The Cardinal and the Deadly*, 40.

Chapter 6: Hope: *The Road* by Cormac McCarthy

1. "Apocalypse," *Online Etymology Dictionary*, accessed October 18, 2017, http://www.etymonline.com/index.php?term=apocalypse.

2. Robert Joustra and Alissa Wilkinson, *How to Survive the Apocalypse* (Grand Rapids: Eerdmans, 2016), 2.

3. Elizabeth H. Rosen, *Apocalyptic Transformation and the Postmodern Imagination* (New York: Lexington, 2008), xii, quoted in Joustra and Wilkinson, *How to Survive the Apocalypse*, 57.

4. Joustra and Wilkinson, *How to Survive the Apocalypse*, 5.

5. Jason Heller, "Does Post-Apocalyptic Literature Have a (Non-Dystopian) Future?," *NPR Books*, May 2, 2015, http://www.npr.org/2015/05/02/402852849/does-post-apocalyptic-literature-have-a-non-dystopian-future.

6. Josef Pieper, *Faith, Hope, Love* (San Francisco: Ignatius, 2012), 92.

7. Charles Pinches, "On Hope," in *Virtues and Their Vices*, ed. Kevin Timpe and Craig A. Boyd (Oxford: Oxford University Press, 2014), 362.

8. Cormac McCarthy, *The Road* (New York: Vintage, 2006), 3.

9. McCarthy, *The Road*, 126.

10. Thomas Aquinas, *Summa Theologiae* I-II, Q. 40, Art. 2, in *Summa Theologiae of St. Thomas Aquinas*, 2nd and rev. ed., 1920, literally translated by Fathers of the English Dominican Province. Available online at http://www.newadvent.org/summa.

11. James K. A. Smith, *Desiring the Kingdom* (Grand Rapids: Baker Academic, 2009), 30.

12. Thomas Aquinas, *Summa Theologiae* I-II, Q. 40, Art. 3.

13. Robert Miner, *Thomas Aquinas on the Passions* (Cambridge: Cambridge University Press, 2009), 219.

14. Thomas Aquinas, *Summa Theologiae* I-II, Q. 40, Art. 5.

15. Pieper, *Faith, Hope, Love*, 100.

16. Pieper, *Faith, Hope, Love*, 105.

17. Claudia Bloeser and Titus Stahl, "Hope," *The Stanford Encyclopedia of Philosophy*, ed. Edward N. Zalta, Spring 2017, https://plato.stanford.edu/entries/hope.

18. Miner, *Thomas Aquinas on the Passions*, 227.

19. McCarthy, *The Road*, 57.

20. McCarthy, *The Road*, 55–57.

21. Pieper, *Faith, Hope, Love*, 98.

22. Pieper, *Faith, Hope, Love*, 113.

23. Thomas Aquinas, *Summa Theologiae* II-II, Q. 21, Art. 1.

24. Thomas Aquinas, *Summa Theologiae* II-II, Q. 21, Art. 2.

25. Thomas Aquinas, *Summa Theologiae* II-II, Q. 20, Art. 2.

26. McCarthy, *The Road*, 5.

27. Thomas Aquinas, *Summa Theologiae* I-II, Q. 40, Art. 7.

28. Thomas Aquinas, *Summa Theologiae* I-II, Q. 40, Art. 7.

29. Thomas Aquinas, *Summa Theologiae* I-II, Q. 40, Art. 7.

30. Glenn Tinder, *The Fabric of Hope* (Atlanta: Scholars Press, 1999), 18.

31. McCarthy, *The Road*, 158.

32. McCarthy, *The Road*, 244.

33. McCarthy, *The Road*, 83.

34. McCarthy, *The Road*, 137.

35. John Piper, "What Is Hope?," *Desiring God*, April 6, 1986, http://www.desiringgod.org/messages/what-is-hope.

36. Pinches, "On Hope," 363.

37. McCarthy, *The Road*, 10.

38. McCarthy, *The Road*, 177.

39. McCarthy, *The Road*, 189.

40. McCarthy, *The Road*, 260.

41. McCarthy, *The Road*, 258–59.

42. McCarthy, *The Road*, 160.

43. McCarthy, *The Road*, 88.
44. Pinches, "On Hope," 353.
45. McCarthy, *The Road*, 230.
46. McCarthy, *The Road*, 130.
47. McCarthy, *The Road*, 88–89.
48. McCarthy, *The Road*, 272.
49. McCarthy, *The Road*, 129.
50. McCarthy, *The Road*, 144.
51. McCarthy, *The Road*, 151.
52. Pieper, *Faith, Hope, Love*, 117–19.
53. Pieper, *Faith, Hope, Love*, 120.
54. Pieper, *Faith, Hope, Love*, 122.
55. Miner, *Thomas Aquinas on the Passions*, 227.
56. Thomas Aquinas, *Summa Theologiae* II-II, Q. 17, Art. 5.
57. Pinches, "On Hope," 356.
58. Miner, *Thomas Aquinas on the Passions*, 228.
59. Pieper, *Faith, Hope, Love*, 101–2.
60. George Saunders, "Tenth of December," in *Tenth of December* (New York: Random House, 2013), 249.
61. Vladimir Nabokov, *Lectures on Literature* (New York: Harcourt, 1980), 375.
62. Nabokov, *Lectures on Literature*, 373.
63. Nabokov, *Lectures on Literature*, 374.
64. McCarthy, *The Road*, 23.
65. McCarthy, *The Road*, 39.
66. McCarthy, *The Road*, 40–41.
67. McCarthy, *The Road*, 280–81.
68. McCarthy, *The Road*, 77.
69. McCarthy, *The Road*, 128–29.
70. Thomas Aquinas, *Summa Theologiae* II-II, Q. 17, Art. 5.
71. Miner, *Thomas Aquinas on the Passions*, 229.
72. Miner, *Thomas Aquinas on the Passions*, 228.
73. Miner, *Thomas Aquinas on the Passions*, 228.
74. N. T. Wright, *Surprised by Hope* (New York: HarperCollins, 2008), 7.
75. Tinder, *Fabric of Hope*, 34.
76. Joustra and Wilkinson, *How to Survive the Apocalypse*, 57.
77. McCarthy, *The Road*, 54.
78. Tinder, *Fabric of Hope*, 31.
79. Alasdair MacIntyre, *After Virtue: A Study in Moral Theory*, 3rd ed. (Notre Dame, IN: University of Notre Dame Press, 2007), 1–2.
80. McCarthy, *The Road*, 16.
81. McCarthy, *The Road*, 278–79.
82. McCarthy, *The Road*, 5.
83. McCarthy, *The Road*, 75.

84. Pinches, "On Hope," 362.

85. Charles Taylor, *A Secular Age* (Cambridge, MA: Belknap, 2007), 20.

86. Taylor, *Secular Age,* 19.

87. Tinder, *Fabric of Hope,* 27.

88. Wright, *Surprised by Hope,* 85.

89. Wright, *Surprised by Hope,* 93–96.

90. Tinder, *Fabric of Hope,* 25.

91. Taylor, *Secular Age,* 18.

92. McCarthy, *The Road,* 246.

Chapter 7: Love: *The Death of Ivan Ilych* by Leo Tolstoy

1. Aristotle, *Nicomachean Ethics,* ed. Roger Crisp, rev. ed. (Cambridge: Cambridge University Press, 2014), 141.

2. Erich Fromm, *The Art of Loving* (New York: Harper and Row, 1962), 9.

3. Josef Pieper, *Faith, Hope, Love* (San Francisco: Ignatius, 2012), 175.

4. Maia Szalavitz, "How Orphanages Kill Babies—And Why No Child Under 5 Should Be in One," *Huffington Post,* June 23, 2010, http://www.huffingtonpost.com/maia-szalavitz/how-orphanages-kill-babie_b_549608.html.

5. Scott Stossel, "What Makes Us Happy, Revisited," *The Atlantic,* May 2013, https://www.theatlantic.com/magazine/archive/2013/05/thanks-mom/309287.

6. Dante Alighieri, *The Divine Comedy,* trans. John Ciardi (London: Penguin, 2003), 894.

7. Pieper, *Faith, Hope, Love,* 174.

8. Wayne Pacelle, *The Bond: Our Kinship with Animals, Our Call to Defend Them* (New York: Morrow, 2011), 135–52.

9. As expressed in Lin-Manuel Miranda's Tony Awards acceptance speech in 2016. Katey Rich, "Watch Lin-Manuel Miranda's Emotional Tony Awards Acceptance Sonnet," *Vanity Fair,* June 12, 2016, https://www.vanityfair.com/culture/2016/06/lin-manuel-miranda-tony-speech.

10. William C. Mattison III, *Introducing Moral Theology: True Happiness and the Virtues* (Grand Rapids: Brazos, 2008), 300.

11. Mattison, *Introducing Moral Theology,* 300.

12. Mattison, *Introducing Moral Theology,* 302.

13. Thomas Aquinas, *Summa Theologiae* II-II, Q. 23, Art. 1, in *Summa Theologiae of St. Thomas Aquinas,* 2nd and rev. ed., 1920, literally translated by Fathers of the English Dominican Province. Available online at http://www.newadvent.org/summa.

14. Thomas Aquinas, *Summa Theologiae* II-II, Q. 184, Art. 1.

15. James S. Spiegel, *How to Be Good in a World Gone Bad* (Grand Rapids: Kregel, 2004), 200–201.

16. Mattison, *Introducing Moral Theology,* 302.

17. Augustine, "Homily 7 on the First Epistle of John: 1 John 4:4–12," trans. H. Browne, in *Nicene and Post-Nicene Fathers,* 1st series, vol. 7, ed. Philip Schaff

(Buffalo, NY: Christian Literature Publishing, 1888), rev. and ed. Kevin Knight. Available online at http://www.newadvent.org/fathers/170207.htm.

18. Mattison, *Introducing Moral Theology*, 292.

19. Thomas Aquinas, *Summa Theologiae* I-II, Q. 62, Art. 3.

20. C. S. Lewis, *The Screwtape Letters, Mere Christianity, Surprised by Joy* (New York: Quality Paperback Book Club, 1992), 102.

21. Augustine, *On Christian Teaching*, ed. R. P. H. Green (Oxford: Oxford World's Classics, 1999), 76.

22. Augustine, *On Christian Teaching*, 21.

23. Leo Tolstoy, *The Death of Ivan Ilych*, trans. Louise and Aylmer Maude (Grand Rapids: Generic NL Freebook, 1886), 256.

24. Tolstoy, *Death of Ivan Ilych*, 267.

25. Tolstoy, *Death of Ivan Ilych*, 266.

26. Tolstoy, *Death of Ivan Ilych*, 255.

27. Elaine A. Robinson, *These Three: The Theological Virtues of Faith, Hope, and Love* (Eugene, OR: Wipf and Stock, 2010), 134.

28. C. S. Lewis, *The Four Loves* (New York: Harcourt Brace Jovanovich, 1960), 87–89.

29. Tolstoy, *Death of Ivan Ilych*, 248.

30. Tolstoy, *Death of Ivan Ilych*, 267.

31. Tolstoy, *Death of Ivan Ilych*, 269.

32. Tolstoy, *Death of Ivan Ilych*, 257.

33. Tolstoy, *Death of Ivan Ilych*, 259.

34. Tolstoy, *Death of Ivan Ilych*, 260.

35. Tolstoy, *Death of Ivan Ilych*, 261.

36. Tolstoy, *Death of Ivan Ilych*, 261.

37. Tolstoy, *Death of Ivan Ilych*, 298.

38. Tolstoy, *Death of Ivan Ilych*, 270.

39. Tolstoy, *Death of Ivan Ilych*, 283.

40. Tolstoy, *Death of Ivan Ilych*, 286.

41. Tolstoy, *Death of Ivan Ilych*, 276.

42. Martha Nussbaum, *Poetic Justice: The Literary Imagination and Public Life* (Boston: Beacon, 1997).

43. Robinson, *These Three*, 143.

44. Paul Bloom, *Against Empathy: The Case for Rational Compassion* (New York: Ecco, 2016).

45. Robinson, *These Three*, 144.

46. Spiegel, *How to Be Good*, 199.

47. Tolstoy, *Death of Ivan Ilych*, 253.

48. Tolstoy, *Death of Ivan Ilych*, 280.

49. Tolstoy, *Death of Ivan Ilych*, 285.

50. Shakespeare, Sonnet 73, in *Norton Anthology of English Literature*, 7th ed., ed. M. H. Abrams (New York: Norton, 2003), 1:1035.

51. Augustine, *Soliloquies* 1, trans. C. C. Starbuck, in *Nicene and Post-Nicene Fathers*, vol. 7. Available online at http://www.newadvent.org/fathers/170301.htm.

52. Tolstoy, *Death of Ivan Ilych*, 286.

53. Tolstoy, *Death of Ivan Ilych*, 271.

54. Tolstoy, *Death of Ivan Ilych*, 283.

55. Tolstoy, *Death of Ivan Ilych*, 284.

56. Tolstoy, *Death of Ivan Ilych*, 286.

57. Benedict XVI, *Caritas in Veritate*, June 29, 2009, para. 5, http://w2.vatican.va/content/benedict-xvi/en/encyclicals/documents/hf_ben-xvi_enc_20090629_caritas-in-veritate.html.

58. Benedict XVI, *Caritas in Veritate*, para. 3.

59. Flannery O'Connor, *Mystery and Manners* (New York: Farrar, Straus and Giroux, 1993), 227.

60. Tolstoy, *Death of Ivan Ilych*, 300.

61. Tolstoy, *Death of Ivan Ilych*, 294–95.

62. Tolstoy, *Death of Ivan Ilych*, 299.

63. Tolstoy, *Death of Ivan Ilych*, 302.

64. John Wesley, "Sermon 149: On Love," in *The Works of John Wesley*, vol. 4, *Sermons, IV, 115–151*, ed. Albert C. Outler (Nashville: Abingdon, 1987), 386.

Chapter 8: Chastity: *Ethan Frome* by Edith Wharton

1. C. S. Lewis, *The Screwtape Letters, Mere Christianity, Surprised by Joy* (New York: Quality Paperback Book Club, 1992), 75.

2. Augustine, *Confessions*, trans. R. S. Pine-Coffin (London: Penguin, 1961), 169.

3. Percy Bysshe Shelley, *The Poetical Works* (London: MacMillan, 1907), 34.

4. Aldous Huxley, *Eyeless in Gaza* (New York: Harper and Brothers, 1936), 289.

5. Augustine, *City of God*, trans. Henry Bettenson (London: Penguin Classics, 1984), 27.

6. This is a crucial distinction in cases of rape and assault when victims feel impure as a result.

7. Rebecca Konyndyk DeYoung, *Glittering Vices: A New Look at the Seven Deadly Sins* (Grand Rapids: Brazos, 2009), 178.

8. Lauren F. Winner, *Real Sex: The Naked Truth about Chastity* (Grand Rapids: Brazos, 2006), 126.

9. Winner, *Real Sex*, 126.

10. Chesterton, "A Piece of Chalk," *Daily News*, November 4, 1905, available at https://www.chesterton.org/a-piece-of-chalk.

11. Edith Wharton, *Ethan Frome* (New York: Scribner, 1979), 4.

12. Wharton, *Ethan Frome*, 3.

13. Wharton, *Ethan Frome*, 11.

14. Konyndyk DeYoung, *Glittering Vices*, 162.

15. David Allen, "The Lust of the Flesh, the Lust of the Eyes, and the Pride of Life—1 John 2:16," *Dr. David Allen,* April 30, 2015, http://drdavidlallen.com/bible/the-lust-of-the-flesh-the-lust-of-the-eyes-and-the-pride-of-life-1-john-216.

16. Wharton, *Ethan Frome,* 27.

17. Wharton, *Ethan Frome,* 72.

18. Wharton, *Ethan Frome,* 30.

19. Wharton, *Ethan Frome,* 31.

20. Wharton, *Ethan Frome,* 33–34.

21. Wharton, *Ethan Frome,* 57.

22. Wharton, *Ethan Frome,* 33–34.

23. Allen, "Lust of the Flesh."

24. Wharton, *Ethan Frome,* 17.

25. Wharton, *Ethan Frome,* 33.

26. Wharton, *Ethan Frome,* 46–47.

27. Wharton, *Ethan Frome,* 124.

28. Wharton, *Ethan Frome,* 130–31.

29. Wharton, *Ethan Frome,* 146–47.

30. Wharton, *Ethan Frome,* 35–36.

31. Hara Estroff Marano and Shirley Glass, "Shattered Vows," *Psychology Today,* July 1, 1998, https://www.psychologytoday.com/articles/199807/shattered-vows.

32. Wharton, *Ethan Frome,* 35–36.

33. Colleen McClusky, "Lust and Chastity," in *Virtues and Their Vices,* ed. Kevin Timpe and Craig A. Boyd (Oxford: Oxford University Press, 2014), 116.

34. Winner, *Real Sex,* 34.

35. Wharton, *Ethan Frome,* 116.

36. Wharton, *Ethan Frome,* 72.

37. Wharton, *Ethan Frome,* 108.

38. Wharton, *Ethan Frome,* 114.

39. Pope John Paul II, *Love and Responsibility* (San Francisco: Ignatius, 1993), 171.

40. "Chaste," *Online Etymology Dictionary,* accessed October 19, 2017, http://www.etymonline.com/index.php?term=chaste.

41. Daniel Goleman, "Long-Married Couples Do Look Alike, Study Finds," *New York Times,* August 11, 1987, http://www.nytimes.com/1987/08/11/science/long-marriedcouples-do-look-alike-study-finds.html.

42. Wharton, *Ethan Frome,* 188.

43. Wharton, *Ethan Frome,* 71.

44. Konyndyk DeYoung, *Glittering Vices,* 177.

45. Frederick Buechner, *Wishful Thinking: A Seeker's ABC* (San Francisco: HarperCollins, 1993), 107.

46. "Yes, Using Facebook May Be Making You More Lonely," *Fox News Health,* March 7, 2017, http://www.foxnews.com/health/2017/03/07/yes-using-facebook-may-be-making-more-lonely.html.

47. Wharton, *Ethan Frome,* 142–43.

48. Winner, *Real Sex*, 52.
49. Winner, *Real Sex*, 57.
50. Winner, *Real Sex*, 69–70.

Chapter 9: Diligence: *Pilgrim's Progress* by John Bunyan

1. "The Joke," Carnegie Hall, April 19, 2016, https://www.carnegiehall.org/Blog/2016/04/The-Joke.
2. "Diligence," *Online Etymology Dictionary*, accessed October 19, 2017, http://www.etymonline.com/index.php?term=diligence.
3. Thomas Aquinas, *Summa Theologiae* II-II, Q. 35, Art. 1, in *Summa Theologiae of St. Thomas Aquinas*, 2nd and rev. ed., 1920, literally translated by Fathers of the English Dominican Province. Available online at http://www.newadvent.org/summa.
4. Peter Kreeft, *Back to Virtue* (San Francisco: Ignatius, 1992), 153.
5. Kreeft, *Back to Virtue*, 154.
6. W. R. Owens, introduction to *The Pilgrim's Progress*, by John Bunyan (Oxford: Oxford World's Classics, 2003), xvii.
7. Bunyan, *Pilgrim's Progress*, 58.
8. Bunyan, *Pilgrim's Progress*, 58–59.
9. C. S. Lewis, "The Vision of John Bunyan," in *The Pilgrim's Progress: A Selection of Critical Essays*, ed. Roger Sharrock (London: MacMillan, 1976), 197.
10. C. S. Lewis, *The Discarded Image* (Cambridge: Cambridge University Press), 1994.
11. J. Paul Hunter, "Metaphor, Type, Emblem, and the Pilgrim 'Allegory,'" in *The Pilgrim's Progress*, ed. Cynthia Wall (New York: Norton, 2009), 408–9.

Chapter 10: Patience: *Persuasion* by Jane Austen

1. "Patience," *Online Etymology Dictionary*, accessed October 19, 2017, http://www.etymonline.com/index.php?term=patience.
2. N. T. Wright, *After You Believe: Why Christian Character Matters* (San Francisco: HarperOne, 2012), 249.
3. Zac Cogley, "A Study of Virtuous and Vicious Anger," in *Virtues and Their Vices*, ed. Kevin Timpe and Craig A. Boyd (Oxford: Oxford University Press, 2014), 99.
4. Gilbert Ryle, "Jane Austen and the Moralists," in *Critical Essays on Jane Austen*, ed. B. C. Southam (London: Routledge & Kegan Paul, 1968), 106–22.
5. Jane Austen, *Persuasion*, ed. William Galperin (New York: Pearson, 2008), 103.
6. C. S. Lewis, "A Note on Jane Austen," in *Selected Literary Essays* (Cambridge: Cambridge University Press, 1969), 175–79.
7. Lewis, "A Note on Jane Austen," 182.
8. Austen, *Persuasion*, 16.
9. Lewis, "A Note on Jane Austen," 179–80.
10. Austen, *Persuasion*, 100.
11. Austen, *Persuasion*, 101.

12. Austen, *Persuasion*, 31.

13. Austen, *Persuasion*, 175.

14. Austen, *Persuasion*, 242.

15. Austen, *Persuasion*, 240.

16. Augustine, "On Patience," trans. H. Browne, in *Nicene and Post-Nicene Fathers*, 1st series, vol. 3, ed. Philip Schaff (Buffalo, NY: Christian Literature Publishing, 1887), rev. and ed. Kevin Knight. Available online at http://www.newadvent.org/fathers/1315.htm.

17. Austen, *Persuasion*, 180–81.

18. Augustine, "On Patience."

19. Austen, *Persuasion*, 17.

20. Austen, *Persuasion*, 116.

21. Austen, *Persuasion*, 84.

22. Austen, *Persuasion*, 97.

23. Alasdair MacIntyre, *After Virtue: A Study in Moral Theory*, 3rd ed. (Notre Dame, IN: University of Notre Dame Press, 2007), 240.

24. Lewis, "A Note on Jane Austen," 185.

25. MacIntyre, *After Virtue*, 240.

26. Lewis, "A Note on Jane Austen," 185.

27. MacIntyre, *After Virtue*, 243.

28. MacIntyre, *After Virtue*, 241.

29. MacIntyre, *After Virtue*, 242.

30. Wright, *After You Believe*, 249.

31. James S. Spiegel, "The Virtue of Patience," *Christian Bible Studies, Christianity Today*, February 23, 2010, http://www.christianitytoday.com/biblestudies/articles/spiritualformation/virtue-of-patience.html.

32. MacIntyre, *After Virtue*, 243.

33. Wright, *After You Believe*, 250.

34. Wright, *After You Believe*, 249.

35. Augustine, "On Patience."

36. Thomas Aquinas, *Summa Theologiae* II-II, Q. 136, Art. 2, in *Summa Theologiae of St. Thomas Aquinas*, 2nd and rev. ed., 1920, literally translated by Fathers of the English Dominican Province. Available online at http://www.newadvent.org/summa.

Chapter 11: Kindness: "Tenth of December" by George Saunders

1. "Memorial Page for Sadie L. Riggs," Geisel Funeral Homes and Crematory, accessed October 21, 2017, http://www.geiselfuneral.com/notices/Sadie-Riggs.

2. Adam Phillips and Barbara Taylor, *On Kindness* (New York: Picador, 2010), 9.

3. Phillips and Taylor, *On Kindness*, 10.

4. "Nice," *Online Etymology Dictionary*, accessed October 21, 2017, http://www.etymonline.com/index.php?term=nice.

5. H. W. Fowler, *A Dictionary of Modern Usage*, 2nd ed. (Oxford: Oxford University Press, 1965), 391.

6. Augustine, *City of God*, trans. Henry Bettenson (London: Penguin Classics, 1972), 851.

7. Thomas Aquinas, *Summa Theologiae* II-II, Q. 36, Art. 1, in *Summa Theologiae of St. Thomas Aquinas*, 2nd and rev. ed., 1920, literally translated by Fathers of the English Dominican Province. Available online at http://www.newadvent.org/summa.

8. "George Saunders's Humor," *The New Yorker*, June 19, 2014, http://www.newyorker.com/books/page-turner/george-saunderss-humor.

9. "George Saunders's Humor."

10. "George Saunders's Humor."

11. Joel Lovell, "George Saunders's Advice to Graduates," The 6th Floor (blog), *New York Times*, July 31, 2013, https://6thfloor.blogs.nytimes.com/2013/07/31/george-saunderss-advice-to-graduates.

12. Phillips and Taylor, *On Kindness*, 12.

13. George Saunders, "Tenth of December," in *Tenth of December* (New York: Random House, 2013), 221.

14. Saunders, "Tenth of December," 224.

15. Saunders, "Tenth of December," 232.

16. Saunders, "Tenth of December," 222.

17. Saunders, "Tenth of December," 227.

18. Saunders, "Tenth of December," 233.

19. Saunders, "Tenth of December," 225.

20. Saunders, "Tenth of December," 233.

21. Saunders, "Tenth of December," 234.

22. Saunders, "Tenth of December," 237.

23. Saunders, "Tenth of December," 240.

24. Saunders, "Tenth of December," 244.

25. Saunders, "Tenth of December," 246.

26. Saunders, "Tenth of December," 248.

27. Saunders, "Tenth of December," 249.

28. Saunders, "Tenth of December," 251.

29. Phillips and Taylor, *On Kindness*, 13.

30. Phillips and Taylor, *On Kindness*, 8.

31. Saunders, "Tenth of December," 251.

32. Phillips and Taylor, *On Kindness*, 12.

33. Phillips and Taylor, *On Kindness*, 5.

34. Phillips and Taylor, *On Kindness*, 11.

35. Saunders, "Tenth of December," 248–49.

Chapter 12: Humility: "Revelation" and "Everything That Rises Must Converge" by Flannery O'Connor

1. Flannery O'Connor, "Revelation," in *The Complete Stories* (New York: Farrar, Straus and Giroux, 1971), 490.

2. Thomas Aquinas, *Summa Theologiae* II-II, Q. 162, Art. 1, in *Summa Theologiae of St. Thomas Aquinas,* 2nd and rev. ed., 1920, literally translated by Fathers of the English Dominican Province. Available online at http://www.newadvent.org/summa.

3. Thomas Aquinas, *Summa Theologiae* II-II, Q. 162, Art. 7.

4. Gregory the Great, *Morals on the Book of Job* 34.47, available at http://www.lectionarycentral.com/gregorymoraliaindex.html.

5. John Chrysostom, "Homily 30 on the Acts of the Apostles," trans. J. Walker, J. Sheppard, and H. Browne, in *Nicene and Post-Nicene Fathers,* 1st series, vol. 11, ed. Philip Schaff (Buffalo, NY: Christian Literature Publishing, 1889), rev. and ed. Kevin Knight. Available online at http://www.newadvent.org/fathers/210130.htm.

6. Peter Kreeft, *Back to Virtue* (San Francisco: Ignatius, 1992), 103.

7. Augustine, "Letter 118 (A.D. 410)," trans. J. G. Cunningham, in *Nicene and Post-Nicene Fathers,* 1st series, vol. 1, ed. Philip Schaff (Buffalo, NY: Christian Literature Publishing, 1887), rev. and ed. Kevin Knight. Available online at http://www.newadvent.org/fathers/1102118.htm.

8. Jane Austen, *Pride and Prejudice* (New York: Bantam, 1981), 35.

9. Eugene Peterson, *Christ Plays in Ten Thousand Places: A Conversation in Spiritual Theology* (Grand Rapids: Eerdmans, 2005), 76.

10. O'Connor, "Revelation," 493.

11. Karl Clifton-Soderstrom, *The Cardinal and the Deadly: Reimagining the Seven Virtues and Seven Vices* (Eugene, OR: Cascade, 2015), 25.

12. Josef Pieper, *The Four Cardinal Virtues* (Notre Dame, IN: University of Notre Dame Press, 1966), 189.

13. O'Connor, "Revelation," 497.

14. O'Connor, "Revelation," 497.

15. O'Connor, "Revelation," 499.

16. O'Connor, "Revelation," 499.

17. Flannery O'Connor, *Mystery and Manners* (New York: Farrar, Straus and Giroux, 1993), 34.

18. O'Connor, "Revelation," 500.

19. O'Connor, "Revelation," 506.

20. O'Connor, "Revelation," 508.

21. O'Connor, "Revelation," 508.

22. O'Connor, "Revelation," 509.

23. James S. Spiegel, *How to Be Good in a World Gone Bad* (Grand Rapids: Kregel, 2004), 38.

24. Simone Weil, *Waiting for God* (New York: Harper Perennial Classics, 2009), 73.

25. Weil, *Waiting for God,* 68.

26. O'Connor, "Revelation," 490.

27. Kreeft, *Back to Virtue,* 102.

28. Weil, *Waiting for God,* 67–68.

29. Spiegel, *How to Be Good,* 39.

30. Flannery O'Connor, quoted in Brad Gooch, *Flannery: A Life of Flannery O'Connor* (New York: Back Bay Books, 2009), 30.

31. O'Connor, quoted in Gooch, *Flannery*, 31.

32. Spiegel, *How to Be Good*, 33.

33. Kreeft, *Back to Virtue*, 100.

34. Spiegel, *How to Be Good*, 30, 37.

35. Craig A. Boyd, "Pride and Humility: Tempering the Desire for Excellence," in *Virtues and Their Vices*, ed. Kevin Timpe and Craig A. Boyd (Oxford: Oxford University Press, 2014), 259–60.

36. Flannery O'Connor, "Everything That Rises Must Converge," in *The Complete Stories* (New York: Farrar, Straus and Giroux, 1971), 411.

37. O'Connor, "Everything That Rises," 407–8.

38. O'Connor, "Everything That Rises," 409.

39. O'Connor, "Everything That Rises," 412.

40. O'Connor, "Everything That Rises," 414–15.

41. O'Connor, "Everything That Rises," 419.

42. André Comte-Sponville, *A Small Treatise on the Great Virtues: The Uses of Philosophy in Everyday Life* (New York: Picador, 2002), 147.

43. Kreeft, *Back to Virtue*, 103.

44. O'Connor, "Everything That Rises," 420.

45. Boyd, "Pride and Humility," 260.

46. Spiegel, *How to Be Good*, 36.

47. Hannah Anderson, *Humble Roots* (Chicago: Moody, 2016), 111.

48. O'Connor, *Mystery and Manners*, 35.

49. O'Connor, *Mystery and Manners*, 81.

50. Flannery O'Connor, *A Prayer Journal* (New York: Farrar, Straus and Giroux, 2013), 38.